EMPLOYMENT LAW

**This book is to be returned on or before
the last date stamped below.**

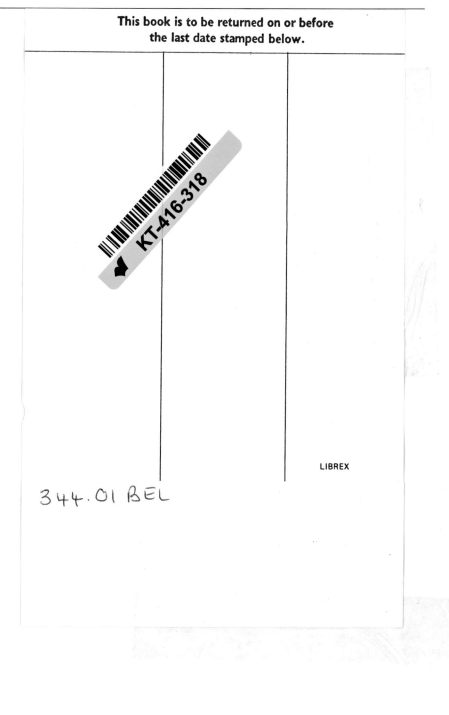

KT-416-318

LIBREX

AUSTRALIA
Law Book Co.
Sydney

CANADA and USA
Carswell
Toronto

HONG KONG
Sweet & Maxwell Asia

NEW ZEALAND
Brookers
Auckland

SINGAPORE and MALAYSIA
Sweet & Maxwell Asia
Singapore and Kuala Lumpur

EMPLOYMENT LAW

Other Titles in the Textbook Series

EMPLOYMENT LAW

Textbook Series

Andrew C Bell

Lecturer in Law, Nottingham Law School

LONDON
SWEET & MAXWELL
2006

Published in 2006 by
Sweet & Maxwell Limited of
100 Avenue Road, London NW3 3PF
(http://www.sweetandmaxwell.co.uk)
Typeset by Servis Filmsetting Ltd, Manchester
Printed in Great Britain by TJ International Ltd, Padstow, Cornwall

No natural forests were destroyed to make this product;
only farmed timber was used and replanted

A CIP catalogue record for this book
is available from the British Library

ISBN–10 0–421–82890–0
ISBN–13 978–0–421–82890–2

DEDICATION

To Angela

PREFACE

Over the past few years, employment law has been perhaps the fastest moving area of English law. In order to conform with EC Directives, the legislature have introduced measures to statutorily regulate many of the issues that in the past have been governed, or sometimes ignored, by the common law. Issues such as discrimination on the grounds of gender reassignment, sexual orientation, religion or belief and, from later this year, age have all been put onto a statutory footing; changes have been introduced into the Disability Discrimination Act; we have at last a statutory definition of harassment; and legislation has been introduced to bring into effect statutory dispute resolution procedures—one effect of which will be to greatly reduce the number of claims heard by employment tribunals, apparently necessary since the tribunal system appears to have become a victim of its own success in terms of availability and ease of access.

This book follows a conventional and logical format, one that is adopted by many of the academic courses at all levels: we start with an overview of the system; consideration of the question of employment status; the contract of employment; issues of discrimination law, including equal pay legislation; other legislation affecting the working relationship; health and safety issues; termination of employment and remedies available, both statutory and at common law; redundancy; transfers of undertaking—the TUPE regulations; restrictive covenants; and chapters covering the basics of collective labour relations—trade unions and industrial action.

Because of the recent statutory incursions into areas previously governed by common law, much of the body of case law in some of these areas built up over the years may no longer be relied upon—or must at least be treated with caution—and in a number of areas we are still awaiting authoritative judgments from the higher courts interpreting or clarifying the legislation. The effect of this must be that, despite the best efforts of the legislators, there will remain for at least a while uncertainty within some of these areas; consequently students and practitioners alike will need to be aware of developments as and when they occur.

Although this book is designed as a stand-alone text aimed at allowing students to gain sufficient knowledge and understanding of employment law to succeed in a degree or post-graduate course, it is not meant to deter students from pursuing further reading; the excellent *Labour Law* by Deakin and Morris, Smith and Wood's *Industrial Law* and the writings of such as Catherine Barnard, Brenda Barrett (particularly in respect of Occupational Stress), Brian Bercusson (the European perspective), Simon Deakin, Keith Ewing, Bob Hepple, Gillian Morris, Michael Rubinstein and Lord Wedderburn will all help the serious student to gain both depth and perspective in the subject.

I would like to thank all those who have helped with the preparation of this book, in particular my wife Angela for her constant support and encouragement. Special thanks also to the team at Sweet & Maxwell, especially Kevin Symons and Joe Marriott, not only for their practical assistance, but also their unfailing courtesy and tolerance.

The law is stated as at May 2006, and any errors and omissions are my own.

Andrew C Bell
May 2006

TABLE OF CONTENTS

TABLE OF ABBREVIATIONS

ACAS   Advisory, Conciliation and Arbitration Service
CAC   Central Arbitration Committee
CO   Certification Officer
CRE   Commission for Racial Equality
DDA   Disability Discrimination Act 1995
DRC   Disability Rights Commission
EA   Employment Act 2002
EADRR   Employment Act (Dispute Resolution) Regulations
EAT   Employment Appeal Tribunal
EC   European Community
ECHR   European Convention on Human Rights
ECtHR   European Court of Human Rights
ECJ   European Court of Justice
EDT   Effective Date of Termination
EOC   Equal Opportunities Commission
EqPA   Equal Pay Act 1970
ERA   Employment Rights Act 1996
ERelA   Employment Relations Act 1999
ETO   Economic, Technical or Organisational Reason
EU   European Union
GOQ   Genuine Occupational Qualification
HSWA   Health and Safety at Work Act 1974
HRA   Human Rights Act 1998
NMWA   National Minimum Wage Act 1998
PIDA   Public Interest Disclosure Act 1998
RRA   Race Relations Act 1976
SDA   Sex Discrimination Act 1975
SI   Statutory Instrument
SOSR   Some Other Substantial Reason

TULR(C)A   Trade Union and Labour Relations (Consolidation) Act 1992
TUPE   Transfer of Undertakings (Protection of Employment)
            Regulations 1981

TABLE OF CASES

TABLE OF STATUTES

TABLE OF STATUTORY INSTRUMENTS

TABLE OF EUROPEAN LEGISLATION

Chapter 1

INTRODUCTION

CHAPTER OVERVIEW

Employment law can be a daunting and frustrating subject.   **CO1**

Daunting because it overlaps into many other areas of law: contract law, welfare law, the law of tort, criminal law and others. Daunting also because its development has been heavily influenced by its historical and social environment; it is a subject about people and their relationships with, and expectations of each other—those relationships, and particularly those expectations, have changed dramatically over the past fifty or so years, and continue to change today.

Frustrating because there are very few—if any—absolutes in employment law. For every rule there are exceptions (*quaere*—is this a rule?); the rules and exceptions must be both learnt and understood. Frustrating because employment law is dynamic, it is constantly developing; those developments may have major impact on specific areas of the law, at times rendering whole sections of case law obsolete and only relevant in a historical context.

The alternative view is that it is the very breadth and dynamism of employment law that make it exciting and give the student, commentator or practitioner the scope to develop their ideas and arguments which themselves may influence the further developments in the law itself.

Employment law is all about people, their relationships and resolving within a legal framework the disputes arising at work—which is where many people spend up to a third of their adult lives.

The sources of the law are similar to most other areas of law, although the impact of European law is greater than in many others. One effect of the influence of EC law has been in recent years a considerable growth in national legislation to give effect both to EC Directives and decisions of the European Court of Justice, and legislation now covers many of the areas that were previously governed by the common law.

Employment law is generally viewed as consisting of two fairly distinct areas: individual and collective; although of course the areas overlap on such issues as collective bargaining and redundancy, and it should be understood that anything affecting the collective will also inevitably impact on the individual. The court system at its lower levels consists of tribunals, an Employment Tribunal and an Employment Appeal Tribunal. Appeals are on issues of law only, and from the employment appeal tribunal would go to the Court of Appeal (Civil Division) and thence to the House of Lords, with references if necessary to the European Court of Justice.

As with other areas of national law, following the implementation of the Human Rights Act, decisions of the European Court of Human Rights must now be taken into account, and the Human Rights Act itself offers as yet not fully explored or tested opportunities for change at both an individual and a collective level.

Brief Historical Overview

1.1 Until less than 150 years ago, workers had few if any rights. The right to hire and fire at will, to set wage levels and working conditions and standards were to all intents and purposes in the hands of the employers. For much of this time, trade unions and their objectives were considered unlawful, and it was not until the 1870s that legislation recognised as legitimate the idea of voluntary collective bargaining. Subsequent legislation and common law developments through to the 1970s both refined and, de facto, expanded the power and scope of the trade unions. It may be argued that the legislation of the hundred years between the 1870s and 1970s did little more that, provide a broad framework within which the trade unions were able to expand and become powerful, and that the successive governments adopted a laissez faire, hands-off approach to much of the area of employment law. That situation was, however, to change with the coming to power of the 1979 Conservative government headed by Margaret Thatcher. In a series of legislation, the ability of the trade unions to regulate their own conduct and organise industrial action was severely curtailed, resulting in a considerable drop in trade union membership over the past 25 years—and an equally considerable drop in the number of working days lost through strike action.

In terms of rights for individual workers, until the 1870s criminal sanctions were available against workers who either left their place of work or refused to work, and even until the 1960s there was little in the way of employment protection legislation. The 1960s saw the introduction of the Contracts of Employment Act 1963 and the Redundancy Payments Act 1965. The 1971 Industrial Relations Act introduced the right not to be unfairly dismissed, and this was followed by the Employment Protection Act 1975. Other notable pieces of legislation were also introduced at around this time, foremost amongst them were the Equal Pay Act 1970 (EqPA), the Sex Discrimination Act 1975 (SDA), the Race Relations Act 1976 (RRA)—it should be remembered that a major influencing factor at this time was the UK's joining in 1972 of the (then) Common Market.

The Labour government in power since 1997 has not sought to reintroduce widespread reform of the "anti-union" legislation introduced during the 1980s. Although legislation was introduced by the Employment Relations Act 1999 (ERelA) requiring trade union recognition by employers in certain circumstances, most of the recent legislation has been directed towards the individual employee, rather than the collective union, and their relationship with the employer; for example, the reduction from two years to one year continuous employment requirement in order to bring a claim for unfair dismissal, and the introduction in the 2002 Employment Act of a statutory dispute resolution procedure affecting both employer and employee.

It is however notable that the past five or ten years have seen a considerable **1.2** growth in statute in many areas of employment law, much of the impetus for this has come from Europe. In the field of discrimination we have seen statute extend the areas of unlawful discrimination to cover gender reassignment (SI 1999/1102), sexual orientation (SI 2003/1661), religion and belief (SI 2003/1660) and a broadening of disability discrimination (SI 2003/1673). Furthermore, the whole area of harassment on the now wider grounds of sex, race, disability and religion has been covered by statute for the first time. Again prompted by Europe, national legislation now affords protection against discrimination towards those working on limited-term contracts (SI 2002/2034) and part-time workers (SI 2000/1551). These changes have already had a considerable impact not only on employers and workers, but also on students of employment law; much of the case law in these areas is now obsolete and of little but historical value: for instance, for the past thirty or more years it was left to the courts to define and develop the law with regard to sexual harassment, this resulted in a mass of often confusing and occasionally contradictory case law all of which attempted to fit an issue which clearly should be unlawful into a statute for which it was never designed. The greater part of this case law may now be ignored as having no relevance in the light of the new statute. The new statute will however give rise to its own body of case law over the next few years as the courts seek to define and limit the application of the new law.

This is not, however, to say that all is either settled or well within the field of employment law. The introduction by the end of 2006 of legislation protecting against age discrimination will almost certainly have wide-ranging effects on a number of issues in this area of law, and there are some issues, notably that of employment status, on which the courts have repeatedly requested parliament to intervene—as yet without success.

THE SOURCES OF EMPLOYMENT LAW

1.3   Unlike some other countries within the European Union, Britain does not have a codified system of employment law. It may be said that there are three main sources of employment law in this country: statute, common law, and European law. Additionally, there are a number of persuasive authorities with a part to play, including Codes of Practice, collective agreements, etc.

Statute

1.3.1   This is the law directly enacted by the UK Parliament, it may take one of two forms: primary legislation—an Act of Parliament, e.g. ERA 1996, ERelA 1999 etc., or secondary legislation—generally a Statutory Instrument, e.g. Working Times Regulations (SI 1998/1833). Both of these forms of legislation are directly enforceable in the UK courts and may be equally relied upon. An Act of Parliament normally either introduces new legislation, e.g. EqPA 1970, or consolidates, perhaps with some changes, existing legislation, e.g. Employment Protection (Consolidation) Act 1978 (since repealed), Trade Union and Labour Relations (Consolidation) Act 1992 (TULR(C)A). Often Acts of Parliament are not, in effect, complete in themselves; they may contain sections allowing the relevant minister to amend (e.g. the minimum wage) or add to (to bring various categories of workers within the definition of employees) the existing Act. Such amendments are by way of the introduction of a Statutory Instrument.

Generally speaking in the field of employment law, a Statutory Instrument is used for one of two things: to amend or update an existing piece of legislation, or to introduce into national legislation a requirement of the EU, i.e. delegated legislation by way of the European Communities Act 1972. Criticism has been levelled at the widespread use of Statutory Instruments—there are several thousands issued each year, although relatively few have direct impact employment law—the two most common answers to such criticism being that the restrictions imposed on Parliamentary debate time do not allow all necessary pieces of legislation to be fully debated by Parliament, and that the complex technicalities of some issues can be better dealt with by a specialist minister or government department than by a full Parliament. Regardless of such criticisms, Statutory Instruments now provide a considerable amount of the legislation in force in employment law.

Common Law

Despite the increase over the past years in statute law, the common law still has   **1.3.2**
considerable importance in the field of employment law. As in other areas of law,
the common law both interprets the statutes and also, in the absence of statute,
e.g. in the area of wrongful dismissal, states the law. Furthermore, because
employment law both draws on a number of other areas of law (the common law
of contract, tort, etc. is relevant) and also is concerned with the relationships
between individuals and organisations, it is often possible to distinguish an otherwise seemingly binding case authority—in a way that is often not possible in such
areas as, e.g. Taxation Law.

European Law

It is certainly arguable that over the past 30 years the most important develop-   **1.3.3**
ment in individual, as opposed to collective, employment law has been the impact
of European law into the UK legal system. It is firmly established that EU law is
supreme over national law, and that in any conflict between the two EU law will
take precedence (*Costa v ENEL* Case C-6/64). Furthermore, national legislation
must be interpreted in accordance with EU law.

   European law may be viewed as taking a number of different forms: the Treaty
itself, the Regulations and Directives issued by the Council and the Commission,
and the decisions of the European Court of Justice.

Treaty Articles, Regulations and Directives

Many Treaty Articles have been shown to be directly effective both vertically (may   **1.3.3.1**
be relied upon in a national court by an individual against the state or an emanation of the state) and horizontally (may be relied upon in a national court by
an individual against another individual). Of particular importance in employment law is Art.141 which states that men and women should receive equal pay
for equal work. Article 141 was shown to be directly effective by the ECJ in the
case of *Defrenne v SABENA* Case 43/75.

   A Regulation issued by the EC "shall have general application. It shall be binding
in its entirety and directly applicable in all Member States" (Art.189 EC Treaty).

   A Directive is an instruction to a Member State to adapt its domestic law to
conform with EU requirements. In the UK, effect is normally given to Directives
by the issuing of a Statutory Instrument under authority of the European
Communities Act 1972. Such a Statutory Instrument may amount to a piece of
stand-alone legislation—as is the Transfer of Undertakings (Protection of
Employment) Regulations 1981, or it may amend an already existing Act—as did
The Employment Equality (Sexual Orientation) Regulations 2003 (SI 2003/1661)
which amended the SDA 1975. A Directive may have direct effect if it is sufficiently

clear and precise, but may only be relied upon by an individual in a national court against the state or an emanation of the state (*Van Duyn v Home Office* Case C-41/74); in other words a Directive may have vertical direct effect only. Normally of course, an individual will have no need to rely on a Directive since national legislation giving full effect to the Directive should have been put in place.

Questions on points of EU law may be referred to the European Court of Justice by any national court under Art.234. Decisions or opinions of the European Court of Justice are in effect binding on national courts, both in the instant case and also as precedent for future cases—although the ECJ itself does not operate a system of binding precedent, and may not therefore be bound by its own previous decisions. It is worth remembering that decisions of the ECJ regarding cases brought by other Member States will thus also form part of binding precedent in UK courts; thus it may well be that a case starting life in a provincial German court will become the leading authority for a legal principle, binding in all courts within the EC.

THE COURT AND TRIBUNAL SYSTEM

1.4   Disputes in employment matters may be resolved in a variety of ways: by Employment Tribunals, by ACAS mediation, by civil courts, by arbitration, by appellate courts or by the statutory dispute resolution procedures.

Employment Tribunals

1.4.1   Employment Tribunals, previously called Industrial Tribunals, have jurisdiction to hear statutory employment rights claims and some common law claims. Most of the claims brought before Employment Tribunals concern unfair dismissal, unlawful deduction from wages, discrimination issues, health and safety issues and disputes between trade unions and their members. In addition they have jurisdiction to hear claims for breach of contract of up to £25,000 outstanding at the termination of employment.

The tribunal is normally composed of a chairman, being either a barrister or solicitor of at least seven years standing, and two lay members. The lay members are drawn from panels comprising those with experience of either side of industry, one having experience perhaps of trade union activities, the other of management or trade association. All three members have equal decision making powers and it is possible, although unusual, for the lay members to outvote the legally qualified chair.

Tribunals were first introduced into Employment Law in 1964 and their jurisdiction, and consequently usage, has since increased considerably. They are designed to be quicker, cheaper, more efficient and more accessible than the conventional court system.

There are a number of advantages and disadvantages to the system, and these include:

a) Informality, lack of ceremony, regalia, etc. Hearings are normally conducted in a room, which although perhaps purpose built, is very similar in size and style to any meeting or small function room.

b) Hearings are normally open to the public, but cases concerning national security, some sex discrimination, and some disability discrimination cases may be heard in private.

c) Representation may be made by the party themselves, by a lawyer, a trade union representative, a friend, etc., although most companies and an increasing number of individuals are legally represented.

d) Legal Aid is not available for first instance tribunal hearings.

e) Costs are rarely awarded, thus there is little financial threat to applicants wishing to bring a claim. However, if the claim has been found at a pre-hearing review to be particularly weak, an applicant may be advised that, should the claim be pursued to full hearing and not be successful, costs and the cost of preparation time, or both, will be awarded against them and a deposit of £500 will be required before the hearing goes ahead (SI 2004/1861).

f) The members of the tribunal are specialist and experienced in employment disputes. Unlike magistrates or judges, members of an employment tribunal hear only cases within one area of law.

g) Certain rules of evidence, e.g. hearsay, do not apply.

h) Although the system is basically adversarial, with each party putting its case and being permitted to cross-examine witnesses, it is usual for the tribunal to put its own questions to the parties and witnesses, and, particularly in cases where an applicant has chosen to represent themselves, to assist a party to sensibly put and explain the issues; in this respect it may be said that the tribunals are more inquisitorial than a conventional court would be.

The procedure for bringing a case to a tribunal is fairly straightforward. The applicant must obtain a form from the tribunal office, complete it and return it. A copy of the form is then sent to the employer who has 28 days in which to respond. Copies of both forms are then sent to ACAS (Advisory Conciliation and Arbitration Service) who will, in most cases, contact the parties in order to effect a settlement before the matter goes to a full hearing—in the Annual Report of the Employment Tribunals Service for 2003–2004 it appears that almost 70 per cent of claims lodged did not reach the full hearing stage, some having been withdrawn following agreement between the parties, but the majority having been settled following ACAS involvement. It is likely that the introduction of the statutory dispute resolution procedures under SI 2004/752 will have the effect of considerably reducing the number of claims made to employment tribunals by ensuring that many of the disputes between employees and employers are fully aired before a hearing can commence.

If no settlement is reached at this stage, a pre-hearing review of each case is then normally carried out by a tribunal chairman, at which time an applicant may be warned that his case appears particularly weak, in which event he may be required to lodge a deposit of £500 if he wishes to proceed to full hearing and also be warned that, should his case be unsuccessful, he may be liable for costs (although such costs will only be awarded if the other party is legally represented).

The tribunal has the authority to require witnesses to attend the hearing, to order disclosure of documents, and to require written answers to questions put by the tribunal. Following the hearing, reasons must be given for the decision reached; if judgment is reached at that time, reasons should be given orally; in reserved judgments, reasons must be given in writing within 14 days of the judgment (SI 2004/1861). Judgments of the Employment Tribunal do not form precedent, but in the absence of other authority may be persuasive.

Appeals against a tribunal decision on a point of law only are to the Employment Appeal Tribunal (EAT), but note that prior to April 2005 appeals could be made to the EAT also on grounds of fact.

Employment Appeal Tribunal

1.4.2   The Employment Appeal Tribunal (EAT) normally sits in London and Edinburgh and has jurisdiction to hear both appeals from Employment Tribunals and against decisions of the Certification Officer in matters relating to trade unions. It has similar standing as and powers to the High Court. The EAT is normally composed of a judge and two lay members—as with Employment tribunals, the lay members will normally have experience of employment matters—and it is possible for the two lay members to outvote the legally qualified chair.

Legal Aid is available for an appeal to the EAT, and, as with Employment Tribunals, representation can be by either a non-legally qualified individual or by a lawyer. Costs are not usually awarded, but the EAT has authority to award costs against a party bringing a particularly weak or vexatious appeal to the other party, whether that other party is legally represented or not.

Arbitration

It is now possible in cases of unfair dismissal only for the parties to agree to take   **1.4.3**
the case to arbitration, rather than to an Employment Tribunal hearing. Since the
introduction of SI 2004/753 parties may agree to the appointment by ACAS of
an arbitrator who will decide whether the dismissal was fair or unfair. The decision will be binding on the parties, who will not then have recourse to a tribunal
hearing. The proposed advantages to this method of dispute resolution are its
informality and confidentiality (proceedings are not open to the public), although
arguably the scheme has not yet been fully advertised.

Chapter 2

EMPLOYMENT STATUS

CHAPTER OVERVIEW

It may seem surprising that in the field of employment law there is no fully work-   **CO2**
able definition of "employee". The question of who is an employee would in most
cases seem an easy one to answer—an employee is someone who is employed by
someone else; unfortunately, descriptions such as this are not in practice helpful.
Take for example the difference between your chauffeur and your taxi-driver: both
will drive you to where you wish to go, and both will be paid for doing so; initially
it may appear that the chauffeur is your employee, whereas the taxi-driver clearly
is not.

   However, the situation may not be as straightforward as that. The chauffeur
may be your or your company's employee, paid a regular salary to drive the
vehicle which is not owned by them. Alternatively, the chauffeur may be an
independent contractor, in business on their own account and perhaps owning
the vehicle—in which case payment is likely to be made on production of an
invoice, probably on a regular basis. Then again, the chauffeur may be working
on a temporary basis through a third-party provider, an agency, in which case
they would be paid by the agency who in turn would be paid by you; in such

cases the vehicle may be owned by either you or provided by the chauffeur. To complicate matters further, the chauffeur may be engaged by you on a full-time basis, a part-time basis or on a casual, as required, basis—and if not engaged by you on a full-time basis, may be engaged by someone else on a similar part-time or casual basis perhaps as a chauffeur or in some other role. The taxi-driver is probably not your employee—although perhaps if engaged by you on a contract basis to exclusively drive you for a period of months, weeks or even hours, it is possible that an employment relationship would be formed—they are probably either self-employed or an employee of a taxi company, although if engaged by the taxi company via an agency the situation may be different again.

It may seem strange that there is no straightforward easy-to-apply method of determining the perhaps most basic of questions in employment law of "who is an employee", but that, as we will see, is the situation. Statute has laid down a basic, but not very helpful, definition and the courts have been charged with interpreting it according to the facts of each case. Unsurprisingly not all of the decisions appear to lie very comfortably with each other; differently constituted courts adopting different guidelines and approaches. The situation is further complicated by the use in recent, and generally European generated, legislation which uses the broader term of "worker" rather than "employee". The effect is that whilst some legislation applies to all workers, many of the fundamental employment rights at a national level only apply to "employees". It is therefore necessary to determine whether an individual is for the purpose of a piece of legislation categorised as an independent contractor, a worker, an employee or something else.

This situation is clearly unsatisfactory, and many calls have been made for the legislature to clarify the position—as yet this has not been done.

To summarise, an individual who performs work for another is very likely to be a worker; workers may be either employees or independent contractors, but on occasion the law may regard them as neither.

EMPLOYEES

2.1   Many of the fundamental rights in employment law are confined to those individuals who are classed as employees, e.g. the right (in certain circumstances) not to be unfairly dismissed (s.94 of the ERA), the right (in certain circumstances) to a redundancy payment (s.135 of the ERA) and the right to minimum notice periods (s.86 of the ERA). The employer is obliged to deduct income tax and National Insurance contributions from an employee's gross wages, and will have a higher duty of care in many situations towards their employees than to others. Additionally, both employer and employee will have rights and responsibilities under the contract of employment.

Section 230(1) of the ERA 1996 gives the definition of an employee as follows:

"In this Act 'employee' means an individual who has entered into or works under (or, where the employment has ceased, worked under) a contract of employment."

Section 230(2) then defines a contract of employment:

"In this Act 'contract of employment' means a contract of service or apprenticeship, whether express or implied, and (if it is express) whether oral or in writing."

It would therefore appear that in order to determine whether an individual is an employee or not, three questions need to be asked:

a) is there an agreement between the parties; and if so

b) is that agreement a contract; and if so

c) is that contract a contract of employment?

The problem arises in that there is no detailed definition or description of a contract of employment, and it has been for the courts to determine which specific aspects of a contract of employment set it apart from other types of contract.

Over the years, the courts have developed and applied various tests in order to decide the question of "who is an employee?" At this point it is helpful to consider separately the approach of the courts when dealing, on the one hand with "typical" workers (those who work on a regular basis, perhaps for a standard or pre-agreed number of hours per week), and on the other with "atypical" workers (those working on a casual, non-regular basis and agency workers). Some of the case law and many of the legal issues are common to both groups of workers, but development of the courts' approach may be better understood if the lines of authority for the two distinct groups are kept separate.

"Typical" Workers

The Tests

The starting point that most texts adopt is the 1880 case of *Yewens v Noakes* **2.1.1** (1880) 6 Q.B.D. 530, in which Bramwell L.J. stated: "A servant is a person subject to the command of his master as to the manner in which he shall do his work." This statement is clearly a product of, and reflects, the society for which it was designed; but as industry became more technical and required more specialist expertise, it became less likely that an individual employer would have the ability to directly control the detailed manner in which each employee performed his task. However, this statement is still today the basis for the "control test".

The test was developed over the years. In 1910, Cozens-Hardy M.R. stated in the case of *Walker v Crystal Palace FC* [1910] 1 K.B. 87 ". . . it may be important to have regard to the fact that the so-called master is carrying on a business for profit." and further when referring to the employee, "He is bound according to the express terms of his contract to obey all general directions of the club."

In 1924, McCardie J. although doubting if the control test would cover all situations, stated in the case of *Performing Right Society Ltd v Mitchell and Booker* [1924] 1 K.B. 762, ". . . the final test, if there is to be a final test, and certainly the test to be generally applied, lies in the nature and degree of detailed control over the person."

As relatively recently as 1957, Streatfield J. stated in *Gibb v United Steel Co Ltd* [1957] 2 All E.R. 110, "The proper test is: Who has the right . . . to control the manner of the execution of the acts of the servant?" It may be noted that the learned judge speaks of the "right" rather than the express "command" of the original test, and this is an issue that had earlier arisen in the case of *Mersey Docks and Harbour Board v Coggins and Griffin* [1946] 2 All E.R. 345 where the House of Lords had considered where the authority to control arose, rather than who actually gave the orders. More recently it has been accepted that in the determination of employment status the issue of control alone will not suffice; as Cooke J. stated in *Market Investigations v Minister of Social Security* [1969] 2 Q.B. 173 ". . . control will no doubt always have to be considered, although it can no longer be regarded as the sole determining factor."

An attempt by Lord Denning in such cases as *Cassidy v Ministry of Health* [1951] 2 K.B. 353 and *Stevenson Jordan & Harrison v MacDonald and Evans* [1952] T.L.R. 101 to introduce an "integration test" met with little lasting success. The test stated that under a contract of service (a contract of employment) the worker is part of the business and his work is an integral part of that business, whereas under a contract for services (a contract under which an independent contractor works), although the work is done for the business, it is not an integral part of that business, but rather an accessory to it. The test not only calls for a value judgement to be made by the court, but also makes allowance neither for the role of ancillary workers, nor for the more recent widespread practices of "contracting out" work by way of competitive tender.

In 1968, the case of *Ready Mixed Concrete (South East) Ltd v Minister of Pensions & National Insurance* [1968] 2 Q.B. 497 was heard by MacKenna J. and resulted in what has become known as the "multiple factor" test. The case concerned an "owner-driver" whose agreement with RMC stated that he was self-employed. He had bought his own lorry on a hire-purchase agreement with an RMC associated finance company, he had been obliged to paint the vehicle in RMC orange and black, he was responsible for maintenance and insurance and other running costs, including petrol, of the vehicle. He was obliged to wear company uniform, and obey all reasonable orders from the company, and was paid at a rate per mile for delivering RMC's product. The question arose as to whether the driver was an employee of RMC or an independent contractor. MacKenna J. applied a three-point test to determine the driver's status. Firstly, did the servant agree to provide his work in consideration of a wage or other remuneration? Secondly, did he agree, expressly or impliedly, to be subject to the other's control to a sufficient degree to make the other master? Thirdly, were the other provisions of the contract consistent with it being a contract of service?

The first point asks, in effect, whether there was a contract in place between the parties; the second point applies the control test; the third point seeks to determine whether the contract between the parties amounted to a contract of employment. The learned judge stated that:

> "if the provisions of the contract as a whole are inconsistent with its being a contract of service, it will be some other kind of contract, and the person doing the work will not be a servant. [The judge may] take into account other matters besides control."

One such matter which was considered was the issue of substitution; it appears that the worker had the power to provide a substitute, rather than undertake the work himself, strongly suggesting that, in view of the personal nature of a contract of employment, the contract under which the owner-drivers worked was not a contract of service. MacKenna J. then referred to, and was apparently influenced by, the American case of *US v Silk* 331 U.S. 704 (1946) which was based on similar facts, quoting from that case, ". . . it is the total situation, including the risk undertaken, the control exercised, the opportunity for profit from sound management, that marks these driver-owners as independent contractors . . .", before himself concluding: "A man does not cease to run a business on his own account because he agrees to run it efficiently or to accept another's superintendence", and holding that the RMC owner-driver was indeed a self-employed independent contractor rather than an employee.

This case was followed by *Market Investigations v Minister of Social Security* [1969] 2 Q.B. 173 which concerned the employment status of part-time market researchers. Cooke J. in reaching his decision referred to case law including the test of MacKenna in *RMC*, but also asked the basic question: "was the worker in business on their own account?" This approach has become known as the "economic reality" test. In the later case of *Lee v Chung and Shun Shing Construction & Engineering Co Ltd* [1990] I.R.L.R. 236, the Privy Council stated that whilst there was no single test for determining employment status, the standard to be applied was best stated by Cooke J. in the *Market Investigations* case.

In the 1990s the courts on occasion adopted a pragmatic or perhaps holistic approach to the question of employment status. Two cases in particular are worthy of some consideration. In the first, *Hall (Inspector of Taxes) v Lorimer* [1994] I.R.L.R. 171, a case concerning income tax assessment on either Sch.D (self-employed) or Sch.E (PAYE employee) basis, the court after comparing—with something seemingly akin to pointillism—the "mechanical tests" to determine employment status, took the view that each case must be decided on its own facts; in that case, the number of different companies the respondent had worked at and the short duration of each engagement were important factors, although they were not factors previously given weight in other authorities. In the second case, *Lane v Shire Roofing Co (Oxford) Ltd* [1995] I.R.L.R. 493, the facts of which showed a number of similarities with the earlier case of *Lee v Chung* (above), the Court of Appeal, whilst referring with approval to the line of authority and various tests defining employment status, were at pains to point out that the facts must be viewed and any tests applied with reference to modern working practices. Both of these cases appear to show a change of approach by the courts, the application of what may be termed a "new economic reality" approach involving a move away from the more formalistic approach of earlier courts. For example, in *Hall (Inspector of Taxes) v Lorimer* on the application of almost any of the recognised tests to any of Lorimer's individual assignments the court would have been expected to find a contract of employment. The court, however, chose to stand back and look at the overall situation, finding in effect that a Sch.E tax basis would be virtually unworkable in reality for a man who in a period of 800 days had performed 580 engagements, each generally lasting for no more than two days. Likewise in *Lane v Shire Roofing* the court appears to have accepted that Lane was previously, and would still have been an independent contractor, but for the economic reality of the construction industry. The court was thus not reluctant to afford him the protection of employment status despite evidence to the contrary.

Self-description

2.1.1.1 In the case of *Construction Industry Training Board v Labour Force Ltd* [1970] 3 All E.R. 220, it was implied that the intention of the parties is not conclusive in determining the employment status of the worker. This was reinforced by Lord Widgery C.J. in *Global Plant Ltd v Secretary of State for Health & Social Security* [1972] 1 Q.B. 139 stating that although the parties cannot by intention make a transaction into something which it is not, yet it is recognised that such an intention is a factor for consideration in these cases. In the case of *Ferguson v John Dawson & Ptns (Contractors) Ltd* [1976] 3 All E.R. 817, even when the worker apparently gave a false name, presumably in order to avoid payment of taxes, and both parties had agreed that he was employed on a self-employed basis, the court, by a majority decision, still held that the company was his employer and that he worked under a contract of employment. As Browne L.J. stated: "The parties cannot by a label decide the true nature of their relationship."

Ferguson is often discussed in conjunction with the later case of *Massey v Crown Life Insurance Co* [1978] I.C.R. 590, in which a manager took professional advice and decided to change his employment status, with agreement from his employer, from employee to self-employed for tax reasons. Some two years later Mr Massey was dismissed and wished to claim for unfair dismissal, an option that was only available to him if he was held to be an employee. Based on the decision in *Ferguson* it perhaps appeared that he had a strong case to succeed. However, the court held him to be self-employed; Lord Denning stating: "Having made his bed as being self-employed, he must lie on it."

Although the decisions in *Ferguson* and *Massey* appear to conflict, it is possible to, if not actually reconcile them, at least to explain them. *Ferguson* concerned a labourer who, arguably, had little option but to work within the system operated by the company—that of supposed self-employment, at the time termed "the lump". Massey, on the other hand, was a professional who had obtained independent advice with a view to changing his status for his own financial benefit. A further difference is the reason that the two cases were brought; Ferguson was trying to obtain compensation for an injury sustained at work, whereas Massey was "merely" trying to obtain financial compensation for his dismissal—although it would perhaps be a mistake to argue that such a reason should influence the courts; in the recent case of *Astbury v Gist Ltd* [2005] W.L. 1104109, a case regarding the employment status of an agency worker, the EAT stated that the question of whether the worker was an employee or not could not vary depending on the reason for bringing the case. Perhaps the major reason for the difference in outcomes between the two cases though concerns the opinions of the judges who heard them. In *Ferguson* the dissenting judgment was from Lawton L.J., who stated: "I can see no reason why in law a man cannot sell his labour without becoming another man's servant, even though he is willing to accept control as to how, when and where he shall work." In *Massey* Lawton L.J. was part of a differently constituted court, composing himself Eversleigh J.L. and Lord Denning M.R., who stated: ". . . if the parties' relationship is ambiguous and is capable of being one or the other, then the parties can remove that ambiguity, by the very agreement itself which they make with one another."

In a recent EAT decision (*Levy McCallum Ltd v Middleton* EAT 9/08/2005 unreported) Serota J. stated what is now the generally preferred position:

> "If parties agree to create a horse but instead create a camel, the fact that they intended to create a horse and even call what they have created a horse is of little assistance in determining whether it is in fact a horse."

Consequently, except perhaps in the most extreme cases, self-description will be merely one of the factors for the courts to consider in arriving at their decision.

Substitution

2.1.1.2   Since the contract of employment is essentially a personal contract, it is reasonable that the issue of substitution should be particularly relevant in determining whether the contract in question is a contract of employment or not. It was a factor of considerable importance in the *RMC* case and the inclusion of a substitution clause in the case of *Express & Echo Publications Ltd v Tanton* [1999] I.R.L.R. 367, even though it was claimed that the clause had never been invoked in practice, was fatal to the claim for employee status. Whilst it is unlikely that most companies would wish to insert a substitution clause into a worker's contract and thereby allow unrestricted use of substitutes at the discretion of their workforce, it appears inequitable that—as in the case of *Tanton*—the mere insertion of such a clause into the working contract may deny employee benefits to a worker who is clearly otherwise entitled to employee status. In the case of *MacFarlane v Glasgow City Council* [2001] I.R.L.R. 7 the EAT held that the insertion of a clause allowing a worker a *conditional* right to substitute was not sufficient to deny employee status. The problem with the inclusion of a substitution clause is that it would appear to contradict the requirement of "mutuality of obligation" (see above) as required by the House of Lords in *Carmichael v National Power Plc* [1999] I.C.R. 1226, without which, their Lordships stated, there cannot exist a contract of employment. It may be possible to argue that such a clause may be struck out under the Unfair Contract Terms Act 1977 which has been deemed to apply to employment contracts (*Johnstone v Bloomsbury Health Authority* [1992] Q.B. 333, *Brigden v American Express Bank Ltd* [2000] I.R.L.R. 94), but as yet there is no authority on this point. The use of s.203 ERA 1996 would also appear to assist, in that it states:

> "(1) Any provision in an agreement (whether a contract of employment or not) is void in so far as it purports—
>
> >   (a) to exclude or limit the operation of any provision of this Act, or
> >   (b) to preclude a person from bringing any proceedings under this Act before an employment tribunal."

The problem here is that normally a worker would need to prove employee status before invoking the prohibition on contracting-out, although note the wording of the section—"whether a contract of employment or not"—which may indicate that the section can be used to prove the status of the actual agreement; as yet there appears to be no definite authority on this point.

2.1.1.3   It may therefore be suggested that a drawing together of the authorities would produce a test along the following lines:

> a) Is there a contract between the parties under which mutuality of obligation exists? (*RMC, Carmichael*).

b) Is there a sufficiency of control exercised by the employer over the worker? (*Yewens, RMC, Carmichael*).

c) Are the other provisions of the contract consistent with it being a contract of employment, e.g. substitution clause, payment of income tax and NI, risk of profit and loss, worker's investment in enterprise, etc. (*Market Investigations, RMC, Carmichael*).

As will be seen, the case of *Carmichael v National Power Plc* [1999] I.C.R. 1226 is strong authority for all of the above propositions. It is a House of Lords case concerning casual workers and issues of continuity of employment, but the legal principles stated in it are applicable to all issues of employment status.

"Atypical" Workers

Atypical workers are those who work, perhaps, a non-standard number of hours per week or on an irregular basis. Casual workers and agency workers may be classed as atypical workers. The very non-standard nature of the working arrangement presents particular difficulties in determining the actual employment status of such workers.

    As with typical workers, issues such as self-description and substitution will also be relevant in determining status.

2.1.2

Casual Workers

A convenient starting point is the case of *Kelly v Trusthouse Forte Plc* [1983] 3 All E.R. 456, and it is worth briefly examining the facts of the case. The company, Trusthouse Forte, relied on the use of casual catering workers to staff its large banqueting functions. They retained two lists of such workers: a list of some 100 regular workers, including Mr Kelly, and a list of some 250 workers who were used less regularly if the regular workers were unavailable or if needs required. Mr Kelly was amongst a number of workers dismissed for trade union activities, and he sought to complain to a tribunal of unfair dismissal. The tribunal had first to decide whether Mr Kelly was an employee or an independent contractor—if the latter, the tribunal would not have jurisdiction to hear his claim. The case was passed on appeal to the Court of Appeal to decide this issue. They adopted the approach of, in effect, drawing up three lists: a list of those factors which indicated employee status, a list of those factors incompatible with employee status, and a list of those factors which were not incompatible with employee status. The factors considered were those indicated in such cases as *RMC* and *Market Investigations*. In holding that Mr O'Kelly was not an employee, the court placed greatest weight on the issue of "mutuality of obligation"—is the company obliged to offer work, if so is the worker obliged to accept the work offered? In Mr

2.1.2.1

O'Kelly's case they argued that there was no mutuality of obligation, the company were not obliged to offer him work and he was not obliged to accept any work offered. It may be argued that Mr O'Kelly was under some obligation to accept work, since he presumably wished to remain on their list of preferred workers, but such moral or factual obligation was insufficient to satisfy the requirement of mutuality of obligation.

This approach was further strengthened by the House of Lords ruling in the later case of *Carmichael v National Power Plc* [1999] I.R.L.R. 43 in which it was stated that before a finding of employee status could be made, there must be a sufficiency of control, there must be mutuality of obligation, and there should be no factors inconsistent with a contract of employment. Their Lordships further stated that the mutuality of obligation must be contractual in nature, in other words it must be based on a contractual arrangement, and a moral or factual obligation would not be sufficient. It would therefore appear to be very difficult for casual workers to establish any on-going employer/employee relationship.

The issue of mutuality of obligation was further explained by the EAT in the case of *Wilson v Circular Distributors Ltd* [2006] I.R.L.R. 38 where Serota J. stated that mutuality of obligation does not require that the employer should be obliged to provide work, merely that he is obliged to provide work *if work is available*. In this particular case there was a contractual term stating that on occasion no work may be available and at such times no payment would be made. The obligation on the part of the employee was that he should accept any work offered.

Global or Umbrella Contracts

2.1.2.2   In the case of *Carmichael*, Mrs Carmichael had an agreement to work on a casual as-and-when required basis, but their Lordships held that this did not amount to a contract of employment, but merely an agreement to enter into short-term contracts of employment when work was available. In that case it was agreed by the parties that during her actual periods of work Mrs Carmichael was an employee of National Power. However, since many of the employment rights require a minimum period of continuous employment (e.g. one year for a claim for unfair dismissal, two years for redundancy payments, and, in Mrs Carmichael's case, two months for receipt of a statement of terms under s.1 of the ERA) it will often be difficult, if not impossible, for casual workers who work on a short contract basis to build up such continuity. This problem is in effect a question of continuity of employment, but on occasion the courts have addressed it as a question of whether there is in existence a global or umbrella contract covering not only the periods of employment but also the intervening periods during which no employment was available.

The concept of a global or umbrella contract is a difficult one to rationalise. It means, in effect, that a contract of employment exists and the individual is an employee of a particular company even though at any given time the individual may be sitting at home not working and drawing unemployment benefits, or indeed working as an employee or perhaps independent contractor for another company. Furthermore, an umbrella or global contract, unless it is expressly identified at such at its inception, can only be identified with hindsight. If, on the other hand, the issue is addressed as one of continuity of employment—that is, for a given purpose (e.g. a claim for unfair dismissal, etc.) are the breaks between the periods of employment sufficient to break an otherwise continuity of employment—it is somewhat easier to understand. A global contract was found in the case of *Airfix Footwear Ltd v Cope* [1978] I.C.R. 1210, and considered in *Carmichael*. In essence, in instances such as *Carmichael*, continuity of employment and the issue of global or umbrella contracts are merely two sides of the same coin.

Agency Workers

The approach of the courts in determining the employment status of agency **2.1.2.3** workers has been and continues to be unsatisfactory. In the, at the time, influential case of *Wickens v Champion Employment* [1984] I.C.R. 356 concerning an attempt by an agency worker to claim unfair dismissal, the court found that no contract of employment existed despite the fact that the written agreement between the parties stated: "The temporary worker is employed under a contract of service". Nolan J. was apparently influenced by the temporary nature of the work in question:

> ". . . it became clear that the contract is not one regulating the relationship on a permanent basis between the employers and the temporaries; it is a document which is entered into afresh each time the temporary worker is assigned a particular task".

And later:

> "The relationship between the employers and the temporaries seems to us wholly to lack the elements of continuity, and care of the employer for the employee that one associates with a contract for service".

Nolan J. concluded his judgment with the words:

> ". . . it would then follow that a casual worker must always be employed under a contract of service unless he has his own business and that, plainly, cannot be the law".

Recent case law has done little to assist the many thousands of agency workers to determine and clarify their status in regard to many of the basic employment rights.

Agency workers share many of the problems of casual workers in seeking to prove the existence of a contract of employment. Although the case of *McMeecham v Secretary of State for Employment* [1995] I.R.L.R. 461 intimated that agency workers may have employee status for the duration of each individual assignment, their problems have been compounded by the decision in *Carmichael v National Power Plc* (see above). Agency workers arc part of a three-cornered arrangement: the worker has a contract with the agency, the agency has a contract with the client firm, the client firm—whilst having no contract with the worker—exercises control over the worker on a day to day basis. It may be possible for the worker to show mutuality of obligation between themselves and the agency, but—since day to day control is exercised by the client company—they will not normally be able to show that they are working under a sufficiency of control by the agency.

The argument was put to the court in the recent "agency" case of *Bunce v Postworth Ltd (t/a Skyblue)* [2005] I.R.L.R. 557 that since the power to control the worker stems from the agency, the agency does have a sufficiency of control; however, the argument failed, Keene L.J. stating: ". . . the law has always been concerned with who in reality has the power to control what the worker does and how he does it". Likewise, although they may be able to show a sufficiency of control on the part of the client company (see for example *Motorola Ltd v Davidson* [2001] I.R.L.R. 4), they are unlikely to be able to prove mutuality of obligation between themselves and the client company since there is no contract between those two parties. This has been demonstrated in such cases as *Montgomery v Johnson Underwood Ltd* [2001] I.C.R. 819 a case concerning a worker who had worked on one particular assignment for the same client company for over two years, and more recently in *Dacas v Brook Street Bureau (UK) Ltd* [2004] I.R.L.R. 358, which also demonstrates both the confusion and problems experienced in this issue. In *Dacas* the tribunal held as a finding of fact that there was both mutuality of obligation and a sufficiency of control between Mrs Dacas and the agency, but then went on to hold that she was not an employee of either the agency or the client company. The EAT, whilst finding itself unable to disturb the tribunal's findings of facts, held that on those facts Mrs Dacas was an employee of the agency. When the case was heard on appeal by the Court of Appeal it was held that there was no mutuality of obligation between Mrs Dacas and the agency, and further that the level of control exercised by the agency over Mrs Dacas was insufficient to satisfy the requirement in *Carmichael*. Interestingly and rather confusingly, one of the judges expressed the opinion that Mrs Dacas was in fact an employee of the client company.

It is however quite apparent to the courts that in many cases the agency worker is also not an independent contractor. This was recognised in the *Montgomery* case, where the court suggested that perhaps Ms Montgomery worked under a contract *sui generis*—but since the court did not define the rights or obligations of such a contract, the nomenclature remains unhelpful.

Provision was made in s.24 of the ERelA 1999, for the Secretary of State to confer on certain groups of workers the rights of employees, but as yet this has not happened with regard to agency workers, despite repeated recommendations by the courts that the question of employment status for agency workers is a matter for legislation.

It should be noted that there are occasions in which an agency may be acting merely as agent for the end-user company, either by effecting an introduction of the worker to the client company and then taking no further part in the relationship—in which case the worker is likely to be an employee of the end-user company—, or by doing nothing more than acting as the client company's personnel and payroll department, or both (such arrangements are likely to be very rare, but see the case of *Astbury v Gist Ltd* [2005] W.L. 1104109, and see also the case of *Ironmonger v Movefield Ltd (t/a Deering Appointments)* [1988] I.R.L.R. 461).

Home-workers

The employment status of home-workers has to a great extent be determined by the Court of Appeal decision in *Nethermere (St Neots) Ltd v Taverna and Gardiner* [1984] I.R.L.R. 240 in which a contract of employment was implied based on the relationship of the parties over a number of years. Stephenson L.J. stated: **2.1.2.4**

> "I cannot see why well founded expectations of continuing homework should not be hardened or refined into enforceable contracts by regular giving and taking of work over periods of a year or more and why outworkers should not thereby become employees . . ."

It is possible to ague that the standard tests for determining employment status were not followed by the court, and it may well be that there are issues of public policy behind this decision, home-workers—those who work at home, rather than from home—are likely to be mainly women and had in the past often suffered from low pay and exclusion from in-company benefits. The implication of a contract, although perhaps a difficult concept to reconcile with the general law of contract, is acknowledged in the s.230 of the ERA 1996 definition of a contract of employment.

Illegality

If an employee knowingly enters into a contract whose purpose is to evade tax or national insurance deductions, or for the commission of an illegal act, that contract may be declared void (*Salvesen v Simmons* [1994] I.R.L.R. 52, *cf. Hyland v JH Barker Ltd* [1985] I.R.L.R. 403). It may be important to distinguish between   **2.1.3** a contract which has been entered into for an illegal purpose and one which although lawfully entered into has been performed in an illegal manner; in the case of *Coral Leisure Group Ltd v Barnett* [1981] I.R.L.R. 204, the employer, in an attempt to defeat an unfair dismissal claim, argued that the contract should be declared void because part of the employee's duties consisted of performing illegal acts. The court held that since those illegal acts had not been specified in the employment contract the contract had not been entered into for illegal purposes—merely that part of the contract had been performed in an illegal way, and therefore the contract was not void (see also on similar facts *Hewcastle Catering Ltd v Ahmed* [1991] I.R.L.R. 473).

If the contract is declared void neither the worker nor the company will have any rights under it. There are relatively few instances in employment law of contracts of employment being declared void, and most concern attempts to defraud the Inland Revenue. It may certainly be argued that in cases such as *Ferguson v John Dawson & Partners (Contractors) Ltd* and *Young & Woods Ltd v West* the court were at liberty to find that the contract was in fact void *ab initio*, but in fact in both of those cases the court identified a valid contract of employment and awarded the worker rights under it.

Fact or Law

2.1.4   Despite dicta to the contrary in the case of *Young & Woods Ltd v West*, Sir John Donaldson M.R. in *O'Kelly v Trusthouse Forte Plc* held:

> "The test to be applied in identifying whether a contract is one of employment or for service is a pure question of law and so is its application to the facts. But it is for the tribunal of fact not only to find those facts but to assess them quantitively and within limits, which are indefinable in the abstract, those findings and that assessment will dictate the correct legal answer. In the familiar phrase, it is all a question of fact and degree".

The Court of Appeal in the case of *The President of the Methodist Conference v Parfitt* [1984] I.R.L.R. 41 pointed out that if the proper course of action in determining employment status was examination and interpretation of a document, then this would amount to a question of law; this approach was confirmed by the House of Lords in *Davies v Presbyterian Church of Wales* [1986] I.R.L.R. 194.

In 1990 the Privy Council confirmed, in the case of *Lee v Chung and Shun Shing Construction & Engineering Co Ltd* [1990] I.R.L.R. 236, that exceptionally where the relationship depended on the true construction of a document it will be a question of law; but where the relationship must be determined by the investigation of factual circumstances the question should be regarded as one of fact. Thus an appellate court should not interfere with a finding of fact unless, to use the words of Lord Simonds in *Edwards v Bairstow* [1956] A.C. 14, the trial court took "a view of the facts which could not reasonably be entertained".

Interestingly, in the *Carmichael* case, the Court of Appeal argued that Mrs Carmichael's status could be determined by the examination of the relevant documents and thus it was open to themselves as the appellate court to interfere with the decision of the lower court; the House of Lords however disagreed and held that it was necessary to consider all the facts surrounding the relationship in order to determine her employment status—thus suggesting that only in very limited circumstances may employee status be viewed as an issue solely of law.

WORKERS

Certain statutes, or parts of statutes, confer rights on workers, rather than merely **2.2** on employees. Section 230(3) of the ERA 1996 defines a worker in the following terms:

> "In this Act 'worker' (except in the phrases 'shop worker' and 'betting worker') means an individual who has entered into or works under (or, where the employment has ceased, worked under)—
>
> a) a contract of employment, or
> b) any other contract, whether express or implied and (if it is express) whether oral or in writing, whereby the individual undertakes to do or perform personally any work or services for another party to the contract whose status is not by virtue of the contract that of a client or customer of any profession or business undertaking carried on by the individual;
>
> and any reference to a worker's contract shall be construed accordingly."

This definition of worker appears in the ERA 1996 in respect of unlawful deductions from wages (s.11), and similar definitions are to be found in the Working Time Regulations 1998 (reg.2), National Minimum Wage Act (NMWA) 1998 (s.54) and in slightly amended forms in both the ERelA 1999 (s.13) and the TULR(C)A 1992 (s.296) in respect of various trade union and disciplinary rights.

The Equal Pay Act 1970 (s.1(6)(a) EqPA) contains an extended definition of "employed" which corresponds approximately to s.11 of the ERA, and the SDA 1975, the Race Relations Act 1976 (RRA), the Disability Discrimination Act 1995 (DDA), The Employment Equality (Religion or Belief) Regulations 2003 and The Employment Equality (Sexual Orientation) Regulations 2003 all define "employment" in similar terms—bear in mind also that discrimination legislation also applies to applicants for employment.

It is clear that since the definition of worker requires that the individual works under a contract, any individual working under an agreement or system which is not a contract will be excluded from the definition. It is also clear that the individual must undertake or perform the work "personally" therefore the inclusion of a substitution clause in the contract (see **2.1.1.2** above) permitting the individual to supply a substitute and thus not perform the work personally may also be fatal to a claim for "worker" status. On these two issues the decision of the ECJ in *Allonby v Accrington and Rossendale College* (Case C-256/01) [2004] I.R.L.R. 224 appears relevant. The court stated that the term "worker" in respect of Art.141 had a meaning within community law and that meaning should not be restricted by national legislation. It therefore appears likely that attempts to restrict the interpretation of the definition by national courts, particularly in cases of equal treatment, may fail.

VOLUNTEERS

2.3 Despite arguments that voluntary workers should be accorded certain minimum rights in terms of health and safety and equality issues, the courts have held that volunteers will normally be neither employees nor workers for the purposes of employment law. The court in *Melhuish v Redbridge CAB* [2005] I.R.L.R. 419 made clear that whether an individual is a volunteer or not depends not on the label but on the substance of the relationship (in effect the self-description issue), and confirmed that true volunteers are neither employees nor workers. If a volunteer were to give a contractual commitment to work for certain periods there may indeed be an argument that their status may be viewed as either worker or employee, but it may be difficult to show that the commitment was indeed contractual in nature (see for example *SE Sheffield CAB v Grayson* [2004] I.R.L.R. 353).

Chapter 3

THE CONTRACT OF EMPLOYMENT

CHAPTER OVERVIEW

The contract of employment is the basis on which an employee is employed. If no **CO3**
contract of employment exists, the individual cannot be categorised as an
employee. As with other contracts, much of the content of the contract is for the
parties to agree—but bear in mind that the doctrine of freedom of contract, whilst
worthy in theory, has little part to play in most contracts of employment. In the
great majority of situations the contract of employment is offered on a "take it or

leave it" basis since, except in times of full employment or for particularly highly skilled or very senior positions, the company—the employer—is in a much stronger position than the individual applicant. Partly to compensate for this imbalance and partly to comply with legislative (usually European generated) requirements, a number of terms are implied into all employment contracts. The courts imply terms principally regarding the duties of the parties, whilst other terms are imposed by various pieces of statute; there are also instances of the courts refusing to uphold seemingly enforceable contract terms, preferring on occasion to adopt an equitable approach rather than following the formal common law path.

It is essential that you recognise that the question of whether a contract of employment exists is a question for the courts to decide (see the previous chapter) and that if an employment contract does exist between the parties, as with all other contracts, its contents are open to scrutiny, interpretation and enforcement by the court. Remember also that for many people the contract of employment is the single most important contract that they will enter into, sometimes outlasting a mortgage agreement or even a contract of marriage. It is therefore necessary that the employment contract should be sufficiently precise that the parties feel secure in their respective duties, rights and obligations, whilst retaining sufficient flexibility to allow it to adapt to changing work environments and employee expectations; a balance that is not easy to achieve.

In many respects, the contract of employment is very similar to any other contract. Usually, a contract of employment will be expressed in writing, but as with many other contracts this need not always be the case. A statutory definition is given as ". . . a contract of service or apprenticeship, whether express or implied, and (if it is express) whether oral or in writing." (s.230(2) of the ERA 1996.)

FORMATION OF THE CONTRACT

3.1   Although basic contract law principles will in most cases be relevant to the formation and operation of a contract of employment, there are a number of areas where employment law has varied those principles. Offer, acceptance, consideration and intention to be legally bound will normally be present at the formation of an employment contract, but on occasion the courts have implied the existence of a contract (see for example the case of *Nethermere (St Neots) Ltd v Taverna and Gardiner* [1984] I.C.R. 612) based on the actions and relationships of the parties, rather than by identifying the individual steps required; considering the statutory definition above this appears a perfectly proper course of action, but one which does not sit well with general contractual principles. Furthermore, it is a rule of contract that an implied term will not take precedence over a clearly stated express term, but the court in *Johnstone v Bloomsbury Health Authority* [1992] Q.B. 333 were not able to agree that an express term for a junior doctor to work excessive hours should take priority over an implied duty of care on the part of the employer. The courts have also warned against the strict use of legal precedent in determining the outcome of cases involving employment relationships, Edmund Davies L.J. stating in the case of *Wilson v Racher* [1974] I.R.L.R. 114:

> "Reported decisions provide useful but only general guides, each case turning upon its own facts . . . (older cases) may be wholly out of accord with current social conditions. What would today be regarded as almost an attitude of Czar—serf, which is to be found in some of the older cases where a dismissed employee failed to recover damages, would I venture to think be decided differently today".

The contract of employment will consist of a number of terms and conditions. These may be either express terms or implied terms. Express terms are those terms which have been agreed between the parties, either orally or in writing—although, as with areas of, for example, consumer law, the courts recognise that in reality the individual often has little say or input into the express terms of the contract, which are often offered on a standard form "take it or leave it" basis. An example of this would be the case of *Jones v Associated Tunnelling Co Ltd* [1981] I.R.L.R. 477, where the court refused to uphold an express term of the contract on the basis that if the term was of little practical significance at the time it was agreed, or in the case of *Jones* at the time it was amended, it may not be realistic to expect the employee to object to it and risk provoking argument, dismissal or rejection of their application (it is worth noting that although there is authority that the Unfair Contract Terms Act 1977 will, at least in part, apply to contracts of employment, it is expressly stated in the Unfair Terms in Consumer Contracts Regulations 1999 that those regulations do not—see below).

Implied terms are those which have not been expressly agreed between the parties, but which the courts accept as being included in the contract for a variety of reasons. The case of *Shirlaw v Southern Foundries (1926) Ltd* [1939] 2 K.B. 206 introduced the "officious bystander" test, wherein the terms are so obvious to an onlooker that they are held to be part of the contract, and therefore do not need to be expressed by the parties. The "business efficacy" test from *The Moorcock* (1889) 14PD 64, restated in *Reigate v Union Manufacturing Co Ltd* [1918] 1 K.B. 592, states that a term may be implied if it is necessary in the business sense to give efficacy to the contract—although it was stated in the House of Lords case of *Lister v Romford Ice and Cold Storage Co Ltd* [1957] A.C. 555 that such a test was more appropriate in situations where both parties are in business, and that a more useful test would be "whether in the world in which we live today it is a necessary condition of the relation of master and man".

Many text-books will include among the implied terms those imposed by statute, one of the main ones being the equality clause imposed by s.1 of the EqPA 1970.

Breach by either party of any of the terms of the contract will, of course, amount to a breach of contract; if the term is held to be a fundamental term of the contract, the breach would allow the injured party to treat the contract as terminated, and act accordingly (for example, if the breach were the fault of the employer s.95(1)(c) of the ERA 1996 would enable the employee to treat the contract as terminated and apply for a finding of unfair dismissal; if the fault were the employee's the employer may be entitled to fairly dismiss the employee (s.98 of the ERA 1996)).

Section 1 Statement

3.1.1   Under s.1 of the ERA 1996, every employer must give to each employee, within two months of the commencement of employment, a written statement of the particulars of employment. Failure to provide the statement within two months allows the employee to complain to an employment tribunal under s.11 of the ERA 1996, and the tribunal may decide what particulars should be included.

This "section 1 statement" must include:

(a) the names of the employer and employee;

(b) the date on which the employment began;

(c) the date on which the employee's period of continuous employment began, which would take into account any previous employment which counts as continuous;

(d) the scale and/or rate of remuneration;

(e) the intervals at which remuneration is paid;

(f) terms and conditions regarding hours of work;

(g) details regarding holidays and holiday pay;

(h) details regarding sickness/ injury and sick pay (here the employee may be referred to separate document);

(i) pension and pension scheme provisions (here the employee may be referred to a separate document);

(j) notice periods;

(k) in the case of temporary positions, the length of contract or expected date of termination;

(l) place(s) of work;

(m) any collective agreements which may affect the terms and conditions of employment (these details may be provided in a separate document);

(n) some further details must be given if the employee is to work outside the UK.

Section 3 of the ERA 1996 states that a "section 1 statement" should also include a note about disciplinary procedures and pensions.

It is common practice for employers to include all of these details in a written contract of employment, which once signed by the parties becomes legally binding. If the employer does not choose to do this, a separate s.1 statement must then be issued; such a statement would not in itself be a contract (unless signed as a contract by the parties (*Gascol Conversions Ltd* v *Mercer* [1974] I.C.R. 420)) but would allow a tribunal to draw strong prima facie evidence of the contents of the employment contract (*System Floors (UK) Ltd* v *Daniel* [1982] I.C.R. 54).

Collective Agreements

A collective agreement is defined by s.178 of the TULR(C)A 1992 as "any agreement or arrangement made by or on behalf of one or more trade unions and one or more employers or employers' associations" and relates to terms and conditions of employment. There is a presumption that such agreements are not binding in law (s.179(1) of the TULR(C)A 1992), but that presumption may be rebutted if the agreement is in writing and contains such a provision (s.179(1)(a) of the TULR(C)A 1992). A collective agreement is brought about by collective bargaining between the union(s) and the employer(s), and although generally not binding on those parties, its contents may be binding between the employer and the employee. **3.1.2**

The results or products of collective bargaining may affect an individual's contract of employment by, in theory, any of three ways. The first and most obvious is by express incorporation into the contract. If a term is agreed upon by the parties whereby the, say, rate of pay is affected by the collective agreement in force between the trade union and the employer, the rate of pay to the employee may be varied accordingly without the need for any further agreement (*Robertson v British Gas* [1983] I.R.L.R. 302). Such a term may be included in the contracts of employment of both union members and non-union members. If the contract of employment does not contain such a clause but collective agreements are in force, or if the contract has not been expressly agreed or reduced to writing, it may be possible for the courts to imply the terms of a collective agreement into an individual employees contract by reference to the s.1 statement, which must contain details of such agreements and which, in the absence of agreement to the contrary, provides strong indication as to what should be included in the employment contract.

The second theory of incorporation into an individual employee's contract is by way of agency—the idea that the trade union is acting as agent for its members as individuals. Although the laws of agency may permit this, in practice it is most unlikely that either the union or its members would wish to be so bound. The case of *Burton Group v Smith* [1977] I.R.L.R. 351 is authority for the presumption that the trade union does not act as agent for its individual members in collective agreements.

Thirdly and finally it may be possible to incorporate the products of collective agreements (or indeed many other terms) into an individual's contract by conduct—in effect as part of custom and practice (see below).

Not all of the issues covered by collective agreements will be appropriate for inclusion in an individual employee's contract of employment, for example the courts have held that procedural issues agreed between the employer and the trade unions, although affecting employees generally may not be suitable for inclusion at an individual level (*British Leyland (UK) Ltd v McQuilken* [1978] I.R.L.R. 245), although it may be open to question exactly what may be meant by "procedural issues".

EXPRESS TERMS

3.2   It is, of course, possible for almost any term to become an express term of the contract, if agreed to by both parties. It appears that the Unfair Contract Terms Act 1977 applies to the contract of employment (*Johnstone v Bloomsbury Health Authority* [1992] Q.B. 333, *Brigden v American Express Bank* [2000] I.R.L.R. 94)—the contract is taken to operate with the employee as the consumer. It should, however, be noted that the wording of the Unfair Terms in Consumer Contracts Regulations 1999 specifically excludes employment contracts.

Mobility Clauses

3.2.1   Apart from the issues raised in the s.1 statement, one of the most common express terms regularly included in contracts of employment is the "mobility clause". This clause purports to allow the employer to move the employee perhaps on either a temporary or even permanent basis to another geographic location. The clause may appear as a standard part of employment contracts even in the case of those employees who in the normal course of events the employer would not wish or even consider moving. The purpose behind the clause is to give the employer flexibility in staff deployment, and is of course particularly useful in situations where the employer operates multiple branches or outlets, or in the case where the business of the employer requires him to operate a mobile or flexible workforce (see also the situation in *High Table Ltd v Horst* [1997] I.R.L.R. 513 regarding redundancy).

The case of *Western Excavating (ECC) Ltd v Sharp* [1978] Q.B. 761 is authority for the rule that an employer cannot be in breach of the employment contract *merely* by invoking a contractual term, whether that term is an implied or an express term and regardless of how "unreasonable" that term may appear.

However, the case of *White v Reflecting Roadstuds Ltd* [1991] I.R.L.R. 331 makes it clear that although the actual invoking of the term may not give rise to a breach of contract, the *manner* in which it is invoked, or indeed the reason for invoking it, may give rise to a breach of the implied term of "mutual trust and confidence" For a further example see the case of *United Bank Ltd v Akhtar* [1989] I.R.L.R. 507, but be aware that the reasoning of the court may have been better explained as in *White v Reflecting Roadstuds.*

Bonus Clauses

3.2.2 It is common in some industries and professions for employees, particularly senior employees, to receive bonuses normally on an annual basis. Such bonuses are usually performance related, and based on either the performance of the company as a whole or on the performance of the individual. Very often the contract of employment will refer to such bonus schemes, but in certain industries the existence of such a scheme may be assumed. Clearly, if the existence of a fixed or fixable level of bonus is expressed in the contract the employee may rely on the contractual term and any non-payment of such a bonus would amount to an unlawful deduction of wages by the employer contrary to s.13 of the ERA 1996. Equally clearly, if the bonus is wholly discretionary under common law, the employee would have no right to claim for non-payment (see for example *Laverack v Woods of Colchester Ltd* [1967] 1 Q.B. 278). On occasion, the position is not clear and a small body of case law has built up over the past few years which may be used as precedent. It is worth considering some of these cases in detail:

Judge v Crown Leisure Ltd [2005] I.R.L.R. 823

Mr Judge was employed at a salary of some £17,000pa. An employee of an associate company was transferred to work alongside him, but at a salary of £35,000pa. At the firm's Christmas party Mr Judge was told by his manager that his salary would be increased to bring him in line with the other employee. When salary increases were announced Mr Judge's amounted to only 1.5 per cent. Mr Judge decided to resign, but was persuaded not to by his manager who increased his bonus for that year from £5,000 to £10,000 and apologised for not being able to keep the promise made earlier. At the next salary review Mr Judge's salary was increased by 2.5 per cent—by which stage the other employee was earning a package of some £43,000. Mr Judge resigned, claiming constructive and unfair dismissal on the grounds that the company had broken its formal promise to increase his salary in line with the other employee. His claim was dismissed by the employment tribunal, whose decision was upheld by the EAT who found that the "promise" was merely a statement that the salaries of the two employees would be equalised at some point in the future, and as yet insufficient time had passed for that promise to have been broken.

The case raises a number of issues which overlap into other areas of employment law. Since bonuses paid amount to "pay" Mr Judge could not argue that he had not received a fairly considerable increase to his pay in the first year, he could not of course bring a claim for equal pay since the pay differential was not based on the grounds of gender, and the case also raises the issue of how the courts may treat things said or done outside of the direct work environment, in this case a Christmas party (on this issue see also the case of *Chief Constable of Lincolnshire Police v Stubbs* [1999] I.C.R. 547, a sex discrimination case).

Cantor Fitzgerald Intl v Horkulak [2004] I.R.L.R. 942

Mr Horkulak worked in a senior position for a firm of brokers. He resigned nine months into a three-year contract claiming constructive dismissal due to a breakdown of mutual trust and confidence. His employment contract contained a clause under which a discretionary bonus would be paid. The High Court awarded him damages for non-payment of this bonus, and the company appealed arguing that the bonus was wholly discretionary. The Court of Appeal found for Mr Horkulak, holding that had he remained in employment the company would have been obliged to exercise its discretion in the payment of the bonus in a just and fair way (otherwise it would have breached the term of mutual trust and confidence), and since Mr Horkulak worked in a senior capacity in a highly competitive industry in which the payment of substantial bonuses was accepted as the norm, he was entitled to treat the bonus as forming part of his overall salary package.

This appears to be an example of the court being prepared to look behind the actual wording used in the contract and determining the practical reality of particular situations.

Taylor v Motability Finance Ltd [2004] EWHC 2619

Mr Taylor was the company's financial director. His contract of employment contained no reference to bonus payments, but it was the practice of the company to operate a discretionary bonus system. Mr Taylor had successfully settled a claim on behalf of the company for some £80m and expected a considerable bonus payment. This was based on a meeting he had prior to the settlement of the claim with the firm's chief executive at which it was apparently suggested that a bonus of some five times his annual salary could be expected. Unfortunately for Mr Taylor, during his work on the claim, the company decided to formalise its bonus structure and imposed a ceiling of 50 per cent of salary on any bonus payment and decided to award this maximum to Mr Taylor. Mr Taylor was apparently unaware of this change, and was dismissed prior to the award actually being made. He claimed before the tribunal that he was entitled to a bonus of 0.5 per cent of the total claim and that the decision to award him only 50 per cent of his salary was made in bad faith. The High Court found for the employer, holding that there was no evidence that the award of 50 per cent of salary was made in bad faith and that such an award amounted to the maximum that could be paid under the company's new bonus structure. The court also made clear that Mr Taylor had been paid for settling the claim by way of his salary, and that any other dispute must be settled by reference to the express and implied terms of his employment contract.

Restrictive Covenants

The other important express term often included in employment contracts is a restrictive covenant or Restraint of Trade clause, which purports to restrict in what capacity and where the employee may work once the contract of employment has been terminated (see Chapter 13). **3.2.3**

VARYING THE TERMS OF THE CONTRACT

As with other contracts, the basic rule is that neither party to the employment contract has the right to unilaterally vary the terms of the contract. However since an employment contract may run for upwards of 40 years it would obviously be inequitable to both parties if no changes or variations were permitted. **3.3**

Variation by Statute

Statute may vary any and all contracts of employment without any assent or agreement of either party, e.g. NMWA 1998, under which the Secretary of State will issue secondary legislation from time to time setting the minimum wage to be paid to all workers. **3.3.1**

Variation by Agreement

The parties to the contract may of course agree to vary the terms of that contract; this may be done on an individual basis, e.g. agreeing to give and receive an increase in salary, or on a collective basis by incorporation into individual contracts of the products of a collective agreement (see above). It should be noted that once the terms of a collective agreement have been incorporated into workers' individual contracts, the removal or amendment of those terms may not of course be done unilaterally (see e.g. *Robertson v British Gas Corp* [1983] I.C.R. 351). Presumably, although it is not clear, should collective bargaining result in less favourable terms for employees and if those employees' contracts contain an express term of incorporation (see above) then the individual contracts may be varied to the detriment of the employee. **3.3.2**

Variation by Means of a Section 4 Statement

A statement under s.4 of the ERA may be used by the employer to vary the original s.1 statement. However, since the s.1 statement is not in itself a contractual document, merely strong prima facie evidence as to the contents of the contract, **3.3.3** changes to that statement cannot directly change the terms of the contract. An employer wishing to change contractual terms by means of a s.4 statement will normally rely on the individual worker(s) not voicing their objection to the changes and being held to have consented to those changes by continuing to work under the amended terms. However, the court in *Jones v Associated Tunnelling Co Ltd* [1981] I.R.L.R. 477 held that the issuing of a s.4 statement cannot by itself be evidence of contract variation, and even if the employee continues to work without voicing their objections, if the term is of no immediate practical importance the court may choose not to uphold it (see also *Burdett-Coutts v Hertfordshire County Council* [1984] I.R.L.R. 91 in which the employees continued to work but under protest).

Variation by Dismissal and Re-engagement

3.3.4   At common law it is open for an employer to dismiss any or all workers and then offer to re-employ some or all of them under a new and different contract—assuming the employer gives either the contractual notice or the minimum notice period required by s.86 of the ERA 1996 (whichever is longer) the employee will have no cause of action against him. However, under ERA 1996, the employees in such a situation may be eligible for redundancy payment (s.135 of the ERA 1996) or a claim of unfair dismissal (s.94 of the ERA 1996). It is likely that dismissal and the offer of re-engagement under a different contract would only come about if the worker had been unwilling to agree to a variation of the original contract, since it amounts to a take it or leave it situation; the company could find itself losing the worker, being involved in paying a redundancy payment or being involved in a claim for unfair dismissal—all of which could be potentially damaging.

The courts recognise that it is necessary on occasion to impose contractual changes due to changes in working practices, modernisation or for other genuine business reasons, and in such cases have been reluctant to find the dismissal unfair and instead to hold that the reason for the dismissal fell within the potentially fair reason of "some other substantial reason" (s.98(1)(b) of the ERA 1996). Lord Denning, in *Hollister v National Farmers Union* [1979] I.C.R. 542, opined that such a dismissal may be fair if it were made for sound business reasons; furthermore, employees are under a duty to adapt (see below).

3.4   IMPLIED TERMS

Duties on the Part of the Employer

3.4.1   It is generally held that an employer must comply with four major implied terms: a duty to pay wages; a duty to exercise reasonable care; a duty to provide a grievance procedure; and a duty of mutual trust and confidence.

Duty to pay wages

Wages are the major consideration for the work done by the employee. Unless   **3.4.1.1**
expressly agreed, wages may not be paid in kind, but must be paid as money.
However, there is no implied right for an employee to be paid in cash; payment
may be made by credit transfer to the employee's bank, by cheque or by wage
packet, etc. Part II of the ERA 1996 protects employees from unauthorised
deductions from wages. It does not, however, apply in the following situations:

i) Where the deduction is made under a statutory provision (s.13(1)(a) of the
ERA 1996).

ii) Where the deduction is made under a provision in the worker's contract
of employment (s.13(1)(a) of the ERA 1996).

iii) Where the worker has consented in writing to the deduction (s.13(1)(b) of
the ERA 1996).

iv) Where the deduction is the reimbursement for an overpayment in wages
(s.14(1)(a) of the ERA 1996), although the deduction will normally only
be permitted by the courts if the original overpayment was a mistake of
fact (rather than a mistake of law), and even so the employer may be
estopped from making the deduction if the employee had been led to
believe the money to be his, had acted on that belief, and the overpayment
had not been the fault of the employee (*Avon County Council v Howlett*
[1983] I.R.L.R. 171).

v) An over-payment of work related expenses (s.14(1)(b) of the ERA 1996)
subject to similar conditions as iv) above.

vi) Where the deduction is made on account of the worker having taken part
in a strike or other industrial action (s.14(5) of the ERA 1996), for application of this see the cases of *Miles v Wakefield Metropolitan District
Council* [1987] I.R.L.R. 193 and *Wiluszynski v Tower Hamlets London
Borough Council* [1989] I.C.R. 493. Both of these cases concern the issue
of partial performance of the employment contract.

In *Miles*, a registrar of births, marriages and deaths refused, as part of
industrial action, to carry out civil marriages on a Saturday morning,
although he attended for work on Saturday mornings and carried out his
other duties fully. His employer had stated that should he not be prepared
to carry out the full range of duties on a Saturday, including civil marriages, he should not attend for work on such days and if he did attend,
he would not be paid. Mr Miles claim for pay on those Saturdays failed.
The court stated that since the employer had made clear that partial performance of his Saturday duties was not acceptable, he was not entitled
to be paid for those periods.

In *Wiluszynski* a similar scenario took place. As part of industrial action Mr Wiluszynski refused to carry out a very small part of his work, although he continued to perform the bulk of his duties conscientiously. His employer had stated that unless he agreed to carry out his full range of duties each week he should not attend for work, and that any work he performed would be treated as voluntary. When Mr Wiluszynski applied to a tribunal to recover his lost wages his application was refused. The employer had made clear that part performance of the contract would not be acceptable, and even though he had performed most of his contracted duties satisfactorily he was not entitled to any wages for the period of the industrial action.

A failure to pay wages is held to constitute a deduction for the purpose of s.13 of the ERA 1996 (*Delaney v Staples (t/a De Montfort Recruitment)* [1992] 1 A.C. 687), but a failure to pay monies in lieu of notice is not. Money in lieu of notice is traditionally held to be damages for wrongful dismissal, and not wages (*Delaney v Staples*). Be aware, however, of the decision in *EMI v Coldicott* [1999] I.R.L.R. 630, where it was held that if the payment of money in lieu of notice is made under authorisation of an express term of the employment contract, the money will be taken to be remuneration arising from the contract rather than being damages for breach of contract—as such, of course, the money will be liable to taxation.

3.4.1.1.1   **Sick Pay:** If the issue of sick pay is not covered by an express term of the contract, the courts have held that there is no presumption of a right to wages when off sick; each case will be considered on its merits (*Mears v Safecar Security Ltd* [1960] Q.B. 54).

Under s.64 of the ERA 1996 in certain particular circumstances only if an employee has been continuously employed for more than one month (s.65 of the ERA 1996) and is suspended from work by the employer on medical grounds he is entitled to be paid remuneration whilst suspended for a period not exceeding 26 weeks.

For periods during which the employee is unable to work due to illness and does not receive a contractual entitlement of sick pay statute has implemented Statutory Sick Pay. After the first three days of sickness the employee will be entitled to receive from the employer an amount (currently just under £70 per week and amended from time to time by statutory instrument) per week which the employer may reclaim from the relevant government department. The scheme operates for a maximum of 28 weeks, after which time the employee may be eligible for other social security benefit.

3.4.1.1.2   **Provision of Work:** Generally there is no obligation on the part of the employer to provide work, as long as wages are paid, as Asquith J. stated in *Collier v Sunday Referee Publishing Co Ltd* [1940] 2 K.B. 647: "Provided I pay my cook her wages regularly, she cannot complain if I choose to take any or all of my meals out". There is contrary dicta from Lord Denning in the case of *Langston v Amalgamated Union of Engineering Workers* [1974] I.C.R. 180 arguing that the approach in *Collier* was out of date and that there was now a "right to work" recognised by the courts. This followed Lord Denning's earlier case of *Nagle v Fielden* [1966] 2 Q.B. 633 in which he stated:

> "The common law of England has for centuries recognised that a man has a right to work at his trade or profession without being unjustly excluded from it. He is not to be shut out from it at the whim of those having the governance of it. If they make a rule which enables them to reject his application arbitrarily or capriciously, not reasonably, that rule is bad. It is against public policy. The court will not give effect to it".

It is however very possible to distinguish *Nagle* on its particular facts, indeed arguably Lord Denning was not propounding a right to work as such, but rather a right not to be unreasonably excluded from a particular trade or profession by a governing body—*Nagle* may also be viewed as an issue of equality rather than a "right to work". Whether English law recognises a right to work is still a moot point, and the preferred position appears to be that *Collier* is still good law—but the courts have identified a number of areas and situations in which the employer may be under a duty to provide work:

i) Where payment is made on a commission or piecework basis (*Devonald v Rosser & Sons Ltd* [1906] 2 K.B. 728). In such a case failure to provide work would amount to the failure to pay wages.

ii) Where an employee is engaged on skilled work and needs to continue to work to maintain or develop that level of skill (*Breach v Epsylon Industries Ltd* [1976] I.C.R. 316).

iii) Where publicity or public exposure is understood to form part of the consideration due to the employee, e.g. an entertainer, actor, etc. (*Turner v Sawdon & Co* [1901] 2 K.B. 653).

iv) If the contract provides, either expressly or impliedly, that the work will be provided, failure by the employer to do so would amount to an actionable breach (*William Hill Organisation Ltd v Tucker* [1998] I.R.L.R. 313). This ties in closely with Lord Denning's statements in *Langston* where he argues in effect that the modern contract of employment in fact implies such a duty on the part of the employer.

Duty to exercise reasonable care

At common law, the employer is under a duty to take reasonable care for the   **3.4.1.2**
health and safety of his employees. The standard of care is "the care which an

ordinary prudent employer would take in all the circumstances" (*Paris v Stepney Borough Council* [1951] 1 All E.R. 42). This duty is owed to employees as individuals (*Paris v Stepney Borough Council*), and consequently a higher standard of duty may be owed to some employees than to others (*James v Hepworth & Grandage Ltd* [1968] 1 Q.B. 94). The employer should provide safe plant and premises, a safe system of work and reasonably competent fellow employees (see Chapter 7).

The employer is also under a duty of care in the provision of references. References given for ex-employees to new or potential employers should be fair and factually accurate. If a reference is written negligently the ex-employer may be liable in tort under the principles in *Hedley Byrne & Co Ltd v Heller & Ptns Ltd* [1964] A.C. 465 to the new or potential employer. However, it was not clear whether the employee would also have a cause of action against the ex-employer for the loss suffered; the House of Lords in the case of *Spring v Guardian Assurance Plc* [1994] I.C.R. 596 held that the ex-employer was under a duty of care to furnish fair and accurate references, and if a reference was given negligently and the giving of that reference caused the loss to the employee the employee would have a cause of action against the ex-employer (for application of this principle see the cases of *Bartholomew v London Borough of Hackney* [1999] I.R.L.R. 246 and *Cox v Sun Alliance Life Ltd* [2001] I.R.L.R. 448).

The issue of the giving of references is not confined to the situation between ex-employers and employees (or employers and ex-employees) but also extends to employers and their current employees. In the case of *TSB Bank v Harris* [2000] I.R.L.R. 157 an employee discovered that her employer had given a misleading reference to a prospective employer and she terminated her employment claiming constructive dismissal on the grounds that her employer had breached the fundamental contract term of "mutual trust and confidence".

Duty to provide a grievance procedure

3.4.1.3   The employer has a duty to both provide and effectively operate a grievance procedure (*WA Goold (Pearmak) Ltd v McConnell* [1995] I.R.L.R. 516). In the case of *Bracebridge Engineering Ltd v Darby* [1990] I.R.L.R. 3 it was held that failure to investigate or take seriously a complaint of sexual harassment constituted a fundamental breach of contract.

The issue of grievance procedures and the conduct of both the employer and the employee have now to a large extent been placed on a statutory basis by the implementation of The Employment Act 2002 (Dispute Resolution) Regulations 2004.

Duty of mutual trust and confidence

3.4.1.4   Sometimes also referred to as a duty to cooperate, or the duty of mutual cooperation. The duty has been defined by the court as an obligation on the employer that he should not "without reasonable and proper cause, conduct [himself] in a manner calculated to or likely to destroy or seriously damage the relationship of confidence and trust between employer and employee" (*Woods v WM Car Services (Peterborough) Ltd* [1981] I.C.R. 666.

Cases to illustrate a breach of this duty include:

- *Isle of Wight Tourist Board v Coombes* [1976] I.R.L.R. 413, where a manager said of his secretary that she was an "intolerable bitch on a Monday morning".

- *Wood v Freelander* [1977] I.R.L.R. 455 where the employer allowed an employee to become the victim of a sustained campaign of sexual harassment.

- *Robinson v Crompton Parkinson Ltd* [1978] I.C.R. 401, where the employer made an unsubstantiated accusation of theft against an employee.

- *Post Office v Roberts* [1980] I.R.L.R. 347, where a senior manager wrote an unfavourable report on an employee without consideration of her work record, which resulted in her being refused promotion.

- *Halford v United Kingdom* [1997] I.R.L.R. 471, in which the European Court of Human Rights held that the monitoring of an employee's phone calls at work by the employer may contravene Art.8 of the ECHR, and since the introduction of the Human Rights Act 1998 (MRA) such an argument may succeed in UK courts—although it is worth considering the particular facts of that case.

- *Malik v BCCI* [1997] I.R.L.R. 462, where the dishonest conduct of the employer (although not aimed at the employee) may amount to a breach of mutual trust and confidence.

It should, of course, be remembered that conduct that may be acceptable in one particular industry or situation, may not be acceptable in another, and in those circumstances may be held to amount to a breach of the duty of trust and confidence.

In recent years the courts have both widened the scope and increased the importance of the implied term of mutual trust and confidence (see, e.g. "constructive dismissal"). The case of *University of Nottingham v Eyett* [1998] I.R.L.R. 646 suggests that, although in previous cases the duty of trust and confidence has been expressed in a negative form, i.e. refraining from conduct likely to harm the relationship, in principle the duty may have a positive form, and in appropriate cases may be breached by a failure on the part of the employer to warn or act (for an early and specific example of such a situation see the case of *Scally v Southern Health and Social Services Board* [1991] I.R.L.R. 522).

Duties on the Part of the Employee

3.4.2 The employee is also bound by a number of implied terms; these are generally held to be a duty of obedience, a duty to adapt, a duty to exercise care and a duty of fidelity or good faith.

Duty of obedience

3.4.2.1 An employee has a duty to obey all reasonable and lawful orders. The employer may not, however:

a) order the employee to do an illegal act (*Morrish v Henlys (Folkestone) Ltd* [1973] I.C.R. 482); nor

b) may the employer order the employee into immediate danger (*Ottoman Bank v Chakarian* [1930] A.C. 277). It appears that the danger must be both "immediate" (*Bouzourou v Ottoman Bank* [1930] A.C. 271) and specific and personal (*Walmsley v UDEC Refrigeration Ltd* [1972] I.R.L.R. 80). The danger may however be either the danger of violence or of illness or disease (*Turner v Mason* (1845) 14 M. & W. 112).

Of particular importance here is the duty to obey work rules and a failure by the employee to do so may lead to a breach of contract by the employee, even though the work rules are not in themselves contractual terms—and may thus be changed by the employer from time to time (although the reason for the change or the manner of implementing the change may lead to the employer breaching the duty of mutual trust and confidence: see for example *Dryden v Greater Glasgow Health Board* [1992] I.R.L.R. 469).

Duty to adapt

3.4.2.2 Generally, an employee has a duty to adapt to new methods and techniques introduced by the employer (see above re variations to the contract), in such cases though, the employer should provide appropriate training or retraining (*Cresswell v Board of Inland Revenue* [1984] I.C.R. 508).

In each case the court must decide whether the changes amount to merely an adaptation of the way in which the job is carried out, or a change of the job itself, in which case the question of redundancy may arise (*North Riding Garages Ltd v Butterwick* [1967] 2 Q.B. 56).

Duty to exercise care

3.4.2.3 The employee has a general duty to exercise reasonable care in the performance of his work.

The practical importance of this usually arises in an action in tort where the employee has acted negligently causing injury to a third party, and the employer is held vicariously liable for the employee's actions. In such a situation the employer may be able to sue the employee for an indemnity, either for breach of contract (*Lister v Romford Ice and Cold Storage Co Ltd* [1957] A.C. 555), or in tort, where both are held to be joint tortfeasors, for either a contribution or a full indemnity. It should be noted that both such actions are extremely rare, and in effect, are contrary to the notion of employer's vicarious liability.

Duty of fidelity or good faith

The courts have held that virtually any act by the employee which is inconsistent with **3.4.2.4** the contract of employment and which does or may cause injury to the employer will amount to a breach by the employee of the duty of fidelity or good faith.

This duty may be broken down into several sub-headings:

(i) Duty to account for secret profits made by the employee in the course of his employment (*Boston Deep Sea Fishing and Ice Co v Ansell*).

(ii) Duty not to compete with the employer whilst in employment (*Hivac Ltd v Park Royal Scientific Instruments Ltd* [1946] Ch. 169), although the courts are reluctant to place any unnecessary restrictions on an individual's spare time.

(iii) Duty regarding competition by ex-employees. With the exception of an express contract term restraining an employee from competition after leaving the employment and a general protection of trade secrets (see Chapter 13), it may be difficult to show a duty of fidelity regarding an employee's actions following the termination of the contract of employment (although, see the Australian case of *Ansell Rubber Co v Allied Rubber Industries* [1967] V.R. 37). Many actions which would constitute a breach of the duty of fidelity if carried out by an employee, may be quite lawful if carried out by an ex-employee. Thus, most breaches of this duty are actually committed by employees prior to leaving his employment either to join another company or to set up business on his own. Examples of this include:

- *Wessex Dairies Ltd v Smith* [1935] 2 K.B. 80, canvassing his employer's customers prior to setting up his own business.
- *Robb v Green* [1895] 2 Q.B. 315, making or memorising a list of the employer's customers prior to setting up his own business.

(iv) duty to co-operate. In the cases of both *Secretary of State for Employment v ASLEF (No.2)* [1972] 2 Q.B. 455 and *Ticehurst v British Telecommunications Plc* [1992] I.R.L.R. 219, the courts have held that actions taken by employees with the intention of disrupting the employer's business may amount to a breach of contract; even though that action may be no more than a "work to rule", which by its very nature means working to the terms of the contract but no further.

WORK RULES

3.5   Although the contract of employment will contain either an express or an implied term that the employee will abide by "the rules", unless individually specified in the contract these rules may not have contractual force in themselves (*Secretary of State for Employment* v *ASLEF (No.2)* [1972] 2 Q.B. 455).

One effect of this is very much in favour of the employer, in that, although breach of the rules by the employee may be a breach of the contract term of duty to obey orders, since the rules themselves do not have contractual force, the employer may change them unilaterally without breaching the contract—assuming that the manner of implementing such a change and the reason for the change do not breach the implied term of mutual trust and confidence (see, e.g. *Dryden v Greater Glasgow Health Board* [1992] I.R.L.R. 469, in which a no-smoking rule was introduced following consultation with staff, notification of forthcoming implementation and offers of assistance to quit smoking, and breach of which was not subject to disciplinary measures until warnings had been given and ignored).

CUSTOM AND PRACTICE

3.6   Since, in most cases, employment contracts today are more formalised than previously and statute now plays a much greater part in defining the terms, in reality, there is very little significance or importance today in the incorporation of terms into the contract of employment through custom and practice. For a term to be incorporated through custom and practice it should be notorious, certain and reasonable. The leading case is *Sagar* v *H Ridehalgh & Son Ltd* [1931] 1 Ch. 310 which indicates that a term should be well known and understood both in the employer's business and also in the region or industry generally before it may be implied into individual contracts through "custom and practice".

The issue of implication through custom and practice was raised in the case of *Dryden v Glasgow Health Board* [1992] I.R.L.R. 469 in which employees had been permitted to smoke at work in areas specifically set aside for this purpose for a number of years. Unfortunately, the court chose not to address this argument fully in its judgment.

STATUTE

3.7   The growth of statute as a source of employment law over the past few years has had considerable impact on the contract of employment. There are perhaps three ways in which statute may affect the actual contract terms:

a) On occasion statute directly imposes a term into the contract of employment, e.g. s.1(1) of the EqPA 1970 imposes an equality clause into the contracts of women, and by virtue of s.1(13) into the contracts of men.

b) Statute may often operate to restrict or negative a contract term, e.g. both the SDA 1975 and Treaty Article 119 would make void any contract term which purported to restrict promotion prospects for women.

c) Whilst breach by the employer of statute will normally be actionable by the employee in its own right, it may also amount to a breach of the duty of mutual trust and confidence.

Chapter 4

EQUAL PAY

CHAPTER OVERVIEW

It is not many years ago that it was not unusual for there to be two salary scales **CO4** for each job: one for men and another for women. The salary scale for women, whilst starting at the same point, would tail off more quickly than the salary scale for men and not go as high. Since the introduction of the Equal Pay Act 1970, which came into effect in 1975, this has no longer been the case. In theory, women and men are now paid the same amount for doing the same or similar work. "In theory" because, despite the legislation, various surveys still suggest that women are paid considerably less than men. This is not to suggest that companies are paying women less than men for performing similar functions—although on occasion this does still appear to be the case—but that there still exists an atmosphere of stereotyping, within which women are restricted from or to particular roles in employment (if you don't believe me, close your eyes and picture an operating theatre, the patient is on the operating table, the surgeon is about to operate and the nurses are ready to assist—what sex was the surgeon, what sex were the nurses?). It seems perfectly natural that the MD is a man and his secretary is a woman, perfectly natural that the staff canteen should be staffed by waitresses, and, of course, consider the gender breakdown of our most senior judges.

There are of course many sociological reasons for such apparent inequalities, and many of those reasons will persist—but equality in employment should not be about operating quota systems, but about equality of opportunity. In that respect I would suggest that the equal pay legislation has played a successful role in its 30 years of existence; it has not yet achieved its aim—that is clear from the number of successful claims still being made—but it has provided the framework within which inequalities may be challenged.

The law regarding equal pay is in principle very basic and straightforward. It states simply that men and women should receive equal pay regardless of gender. However, aspects of the legislation and much of the case law have succeeded in complicating and at times confusing this otherwise simple doctrine.

Equal pay legislation in the UK is twofold: national legislation—the EqPA 1970 as amended; and Art.141 of the Treaty of Rome, along with the explanatory EU Directives Nos 75/117 and 76/207.

In the case of *Pickstone v Freemans Plc* [1988] I.R.L.R. 357, the House of Lords stated that the EqPA 1970 must be interpreted purposively in line with Art.141 and Directive 75/117. Normally, therefore, a national court will have no need nor authority to consider Art.141 if the EqPA 1970 provides a full and adequate remedy (*Blaik v Post Office* [1994] I.R.L.R. 280).

THE EQUAL PAY ACT 1970 (AS AMENDED)

4.1   The Equal Pay Act 1970 applies to all of those workers who are "employed". Section 1(6)(a) of the EqPA 1970 states: "employed means employed under a contract of service or of apprenticeship or a contract personally to execute any work or labour, and related expressions shall be construed accordingly". The definition is therefore wider than the s.230 of the ERA 1996 definition of "employee" and covers both employees and those independent contractors personally undertaking the work.

Although the language of the Equal Pay Act is framed so as to address women, s.1(13) makes clear that the legislation applies equally to both women and men.

Section 1 of the Act imposes into every woman's contract of employment an equality clause, under which if any term of the woman's contract is less favourable than the corresponding term in the man's contract, the woman's contract shall be modified to correspond with the man's.

It is possible for a woman or a man to bring a claim for equal pay under any of three heads within the EqPA 1970. In each case it is necessary for the applicant to select a comparator who must be of the opposite sex. The choice of comparator is for the applicant to make (*Picksone v Freemans Plc*), but may not be a hypothetical comparator although it may be a predecessor (*Macarthys Ltd v Smith* [1980] I.C.R. 672) or a successor (*Diocese of Hallam Trustee v Connaughton* [1996] I.R.L.R. 505). The applicant may choose either a single comparator or multiple comparators (*Hayward v Cammell Laird Shipbuilders* [1988] I.C.R. 464). If the applicant is unable to name a comparator, they may be granted discovery to enable them to obtain sufficient details—however such discovery may not be used as a "fishing trip" permitting an applicant to trawl through personnel records in search of likely comparators, etc. (*Leverton v Clwyd County Council* [1989] I.C.R. 33). It is also necessary that both the applicant and the comparator(s) are employed either by the same employer at the same establishment, or by the same or associated employer at an establishment at which "common terms and conditions of employment are observed" (*Leverton v Clwyd County Council*). The House of Lords in *British Coal Corporation v Smith* [1996] I.R.L.R. 404 took a broad approach to this, stating that it was sufficient that the terms should be "substantially comparable". On the issue of choice of comparators, it is worth considering the recent case of *South Ayrshire Council v Morton* [2002] I.R.L.R. 256, which permitted employees of one Local Education Authority to choose as comparators employees of another Local Education Authority, and which may extend the range available to certain applicants; although be aware of the Court of Appeal decision in *Robertson v Department of Environment, Food and Rural Affairs* [2005] I.R.L.R. 363, in which it was held that members of one government department may not use members of a different government department as comparators, since each government department has the authority to agree many of the terms and conditions of its civil servants. It would therefore appear that dicta from such as *Lawrence v Regent Office Care Ltd* [2002] I.R.L.R. 822 and *South Ayrshire v Morton* will only be relevant to situations involving authorities controlled by a particular government department, and that cross-departmental claims, and almost certainly similar private sector claims, will be excluded.

The three heads of claim are: *like work*, *work rated as equivalent*, and *work of equal value*.

Like Work

Sections 1(2)(a) and 1(4) of the EqPA 1970 state that an applicant may bring a   **4.1.1** claim if the work they do is "the same" as or of "a broadly similar nature" to the work done by their chosen comparator; and the work will be of a broadly similar nature if any differences are of no practical importance. In the case of *Capper Pass Ltd v Lawton* [1977] I.C.R. 83, the EAT adopted a "broad brush approach" in holding that the work done by the applicant, the directors' cook, was sufficiently similar to the work done by cooks in the works canteen for the claim to succeed.

Likewise, in the case of *Shields v E Coombes (Holdings) Ltd* [1978] I.C.R. 1159 where male counter-hands were paid more than females since, according to the employer, the males acted not only "as a deterrent to attack . . . or other trouble" but also to deal with any such trouble until the police arrived, the Court of Appeal held that since in the previous three years there had been no such trouble, the additional responsibilities of the males were of no practical importance. Consequently, the applicant's claim succeeded. It is of course possible that the very presence of the men had the effect of deterring trouble, and this may well have increased the value of the men over the women from the perspective of the employer; but even so, it would not have affected the actual work undertaken by the men since in practice they were not called upon to deal with any trouble.

Consequently, in the case of *Dugdale v Kraft Foods Ltd* [1976] I.R.L.R. 368 the fact that men were required to work night shifts and the women were not was not held by the EAT to amount to a material difference such as to account for a difference in rates of pay. It is, however, perfectly proper for an employer to pay staff an additional allowance for working unsociable hours (overtime, night shifts, weekend work, etc.), provided that the allowances are a genuine reflection of the additional inconvenience and not merely a way of increasing the men's pay. If both men and women work both day and night shifts, it is arguable that the employer may then pay one rate for day-shift work and another higher rate for night-shift work, since the difference in pay in such a situation would not amount to a difference based on the sex of the worker, and the principles in *Glasgow City Council v Marshall* [2000] I.R.L.R. 272 would apply.

However, in cases where differences relate to genuine differences in levels of responsibility or the consequences of mistakes, these differences may be sufficient to defeat a claim, as in the case of *Eaton Ltd v Nuttall* [1977] I.C.R. 272, where two people, one man and one woman, although carrying out a basically similar job, were dealing with material of different values.

A three stage approach was set out by Bridge L.J. in *Shields v Coombes* for claims based on like work:

> "First, was their work of the same or a broadly similar nature? Second, if so, were any differences between the things she did and the things he did (regard being had to the frequency, nature and extent of such differences) of practical importance . . . Third . . . Can the employer then prove that any variation between the woman's contract and the man's is genuinely due to a material difference (other than the difference of sex) between her case and his?"

Work Rated as Equivalent

4.1.2   If a job evaluation scheme has been carried out and agreed by the parties (*Arnold v Beecham Group* [1982] I.R.L.R. 307) it may be relied upon to found a claim for equal pay. The job evaluation study must, of course, be objective (*Rummler v Dato-Druck GmbH* [1987] I.C.R. 774) and should take into account such factors as effort, skill, decision in terms of the demands made on the worker (s.1(4) of the

EqPA 1970). The court in *Eaton v Nuttall Ltd* confirmed the guidance laid out in the ACAS Guide No.1. Proper implementation and operation of a job evaluation scheme will also provide an employer with a valid defence to claims of equal pay.

Work of Equal Value

Following the case of *EC Commission v United Kingdom* Case 165/82, legislation **4.1.3** was introduced to bring the EqPA 1970 into line with Art.141 and Directive 75/117, this resulted in the Equal Pay (Amendment) Regulations 1983 bringing into effect the third head of claim—work of equal value.

s.1(2)(c) of the EqPA: "where a woman is employed on work which . . . is, in terms of the demands made on her (for instance under such headings as effort, skill and decision), of equal value to that of a man in the same employment . . ."

It is for the applicant to choose under which head they wish to bring their claim, although they must consider whether a claim under "like work" would be more appropriate; they may wish to claim under "equal value" even if prima facie there is an available comparator to enable a claim under "like work" (*Pickstone v Freemans Plc*). This prevents the employer from employing a token male on like work and so avoiding the purpose of the legislation. The issue of the "token male" defence is that if a particular job within a company is done exclusively by women it is not open to those women to bring a claim for equal pay under the head of "like work"—since there are no male comparators—and they would therefore bring their claim under the head of "work of equal value" naming as a comparator a male performing a different job, but which may be argued to be equivalent, etc. If, however, the company employ one man, the "token man", to do the same job as the women the company may then argue that the level of the women's pay is not based on their gender since it is also paid to men performing the same task. Theoretically such an argument would succeed in cases of "like work" and also if the company, rather than the applicant, was able to choose the comparator.

The procedure involved in an equal value claim is as follows. Once the claim form has been submitted to the tribunal office, a copy forwarded to the employer and the employer's response has been received, as with other tribunal claims, ACAS will normally intervene contacting the parties to try to conciliate and reach a settlement. If such a settlement is reached it will be binding, and the matter will go no further. If the ACAS intervention is not successful the issue will normally go to a tribunal to decide initially whether there are, prima facie, reasonable grounds for determining that the work is of equal value. If the tribunal finds that there are no such grounds it may dismiss the case at this stage. If, however, it is held that there are such grounds to proceed the employer may at this stage raise a defence of "genuine material factor". If the employer does raise such a defence at this stage and the defence is successful, the case will be decided on this basis; if the defence is not successful, it is not open to the employer to raise the defence again at a full hearing stage. If the defence fails at this stage the tribunal may then commission an independent expert to carry out a study of the work in question and report to the tribunal. The tribunal would then adjourn, probably for several months, while the expert report is prepared. Although much of the overall format of the expert's procedure is set out in SI 2001/1171, there is no single method of job evaluation laid down by statute and it is for the individual expert to determine the format of their own investigation; this may take the form of interviews with both parties, requiring disclosure via the tribunal of various documents and the production of job descriptions, along with a conclusion. The tribunal will then sit to consider the expert's report. Although it is usual for the tribunal to accept the expert's report in full, it does not have to—there are occasions where parts of the report have been ignored (*Wells v F Smales & Sons Ltd* (1985) 281 I.R.L.I.B. 11), or where the report's conclusion has been rejected entirely (*Tennants Textile Colours Ltd v Todd* [1989] I.R.L.R. 3). At this hearing, if the report is accepted, evidence from the parties will also be heard, cross-examination permitted, and the company may, if it has not already done so, put forward a defence of genuine material factor.

GENUINE MATERIAL FACTOR DEFENCE

4.2   A claim for equal pay may be defeated "if the employer proves that the variation [in pay] is genuinely due to a material factor which is not the difference of sex . . ." (s.1(3) of the EqPA 1970).

The Act goes on to state that in the case of claims for "like work" or "work rated as equivalent" the material factor *must* be a material difference, whereas in a claim for "equal value" the material factor *may* be such a material difference. This would seem to suggest that wider defences are open for claims of "equal value". However case law does not support this contention, and it is probably safe to assume that defences for all three heads of claim are to be treated in the same way. Those material factors which refer specifically to the individual worker will not normally present any problems to the tribunal. It is quite acceptable that factors such as length of service, seniority, responsibility or qualifications may be acceptable as defences.

However, problems may arise with factors which are due to the operation of the employer's business or more general market factors. It is worth considering some of these in some detail:

- Red-circling, where an internal reorganisation reduces the grade of some workers but allows them to retain their previous salary scale. If the red-circling is discriminatory or has been brought about by some past discrimination it will not be permitted as a valid defence (*Snoxell v Vauxhall*

Motors Ltd [1977] I.C.R. 700). In any event, red-circling should not exist any longer than is necessary.

- Collective agreements may be accepted as defences, but they must be genuinely operated, transparent in classification systems and not tainted by any discriminatory attitudes. It is for the employer to rebut any suggestions of discrimination and explain how any job evaluation study worked (see *Rummler v Dato-Druck GmbH* Case 237/85 [1986] E.C.R. 2101, *Danfoss* Case 109/88 [1989] I.R.L.R. 532).

- Performance related pay, commission based, piecework or target related. It is for the employer to show objective justification for any pay differences between men and women, in much the same way as for collective agreements (*Royal Copenhagen* Case C-400/93 [1995] I.R.L.R. 648).

- Part-time working. Traditionally most part-time workers have been women, thus discrimination against part-timers is indirect discrimination against women, and will be prima facie unlawful. However, discrimination in fringe pay, e.g. overtime and shift allowances may be permissible if it can be objectively justified (*Calder v Rowntree Mackintosh Confectionary Ltd* [1993] I.R.L.R. 212, *Degnan v Redcar and Cleveland Borough Council* [2005] I.R.L.R. 615).

- Market forces. At first glance, it would appear that a "market forces" defence should succeed. If a company is able to attract a class or group of people to work for less than others it would make sound financial sense to do so. However, considering the inequalities of bargaining power in employment and the fact that traditionally men have been able to command higher wages than women, to allow such a *carte blanche* defence would obviously seriously undermine both domestic and EU legislation. The approach of the courts is demonstrated in the following cases:

Rainey v Greater Glasgow Health Board [1987] I.C.R. 129: the House of Lords held that market forces may constitute a defence if they amounted to a genuine, objective reason. Although this decision has been criticised, it may be justified if viewed as a form of red-circling, particularly if viewed in the light of the following case.

Benveniste v University of Southampton [1989] I.R.L.R. 122: where the court held that market forces could only amount to a genuine material factor defence for as long as those particular facts existed. Once the market or financial constraints eased, the defence would no longer be available.

Enderby v Frenchay Health Authority [1994] I.C.R. 112: in which the ECJ stated that it was "for the national court to determine, if necessary by applying the principle of proportionality, whether and to what extent the shortage of candidates for a job and the need to attract them by higher pay constitutes an objectively justified economic ground for the difference in pay . . ."

***Ratcliffe v North Yorkshire County Council* [1995] I.R.L.R. 439:** where the House of Lords held that the employer could not cut the wages of employees in order to compete with an external contractor for a competitive tender, thus denying a market forces defence.

Equal Pay—not Fair Pay

4.3   Not all cases which at face value appear to fall within the scope of equal pay legislation will in fact do so, even if it appears to concern a person of one sex doing a similar job to, but being paid less than, a person of the other sex. An example of this may be seen in the case of *Glasgow City Council v Marshall* [2000] I.R.L.R. 272 in which there were eight applicants in the case, seven female and one male. All were instructors in special schools in Scotland and claimed equal pay with teachers working in the same schools. The female instructors named a male teacher as comparator and the male instructor named a female teacher. It was accepted that although teachers had higher qualifications than the instructors, both groups performed the same or broadly similar work. It was therefore for the employers to establish a s.1(3) defence, which they did by arguing both that the pay structure was the result of collective negotiations, and also by introducing statistical evidence to show that the pay structures did not discriminate on the grounds of gender. The House of Lords held that the claim would fail since all instructors, both male and female, were paid the same "instructor" rate as agreed by collective bargaining, and all teachers, whether male or female were paid at the same agreed "teacher" rate—thus, it was held, differences in pay were not the result of discrimination on the grounds of sex. The House of Lords laid down a four-stage approach:

(i) the explanation for differences in pay must be genuine;

(ii) as a question of causation, the less favourable treatment complained of is due to the reason given in that explanation;

(iii) the reason is not the difference of sex, either directly or indirectly; and

(iv) that the factor relied upon is a material difference between the woman's case and the man's case.

As Lord Slynn stated: "This is plainly in essence a claim that the pay is not fair; and not a claim that the pay is unequal because of discrimination between the sexes. As such, it does not fall within the Equal Pay Act 1970."

WHAT IS PAY?

Section 1 of the EqPA 1970 states, in relation to like work, work rated as equival-   **4.4**
ent and work of equal value:

> "(i) if . . . any term of the woman's contract is or becomes less favourable
> to the woman than a term of a similar kind in the contract under
> which that man is employed, that term of the woman's contract shall
> be treated as so modified as not to be less favourable, and
>
> (ii) if . . . at any time the woman's contract does not include a term cor-
> responding to a term benefiting that man included in the contract
> under which he is employed, the woman's contract shall be treated as
> including such a term."

Consequently, the courts have held the following:

- Each term in the contract should be equalised, not just the overall
  package—despite initial fears of "leap-frogging" (*Hayward v Cammell
  Laird Shipbuilders*). Problems may arise in terms of fixed bonus payments
  and attendance allowances in claims for work of equal value. In the case
  of *Degnan v Redcar and Cleveland Borough Council* [2005] I.R.L.R. 615
  the Court of Appeal held that both the fixed bonus payments and the
  attendance allowances were to be treated as forming part of the rate of
  pay in order to determine the hourly rate of the comparators—in this case
  to have treated the bonus and attendance payments as separate issues
  would have disadvantaged the part-time workers whose contracts did not
  contain such a term, but the danger for the courts in this approach is that
  it may come dangerously close to the "lumping together" of terms contrary to the *Hayward* principal.

- Occupational pensions are pay (*Barber v Guardian Royal Exchange* [1990]
  I.C.R. 616). This covers all benefits paid under an occupational pension
  scheme, but does not apply to state pension schemes. Although accepting
  that occupational pensions amount to pay, the Privy Council in *Air
  Jamaica v Charlton* [1999] 1 W.L.R. 1399 were of the opinion that they
  were governed by Trust Law rather than Employment Law.

- The right to join an occupational pension scheme is covered by Art.141
  (*Bilka-Kaufhaus GmbH v Weber von Hartz* [1986] I.R.L.R. 317)—a decision which affected many thousands of UK part-time employees who had
  previously been excluded from such schemes.

- Sick pay is pay (*Rinner-Kuhn v FWW Spezial-Gebaudereinigung GmbH*
  [1989] I.R.L.R. 493).

- Pay for attending training courses is pay (*Arbeiterwohlfahrt der Stadt Berlin eV v Botel* [1992] I.R.L.R. 423).

- Rules governing pay increments are pay (*Nimz v Freie und Hansestadt Hamburg* [1991] I.R.L.R. 222).

- Ex gratia termination payments are pay (*Barber v Guardian Royal Exchange*).

- Redundancy payments are pay (*Barber v Guardian Royal Exchange*).

- Compensation for unfair dismissal is pay (*R. v Secretary of State Ex p. Seymour-Smith and Perez* [1999] E.C.J.).

However, social security payments, including for example unemployment benefit, state pensions, etc., would fall outside the ambit of Art.141 or EqPA 1970.

LIMITATION PERIOD

4.5   Although the EqPA 1970 set a two-year limitation period for claiming arrears of pay, following the ECJ case of *Levez v TH Jennings (Harlow Pools) Ltd* [1999] I.R.L.R. 26, in which it was successfully argued that a two-year limit would offend against the principle of effectiveness, in that it was less favourable than the six-year limitation period governing other actions such as claims for discrimination, a six-year limitation period is now applied (s.2ZB of the EqPA).

Many of the issues referred to above are demonstrated in the case of *Hayward v Cammell Laird Shipbuilders* [1988] I.C.R. 464. Ms Hayward, who was employed as a cook, brought a claim for equal pay, by claiming that her work was of equal value with that of male painters, joiners and insulation fitters employed by the same company. The company argued that although her basic rate of pay was below that of her comparators, she received a number of fringe benefits, which in real terms brought her overall pay package to a comparable level. The Court of Appeal accepted the company's argument, but her appeal was allowed by the House of Lords who held that the individual components of the pay packages of Ms Hayward and her comparators should be equalised, not just the overall total. This approach was confirmed by the ECJ shortly afterwards in *Barber v Guardian Royal Exchange* [1990] I.C.R. 616. One of the problems with such an approach for employ-ers is the issue of leap-frogging; if the individual components of pay are equalised it may then be open to the male comparators to bring an equal pay claim to receive the same level of fringe benefits as the original applicant. It is therefore very import-ant for an employer when determining salary packages to consider this aspect.

The case of *Hayward v Cammell Laird*, which was one of the first to be brought under the head of "equal value" is a useful one, since it is good authority for several propositions: an applicant may choose their own comparator; an applicant may choose multiple comparators if they wish; individual components of pay should be compared and equalised, not just the overall package; the supposed danger of "leap-frogging" does not constitute a defence. A restriction to the *Hayward* approach was however identified in *Degnan v Redcar and Cleveland Borough Council* where the Court of Appeal refused to allow the applicant to choose multiple comparators for the purpose of equalising components of her pay with individual components of the different comparators—to have allowed otherwise would have enabled her to have picked the most advantageous components from a range of comparators' pay structures and have claimed a salary package in excess of any of her comparators.

REMEDIES

It is not the role of the employment tribunal to fix wage levels or to adjust wages **4.6** based on fairness (see *Glasgow City Council v Marshall* above). Their role is to determine whether any factor in the equality clause imposed into every employment contract by the EqPA 1970 has been breached and if so to remedy that breach. The applicant must normally bring a claim within six months from the date on which employment ended (s.2(4) of the EqPA 1970), or if the applicant is a minor or of unsound mind within six months of those circumstances ending (s.11(2A)0 EqPA), or where an employer has deliberately concealed from the applicant information "without knowledge of which the woman could not reasonably have been expected to institute the proceedings" (s.2ZA(2) of the EqPA 1970) within six months of the information being discovered. Subsequent to SI 2003/1656 it is now possible for a successful applicant to recover pay arrears for six years prior to the commencement of proceedings (s.2ZB of the EqPA 1970).

The tribunal has no jurisdiction under either the EqPA 1970 or Art.141 to award the applicant proportionate arrears of pay by deciding that the applicant's work is either more valuable or less valuable than the comparator's and making an award on that basis. At the same time the ECJ firmly rejected the defence raised by the employer in *Murphy v Bord Telecom Eireann* [1988] I.R.L.R. 267 that although the women were paid less than men, their work was of higher value, so could not be compared.

Chapter 5

DISCRIMINATION

CHAPTER OVERVIEW

The law relating to unlawful discrimination in employment has been one of the **CO5** fastest growing areas of English law over the past few years. Much of the impetus has been generated by either EC Directives or decisions of the European courts, both the European Court of Justice and the European Court of Human Rights, although national legislation by way of the Race Relations Act 1976 has led the way in terms of racial discrimination.

Legislation is now in place to make unlawful discrimination on the grounds of:

Sex—gender, sexual orientation, gender reassignment.

Race—colour, race, nationality, ethnic or national origins.

Disability—both physical and mental impairments.

Religion or Belief—both religious and philosophical belief.

And from October 2006, discrimination on the grounds of age will become unlawful. The Employment Equality (Age) Regulations 2006, at the time of writing still at draft stage, propose to prohibit discrimination in employment on the grounds of age and will probably adopt a format similar in style to the recent religion and belief legislation, and probably allow employers defences of justification and genuine occupational requirements. The Regulations will remove the upper age limit for unfair dismissal and redundancy claims, along with statutory sick pay and statutory maternity, adoption and paternity pay.

Some legislative protection is given to those with criminal records, under the Rehabilitation of Offenders Act 1974, and in Northern Ireland it is unlawful to discriminate on the grounds of religion or political opinion (Fair Employment (Northern Ireland) Act 1989).

One important aspect of the recent legislation is the specific inclusion of harassment as a form of direct discrimination. Previously the term "harassment" was not mentioned in any of the discrimination legislation and it was for the courts to try to both define the term and to fit it into the existing statute. Generally they were successful, but owing to the wording of the statute it was necessary to find that the victim had been subjected to a detriment based on the victim's (since most cases arose through sexual harassment) gender. This, as pointed out by the House of Lords in the *MacDonald* case ([2003] I.C.R. 937), was not always easy; if for example an employer, either directly or vicariously, referred to a female employee as "a silly cow" that being gender-specific language may on the face of it amount to sexual harassment, but if that employer also referred to male employees as "silly gits" it is difficult to see how the female employee had suffered a detriment in comparison to male employees—which was a requirement of the statute. If the actual words used were held in themselves to amount to a detriment, as the courts generally did, then the male employees, not being in receipt of gender specific words, would have no equivalent cause of action—a situation which was recognised as being inequitable. The new legislation has put an end to this situation, along with many of the other problems faced by the courts over the past thirty or so years. To understand more fully these problems, although now of historical interest only, it is worth reading the judgments of the various courts in the *MacDonald* case as they attempted to grapple with the realities of life in the face of lack of legislative intervention.

A major result of the new legislation in discrimination is that much of the existing case law is now either redundant or only to be relied upon with caution; we are awaiting authoritative judgments from the higher courts.

Historical Overview

Although there was an amount of anti-discrimination legislation in place in the UK prior to 1970 its scope was very limited and its effect not considerable. The first major piece of relevant legislation was the Equal Pay Act 1970, although its introduction was delayed until 1975 in order to give employers sufficient time to amend their working practices and wage policies. The Sex Discrimination Act followed in 1975, and the Race Relations Act, which closely followed the SDA 1975 in format, in 1976. It was not until 1995 that any, supposedly, comprehensive legislation concerning disability discrimination was passed—the Disability Discrimination Act 1995. All of these Acts have been extensively modified since their introduction. The impetus for much of the anti-discrimination legislation in the UK has been the need to comply with Art.141 (formerly Art.119) of the EC Treaty regarding equal treatment. The Treaty of Amsterdam introduced Art.13 EC concerning discrimination on the grounds of sex, race, ethnic origin, religion, disability, age and sexual orientation. This has given rise to two important EC Directives, the Race Directive 2000/43/EC and the Employment Directive 2000/78/EC. The UK purports to have complied with these Directives by the introduction of secondary legislation amending the SDA 1975, RRA 1976 and DDA 1995 over the past three years. The one area still to be addressed by national legislation in order to comply with the Directives is that of age discrimination, in which the UK has until December 2006 to introduce the relevant changes.

5.1

The implementation in 2000 of the Human Rights Act 1998 would have been expected to produce important changes in the field of discrimination in employment. In particular Art.14 of the European Convention of Human Rights confers the right to enjoy other ECHR rights without discrimination, and defines discrimination more widely than UK national legislation recognises; however, those "other ECHR rights" do not include the right to employment. Were the UK to ratify Protocol 12 of ECHR, the right of enjoyment would then include "any right set forth by law", which of course would include employment issues. As yet the UK has not ratified Protocol 12.

EQUAL OPPORTUNITIES COMMISSION (EOC), THE COMMISSION FOR RACIAL EQUALITY (CRE) AND THE DISABILITY RIGHTS COMMISSION (DRC)

5.2   The EOC was set up under the SDA 1975, and the CRE under the RRA 1976. Both have powers under the relevant Act to conduct formal investigations, to issue non-discrimination notices, to act in the case of discriminatory advertisements, to seek injunction through the civil courts to restrain persistent offenders, and to assist individuals in bringing actions. In 1999, the DRC was formed under the DDA 1995 to perform a similar function to the EOC and CRE. All three commissions are charged with reviewing and recommending on policy and legislative issues. The government White Paper—"Fairness for All"—proposes a single commission to take over all discrimination and human rights issues and this is likely to come about with the passing of the Equality Bill sometime in 2006.

STATUTE

5.3   Since the RRA 1976 follows the SDA 1975 very closely, and much of the case law is interchangeable, it is convenient to examine both sex and race discrimination together, and to look at disability discrimination and other areas of anti-discrimination legislation separately.

5.3.1   Sex and Race Discrimination

Scope of the existing legislation

5.3.1.1   Both the Sex Discrimination Act 1975 and the Race Relations Act 1976 cover all aspects of employment, from the recruitment process, through the working relationship, to the termination.

    Both the SDA and the RRA apply not only to those working under a contract of service, i.e. "employees", but also to those under a contract to personally execute any work or labour, i.e. "self-employed independent contractors" (s.82 of the SDA 1975, s.78 of the RRA 1976). There is no minimum qualifying period necessary in order to gain protection under the legislation, indeed, as stated above, the Acts will apply even before the employment relationship is confirmed.

The Sex Discrimination Act 1975

5.3.1.2   Although the SDA is phrased so as to apply to discrimination against women, it applies equally to discrimination against men (s.2(1) of the SDA 1975), with the exception of special treatment afforded to women in connection with pregnancy and childbirth (s.2(2) of the SDA 1975).

The SDA covers not only discrimination on the grounds of gender, but also discrimination against married persons and civil partners (s.3 of the SDA 1975), although it does not cover discrimination against unmarried persons.

The Race Relations Act 1976

The RRA covers discrimination on racial grounds. "Racial grounds" are defined as "colour, race, nationality or ethnic or national origins" (s.3(1) of the RRA 1976). The court in *Redfern v Serco* [2005] I.R.L.R. 744 confirmed that the term "racial grounds" applies equally to the racial characteristics of the person treated or another person, in other words discrimination on "racial grounds" may cover discrimination aimed at a third party (see also *Weathersfield Ltd (t/a Van & Truck Rentals) v Sargent* [1999] I.R.L.R. 94).

There is much case law to define more precisely the term "ethnic origin". The House of Lords in the case of *Mandla v Dowell Lee* [1983] I.R.L.R. 209 laid down a number of conditions to be considered for any group wishing to bring themselves within the protection of the Act. Both of these the House of Lords held to be essential:

i) a long shared history, of which the group is conscious as distinguishing itself from other groups, and the memory of which it keeps alive; and

ii) a cultural tradition of its own, including family and social customs and manners, often but not necessarily associated with religious observance.

These five conditions were held by the House of Lords to be important factors, but not essential:

iii) a common geographical origin or descent from a small number of common ancestors;

iv) a common language, that need not be exclusive to the group;

v) a common literature;

vi) a common religion, different from neighbouring or surrounding groups; and

vii) being a minority or oppressed or dominant group within a community.

Applying this "test" it was held in *Mandla v Dowell Lee* that Sikhs are an ethnic group.

Subsequent case law has decided the following:

• Jews are an ethnic group (*Seide v Gillette Industries* [1980] I.R.L.R. 427)

- Gypsies (but not "new age travellers") are an ethnic group (*CRE v Dutton* [1989] I.R.L.R. 8)

- Rastafarians are not an ethnic group (*Dawkins v Dept of the Environment* [1993] I.R.L.R. 284)

- Jehovah's Witnesses are not an ethnic or racial group (*Lovell-Badge v Norwich City College* Case 1502237/97)

- RRA 1976 covers the Welsh (*Gwynedd County Council v Jones* [1986] I.C.R. 833)

- Both the Scots and the English are covered by the RRA by reference to "national origins" but not by "ethnic origins" (*Northern Joint Police Board v Power* [1997] I.R.L.R. 610, *Boyce v British Airways* [1997], unreported).

It should be noted that Sikhs, Jews, Jehovah's Witnesses and (presumably) Rastafarians are also protected on the grounds of religion or belief (Employment Equality (Religion or Belief) Regulations 2003).

Positive Discrimination

5.3.2   There is a difference between *positive action* and *positive discrimination*. Examples of positive action would be when an organisation seeks to promote applications for recruitment from certain, perhaps under-represented, sectors of society, e.g. ethnic minorities; or when a company actively encourages sections of its workforce, perhaps women, to attend training courses and seek promotions to positions in which they are under-represented. Such positive action is quite lawful (see for example reg.25 of the The Employment Equality (Religion or Belief) Regulations 2003), as long as the actual selection is made on merit and not on the basis of sex or origin.

Positive discrimination, for example restricting applications for a particular job to women only because women may be under-represented in that position or at that level, however, is generally not lawful (see for example *Jepson and Dyas-Elliott v Labour Party* [1996] I.R.L.R. 116, decided prior to the Sex Discrimination (Election of Candidates) Act 2002). Discrimination in favour of one sex or any particular ethnic group will amount to discrimination against the other sex or other ethnic groups, and thus be contrary to the SDA 1975 or RRA 1976.

However, Art.2(4) of the Equal Treatment Directive allows for the introduction of "measures to promote equal opportunity for men and women, in particular by removing existing inequalities which affect women's opportunities". The ECJ have considered the extent to which this may allow positive discrimination in two cases. In the case of *Kalanke v Freie Hansestadt Bremen* [1995] I.R.L.R. 660, the court held that a rule which automatically gave priority to an equally qualified woman for a position in which women were under-represented, was contrary to the Equal Treatment Directive and would not fall within Art.2(4) of the Directive.

In the later case of *Marschall v Land Nordrhein Westfalen* [1998] I.R.L.R. 39, the ECJ appear to have adopted a different approach, stating that such a rule may not breach the Equal Treatment Directive if there is a guarantee that all candidates will be subject to an objective assessment which takes into account all the factors specific to the individual candidate, and the criteria used in the assessment are not in themselves discriminatory. It may be argued that the reasoning in *Marschall* is, in itself, self-defeating; but it perhaps reflects a wider current European view that some positive discrimination in certain circumstances may not be harmful.

Under the Treaty of Amsterdam, amendments to Art.141 allow member states to adopt measures that provide for "specific advantages" to an under-represented sex in order to achieve full equality in practice. Such measures may therefore amount to positive discrimination, and indicate a pragmatic approach by the EU in seeking to achieve equality between men and women.

Sexual Orientation

The Court of Appeal in *R v Ministry of Defence Ex p Smith* [1996] 1 All E.R. 257 **5.3.3** stated that the legislation was aimed at gender discrimination, not orientation discrimination. In the case of *Smith v Gardner Merchant Ltd* [1998] I.R.L.R. 510, the Court of Appeal held that the SDA 1975 would apply in the case of a male homosexual harassed because of his sexual orientation if it could be shown that a female homosexual would not have been similarly treated—in other words if his treatment was because he was a man. In the case of *Advocate General for Scotland v MacDonald; Pearce v Mayfield Secondary School Governing Body* [2003] I.C.R. 937, the events of which occurred prior to the implementation of SI 2003/1661, see below, the House of Lords confirmed that the SDA 1975 did not cover sexual orientation, despite some inventive arguments from the EAT.

However, from December 2003 the position has become clearer; the introduction of The Employment Equality (Sexual Orientation) Regulations 2003 (SI 2003/1661) giving effect to the EC Directive on discrimination makes both direct and indirect discrimination on the grounds of sexual orientation unlawful (reg.3), along with discrimination by way of victimisation (reg.4) and harassment on the grounds of sexual orientation (reg.5). Sexual orientation is defined in reg.2(1) as:

"sexual orientation towards—

(a) persons of the same sex;
(b) persons of the opposite sex; or
(c) persons of the same and of the opposite sex".

Gender Reassignment

5.3.4   The law concerning transsexuals, those who have undergone, or intend to undergo gender reassignment has also been covered by legislation. The ECJ in *P v S and Cornwall County Council* [1996] I.R.L.R. 445 ruled that the Equal Treatment Directive would apply in such situations. Likewise, the EAT decision in *Chessington World of Adventure v Reed* [1998] I.R.L.R. 56 makes it clear that the SDA 1975 will apply in the case of discrimination against transsexuals. The relevant legislation is The Sex Discrimination (Gender Reassignment) Regulations 1999 (SI 1999/1102) amending the SDA 1975 to specifically include discrimination on the grounds of gender reassignment, in so far as the applicant "intends to undergo, is undergoing or has undergone gender reassignment" (s.2A(1) of the SDA 1975).

Under both the SDA 1975 and the RRA 1976 there are four forms of discrimination: *direct discrimination, indirect discrimination, victimisation* and *harassment*.

Direct Discrimination

5.3.5   A person discriminates against another if on the grounds of the other's sex or race the person treats the other less favourably than they treat or would treat other persons of a different sex or race (s.1 of the SDA 1975 and RRA 1976).

Case law has defined this as the "but for" test—would the victim have been treated differently but for their sex or race? (*James v Eastleigh Borough Council* [1990] I.R.L.R. 288)

The motive for the discrimination is irrelevant (*James v Eastleigh*), thus direct discrimination brought about by good intentions or even unintentionally is still discrimination for the purposes of both Acts (although on this point it may be worth considering dicta in *Advocate General for Scotland v MacDonald; Pearce v Mayfield Secondary School Governing Body* [2003] I.C.R. 937, HL).

Segregation on racial grounds constitutes direct discrimination (s.1(2) of the RRA 1976), but allowing segregation to occur is apparently not actionable (*Pel Ltd v Modgill* [1980] I.R.L.R. 142).

There is case law to suggest that the *de minimis* rule should apply to discrimination—that is, if the act complained of is trivial, it need not constitute actionable discrimination (*Peake v Automotive Products* [1978] Q.B. 233), however in recent years the courts have been reluctant to accept, let alone extend, this principle in practice. In the case of *Gill v El Vino Co Ltd* [1983] I.R.L.R. 206, Eveleigh L.J. stated:

> "I find it very difficult to invoke the maxim *de minimus non curat lex* in a situation where that which has been denied to the plaintiff is the very thing that Parliament seeks to provide, namely facilities and services on an equal basis".

Harassment

Previously, neither the SDA 1975 nor the RRA 1976 contained any specific ref- **5.3.6**
erence to harassment, and the courts found it necessary to define harassment as
direct discrimination and develop the concept via, at times confusing and contradictory, case law. Implementation of the EC Equal Treatment Framework
Directive (2000/78/EC) and Race Directive (2000/43/EC) have resulted in national
legislation for the first time defining harassment.

The RRA 1976 now states:

> "Section 3A Harassment
>
> (1) A person subjects another to harassment in any circumstances rele-
> vant for the purposes of any provision referred to in section 1(1B)
> where, on grounds of race or ethnic or national origins, he engages in
> unwanted conduct which has the purpose or effect of—
>
>> (a) violating that other person's dignity, or
>> (b) creating an intimidating, hostile, degrading, humiliating or
>> offensive environment for him.
>
> (2) Conduct shall be regarded as having the effect specified in paragraph
> (a) or (b) of subsection (1) only if, having regard to all the circum-
> stances, including in particular the perception of that other person, it
> should reasonably be considered as having that effect".

The SDA 1975 has been amended since October 1, 2005 by SI 2005/2467—The
Employment Equality (Sex Discrimination) Regulations 2005— with the insertion of a new section:

> "Harassment, including sexual harassment
> 4A.
>
> (1) For the purposes of this Act, a person subjects a woman to harass-
> ment if—
>
>> (a) on the ground of her sex, he engages in unwanted conduct that
>> has the purpose or effect—
>>> (i) of violating her dignity, or
>>> (ii) of creating an intimidating, hostile, degrading, humiliat-
>>> ing or offensive environment for her,
>>
>> (b) he engages in any form of unwanted verbal, non-verbal or
>> physical conduct of a sexual nature that has the purpose or
>> effect—
>>> (i) of violating her dignity, or

(ii) of creating an intimidating, hostile, degrading, humiliat-
ing or offensive environment for her, or
(c) on the ground of her rejection of or submission to unwanted
conduct of a kind mentioned in paragraph (a) or (b), he treats
her less favourably than he would treat her had she not rejected,
or submitted to, the conduct.

(2) Conduct shall be regarded as having the effect mentioned in sub-
paragraph (i) or (ii) of subsection (1)(a) or (b) only if, having regard
to all the circumstances, including in particular the perception of the
woman, it should reasonably be considered as having that effect."

Subsection 3 applies to harassment on the grounds of gender re-assignment.

Subsection 5 makes clear that the legislation applies equally to men and
women.

The new legislation appears comprehensive, but as always it will be for the
courts to interpret in terms of application. It is clear, however, in terms of sexual
harassment that the issues raised by the House of Lords in *Advocate General for
Scotland v MacDonald; Pearce v Mayfield Secondary School Governing Body*
[2003] I.C.R. 937 concerning the ambiguity of the term "sexual harassment" and
the implied question of motive have been addressed.

It is not yet clear how much relevance and weight the courts will place on existing case law when interpreting the new legislation, but it is likely that the two
issues referred to below will be relevant:

- a single act, if sufficiently serious, may constitute harassment (*Bracebridge Engineering Ltd v darby* [1990] I.R.L.R. 3).

- a single verbal comment, if sufficiently serious, may constitute harassment (*In Situ Cleaning Co Ltd v heads* [1995] I.R.L.R. 4).

In this respect, bear in mind that if the harassment consists of a "course of
conduct" action may be possible under the Protection from Harassment Act 1997
which creates both civil and criminal liability. The recent Court of Appeal ruling
in *Majrowski v Guys and St Thomas' NHS Trust* [2005] I.R.L.R. 340 indicates that
an employer may be vicariously liable under the Act for actions of their employees undertaken in the course of business.

Detriment

5.3.6.1   Firstly, s.6 of the SDA 1975 and s.4 of the RRA 1976 both state that the discrimination must subject the victim to either dismissal or "any other detriment".
In the case of *De Souza v Automobile Association* [1986] I.R.L.R. 103, the Court
of Appeal held that to prove racial harassment it was not sufficient to racially
insult a coloured employee, even if that insult caused him distress, it would be

necessary to prove that the employee was subjected to some "other detriment"—under the now existing legislation this is no longer necessary, it is the actual racial harassment which is actionable (s.4(2A) of the RRA 1976). In the case of *Snowball v Gardner Merchant Ltd* [1987] I.C.R. 719, the EAT allowed evidence to be admitted to show that due to the victim's attitude towards sexual matters, the harassment may not in itself have caused a detriment. However, the later case of *In Situ Cleaning Co Ltd v Heads* [1995] I.R.L.R. 4 doubted this line of reasoning by stating that detriment means no more than disadvantage, and thus the harassment itself becomes the detriment. In effect this reasoning is supported by the new amendment to the SDA 1975 which makes the actual sexual harassment actionable in its own right (s.6(2A) of the SDA 1975), although it is likely that evidence of the type admitted in *Snowball v Gardner Merchant* will still be necessary in determining the level of compensation to be awarded. This was the case in *Wileman v Minilec Engineering Ltd* [1988] I.R.L.R. 144 in which details of the victim's apparent attitude to sex and nudity were permitted to be brought as evidence that she had suffered little injury through the harassment. This issue is not without its problems, on the one hand since sexual harassment must be viewed at least in part subjectively, that is from the point of view of the victim, the court must attempt in order to determine the level of compensation payable to gauge the level of detriment suffered by the victim, since to do otherwise would in effect lead to a "scale of charges" for harassment; on the other hand, the allowing of such evidence must at times deter victims from bringing or pursuing such claims, in that they may at times feel it is they, rather than the aggressor, who are "on trial".

Comparators

The final issue to be considered is that of the comparator. Unlike a claim for equal pay, an action for direct discrimination does not require that the complainant must identify an actual comparator. In all but one situation, it was sufficient to apply the "but for" test and compare the action taken against the complainant with the action that would have been taken against a hypothetical comparator. **5.3.6.2**

It is also arguable that the definition of harassment in the new legislation makes the need for any comparator redundant. The actual wording of the newly inserted sections makes no mention of comparison, but the use of gender-specific terms ("woman", "she", etc.) and the inclusion of the issue in (in the case of sexual harassment) a statute which until very recently could have been described as "discrimination on the grounds of gender" may perhaps imply otherwise.

The situation (mentioned above) that was the exception to the comparator issue is that of pregnancy and childbirth. Previously the courts had considered that the proper comparator for a pregnant woman should be a sick man. However, the ECJ in the case of *Webb v EMO Air Cargo Ltd* [1994] I.R.L.R. 482 held that "pregnancy is not in any way comparable with a pathological condition", thus there is no requirement for a comparator, either real or hypothetical. The ECJ also held that discrimination on the grounds of pregnancy amounted to direct discrimination.

A note of caution was however sounded by the House of Lords when the case was returned from the ECJ; Lord Keith did suggest that the dismissal of a pregnant woman may not be unlawful if the employee had been hired on a fixed-term contract, rather than on an open ended, ongoing basis. Lord Keith's reasoning appears to be that in such a situation the woman would not be dismissed on account of the pregnancy, but because of her unavailability to complete the contract for which she was engaged. In the case of *Carunana v Manchester Airport Plc* [1996] I.R.L.R. 378, the court chose to treat this exception as applying only where the woman would not be available for any part of the contract.

Victimisation

5.3.7   Victimisation occurs when an employer takes action amounting to discrimination against an employee, because the employee has brought proceedings, given evidence, or done anything under SDA 1975, RRA 1976, EqPA 1970, or ss.62–65 of the Pensions Act 1995, or intends to do so (s.4 of the SDA 1975, s.2 of the RRA 1976). For an example see the case of *Aziz v Trinity Street Taxis Ltd* [1988] I.C.R. 534. The later case of *Nagarajan v London Regional Transport* [1999] I.R.L.R. 572 makes it clear that it is not necessary that the respondent acted with the intention of victimising, it is sufficient that they did the act complained of and that the act was an important cause of the decision.

Indirect Discrimination

5.3.8   Indirect discrimination is defined in s.1(1)(b) of the SDA 1975 and s.1(1)(b) of the RRA 1976 as applying a requirement or condition to all employees or potential employees, but the proportion of any particular sex or race who can comply with the condition is considerably smaller than the proportion of those from outside that sex or race who can comply, and the employer cannot justify that requirement, and the complainant's inability to comply with the requirement is to their detriment. This definition was valid in an employment context until the recent amendments to both the RRA 1976 and SDA 1975, and appears still to be valid in terms of certain aspects of the RRA 1976 (see below) and to situations not covered by s.1(3) of the SDA 1975 and s.1(1B) of the RRA 1976 (both concerning discrimination in the employment field).

The phrase "can comply" was considered in the case of *Mandla v Dowell Lee* [1983] I.C.R. 385, where Lord Fraser was of the opinion that it should not be given its literal meaning, i.e. "can physically", but should be taken to mean "can in practice" or "can consistently with the customs and cultural conditions of the racial group".

However, the recent changes to both the SDA 1975 and the RRA 1976 have amended that definition in relation to discrimination in the employment field.

The relevant section in the SDA 1975 is s.1(2)(b) which now reads:

> "(b) he applies to her a provision, criterion or practice which he applies or would apply equally to a man, but—
>
> > (i) which puts or would put women at a particular disadvantage when compared with men,
> >
> > (ii) which puts her at that disadvantage, and
> >
> > (iii) which he cannot show to be a proportionate means of achieving a legitimate aim."

The equivalent section in the RRA 1976 is s.1(1A) which reads:

> ". . . he applies to that other person a provision, criterion or practice which he applies or would apply equally to persons not of the same race or ethnic or national origins as that other, but—
>
> > (a) which puts or would put persons of the same race or ethnic origin or national origins as that other at a particular disadvantage when compared with other persons,
> >
> > (b) which puts that other at that disadvantage, and
> >
> > (c) which he cannot show to be a proportionate means of achieving a legitimate aim.

As yet there is very little authoritative case law to determine how the courts will interpret the new definition, although some of the problems associated with the previous definitions (see for example "pool of comparators" below) should now no longer be relevant.

On the issue of justification in a case of indirect sex discrimination (*Hardys & Hansons Plc v Lax* [2005] I.R.L.R. 726), the Court of Appeal held that "objective justification" means nothing more than "reasonable necessity" and it is for the tribunal to determine whether in the particular circumstances, having examined the working practices of the employer along with their commercial and business needs, the practice is reasonable.

There is however a problem concerning indirect discrimination within the RRA 1976. The original definition contained within s.1(1) applies to discrimination "on racial grounds", which is defined in s.3(1) as "colour, race, nationality or ethnic or national origins", whereas the definition within s.1(1A) above makes no mention of colour or nationality. This is because the wording of s.1(1A) is taken from the EC Directive which makes no direct reference to either colour or nationality. It therefore appears that the courts will have to apply the original definitions in such cases, which may lead to inconsistencies.

5.3.8.1   Pool of Comparators: Prior to the amendments to both the RRA 1976 and the SDA 1975 it was necessary in order to prove indirect discrimination to show that the proportion of persons to which the complainant belongs who could not comply with the imposed requirement was considerably smaller than the proportion of persons from outside the complainants group who could comply. Thus it was necessary to identify a pool of comparators. Although in most situations it should now no longer be necessary to adopt this approach, in the case of indirect discrimination on the grounds of colour or nationality it would appear that this approach must still be followed.

The Court of Appeal in *Jones v University of Manchester* [1993] I.C.R. 474 warned against sub-dividing or otherwise manipulating the pool in order to bring about a particular result. It held that the relevant pool is the number of persons referred to in the legislation, i.e. the number of persons to whom the requirement has been or would be applied to by the employer.

5.3.8.2   Examples of indirect discrimination have included:

- Discrimination against part-time workers, the majority of whom are women (*R v Secretary of State for Employment, Ex p. EOC* [1994] 2 W.L.R. 409, which resulted in the removal of hour thresholds for certain employment rights by SI 1995/31).

- An age restriction "must be between 17–28" was indirectly discriminatory against women because of family commitments (*Price v Civil Service Commission* [1978] I.C.R. 27).

- A rule that the successful candidate should not have young children was held to be indirectly discriminatory against women (*Thorndyke v Bell Fruit Ltd* [1979] I.R.L.R. 1).

- A contractual requirement to work full-time may be indirectly discriminatory against women (*Home Office v Holmes* [1984] I.C.R. 678, although see the later case of *Greater Glasgow Health Board v Carey* [1987] I.R.L.R. 484).

- The inclusion of a mobility clause in the employment contract may be discriminatory against women (*Meade-Hill v British Council* [1995] I.R.L.R. 478).

The Issue of Proof

5.3.9   Effect was given to the Burden of Proof Directive 97/80/EC by the insertion of s.63A of the SDA 1975, s.54A of the RRA 1976, reg.29 of the Employment Equality (Sexual Orientation) Regulations 2003 and reg.29 of the Employment Equality (Religion or Belief) Regulations 2003. The effect is that it is no longer necessary for the complainant to prove their case, merely to establish the facts of the complaint. The burden of proof then moves to the person alleged to have discriminated, to rebut the presumption of discrimination. If they are not able to do so, the tribunal should then find discrimination. Following the implementation of the regulations there was some confusion as to how exactly they should be applied until guidance was given in their operation in the case of *Barton v Investec Henderson Crosthwaite Securities Ltd* [2003] I.C.R. 1205, but later tribunals have tended to modify that guidance with the effect that employers have at times been placed under a less strict burden. In the recent case of *Igen Ltd v Wong* [2005] I.R.L.R. 258 the Court of Appeal has reiterated and strengthened the *Barton* guidelines. The format is that the appellant makes out a prima facie case by proving facts which in the absence of a satisfactory explanation will amount to discrimination. The burden then shifts to the respondent who must show on the balance of probabilities that the treatment was "in no sense whatsoever" on the grounds of the alleged discrimination. The tribunal should expect "cogent evidence to discharge that burden of proof". Prior to the hearing, the complainant is entitled to send a questionnaire to the respondent requiring them to explain, amongst other things, why they received the particular treatment complained of. The format of the questionnaire is laid down by statute (depending upon the head of discrimination concerned), and failure by an employer to reply or in the event of equivocal answers the tribunal is entitled (again by statute depending upon the head of discrimination complained of) to draw "any inference from that fact that it considers it just and equitable to draw, including an inference that he committed an unlawful act".

Statistical evidence may be used by the tribunal in cases of indirect discrimination, generally it will be necessary in cases requiring the pool of comparators application and may continue to apply to the later definition (s.1(2)(b)(i) of the SDA 1975, s.1(1A)(a) of the RRA 1976, etc.). Statistical evidence may also be used in cases of direct discrimination following *West Midlands Passenger Transport Executive v Singh* [1988] I.C.R. 614 to point towards imbalances between the sexes, races, etc. which may indicate issues of discrimination. Such evidence may also be used towards rebutting an employer's argument that they had in place an effective equal opportunities policy.

Dress Codes

Whilst on the one hand the employer may issue rules regarding dress and uniform, and whilst these rules will normally form part of the work rules—breach of which may put an employee in breach of the employment contract—on the other hand, the rules themselves must not contravene discrimination laws.   **5.3.10**

Dress codes and sex discrimination

In terms of sex discrimination, the courts have adopted the approach that dress rules will not normally breach discrimination law if they apply a similar standard   **5.3.10.1** of conventionality to both men and women (*Smith v Safeway Plc* [1996] I.R.L.R. 456 interpreting *Schmidt v Austick Bookshops Ltd* [1977] I.R.L.R. 360), arguably as standards of conventionality naturally change over time there may be limited value in factual case law as future precedent. An issue that was raised in *Schmidt* was further examined in the case of *Burrett v West Birmingham Health Authority* [1994] I.R.L.R. 7, namely that although the dress codes for men and women were different, it could not be said that the appellant had been sufficiently disadvantaged to amount to a "detriment". In the case of Ms Burrett who was a nurse whose uniform included a cap, whereas the male nurses uniform did not, she was later disciplined for not wearing the cap—which the court accepted was a detriment—the court did not accept however that this detriment was brought about by discriminatory action of the employer, but by her refusal to obey a lawful instruction, part of her work rules.

Dress codes and race discrimination

5.3.10.2 Case law concerning racial discrimination is not quite so straightforward. Each case must be considered on its own facts and merits: in one case a ban on beards was not held to be unlawful discrimination against Sikhs (*Singh v Rowntree Mackintosh Ltd* [1979] I.R.L.R. 199, a case concerning health and safety measures in a food handling operation), whereas in another case a Sikh woman, dismissed for carrying a dagger contrary to the employer's work rules, was unlawfully discriminated against (*Kaur v Butcher & Baker Foods Ltd* Case 1304563/97 concerning a rule prohibiting jewellery in a food handling operation).

Vicarious Liability

5.3.11 An employer may normally be held vicariously liable for acts committed by their employees in the course of their employment (s.41 of the SDA 1975, s.32 of the RRA 1976). Under earlier case law, it was possible for an employer to avoid liability by arguing that it was no part of the employees' job or duty to commit the acts complained of, and consequently, such acts were not committed in the course of employment (see *Irving v Post Office* [1987] I.R.L.R. 289).

However, the Court of Appeal in *Jones v Tower Boot Co Ltd* [1997] I.R.L.R. 168 rejected this approach, stating that the restrictive tortious definition of "in the course of employment" should not apply to cases of discrimination, but that the words should be given the broader definition a layman would apply to them (*Jones* is an interesting case to read in respect of the ways the lower courts sought to avoid the earlier binding decision in *Irving*). This purposive approach has been followed in such cases as *Chief Constable of the Lincolnshire Police v Stubbs* [1999] I.R.L.R. 81, where the EAT held that, since work related social functions are an extension of employment, a male police officer who sexually harassed a female colleague at both an after work gathering and at an organised leaving party was acting "in the course of his employment".

The principles of vicarious liability in discrimination cases had also been extended by the EAT decision in *Burton and Rhule v De Vere Hotels* [1996] I.R.L.R. 596, in which it was held that an employer "subjects" an employee to the detriment of harassment when, in circumstances which he can control, he causes or permits the discrimination or harassment to take place—however, in *Advocate General for Scotland v MacDonald*, the House of Lords disapproved *Burton* on this issue, holding that an employer should only be liable for acts of their own employees, and not for actions of third parties.

Defences

It is a complete defence under s.7 of the SDA 1975 and s.5 of the RRA 1976 to a complaint of sexual or racial discrimination that the discrimination occurred where sex or race is a genuine occupational qualification. Genuine occupational qualifications exist under the SDA 1975 (including gender reassignment), but in terms of sexual orientation under SI 2003/1661, and religion or belief under SI 2003/1660 a potentially broader term of "genuine occupational requirements" is used. The RRA 1976 uses both terms.   **5.3.12**

The courts have tended to interpret the words "genuine occupational qualification" strictly, some examples are:

- For reasons of authenticity in dramatic performances (s.7(2)(a) of the SDA 1975).

- For reasons of authenticity where food or drink is provided (s.5(2)(c) of the RRA 1976, e.g. a Chinese waiter/waitress in a Chinese restaurant).

- The refusal to employ a female assistant in a menswear shop was held to be unlawful, since any intimate contact with customers could be undertaken by other male staff (*Wylie v Dee & Co (Menswear) Ltd* [1978] I.R.L.R. 103).

- The refusal to employ a male assistant in a women's dress shop was held to be unlawful, since any intimate contact with customers could have been performed by other female staff (*Etam Plc v Rowan* [1989] I.R.L.R. 150).

In terms of defences for indirect discrimination, the SDA 1975 allows the defence of justification: "which he cannot show to be justifiable irrespective of the sex of the person to whom it is applied . . ." (s.1(2)(b)(ii) of the SDA 1975); whilst the RRA 1976 talks of "proportionality": ". . . which he cannot show to be a proportionate means of achieving a legitimate aim" (s.1(1A)(c) of the RRA 1976).

The best defence for an employer is that they have in place a comprehensive and effective equal opportunities policy—but such a policy must be properly promulgated and enforced among the workforce (*Balgobin v London Borough of Tower Hamlets* [1987] I.R.L.R. 401).

DISABILITY DISCRIMINATION

5.4   The Disability Discrimination Act 1995 has been amended by SI 2003/1673 with effect from October 2004 to give effect to the relevant parts of Council Directive 2000/78/EC; some of the changes are minor, consisting of little more than renumbering of sections, but others have much wider and more important consequences, for example the exemption which existed for employers of under 15 employees has now been removed. One outcome of these changes is that much of the existing case law is now obsolete, statute having moved on.

Under s.3A of the Disability Discrimination Act 1995 (DDA),

"a person discriminates against a disabled person if—(a) for a reason which relates to the disabled person's disability, he treats him less favourably than he treats or would treat others to whom that reason does not or would not apply, and (b) he cannot show that the treatment in question is justified."

However, the Act goes on to state that such treatment cannot be justified if it amounts to direct discrimination (s.3A(4)). Direct discrimination is defined in s.3A(5):

"A person directly discriminates against a disabled person if, on the ground of the disabled person's disability, he treats the disabled person less favourably than he treats or would treat a person not having that particular disability whose relevant circumstances, including his abilities, are the same as, or not materially different from, those of the disabled person".

There is no requirement that the discrimination must be deliberate or intentional. The comparator in a direct disability discrimination claim should be someone without the claimant's disability, but with similar "relevant circumstances" and abilities.

Disability is defined as being a physical or mental impairment which has a substantial and long-term adverse effect on the ability to carry out normal day-to-day activities (s.1(1) of the DDA 1995). Schedule 1, s.4(1) states that an impairment is to be taken to affect the ability of the person concerned to carry out normal day-to-day activities only if it affects one of the following.

(a) mobility;

(b) manual dexterity;

(c) continence;

(d) physical co-ordination;

(e) ability to lift, carry or otherwise move everyday objects;

(f) speech, hearing or eyesight;

(g) memory or ability to concentrate, learn or understand; or

(h) perception of the risk of physical danger.

Schedule1, s.6(1) states:
"An impairment which would be likely to have a substantial adverse effect on the ability of the person concerned to carry out normal day-to-day activities, but for the fact that measures are being taken to treat or correct it, is to be treated as having that effect".

Although the statute provides guidance and the tribunal is likely to have the benefit of medical advice, the decision on whether an individual qualifies for protection under the Act is a question of fact for the tribunal based on the facts of the individual case: in the case of *Whitbread Hotel Co Ltd v Bayley* EAT 03/04/06, the court held that a clinical diagnosis of severe dyslexia amounted to a disability for the purpose of the Act, whereas, in *Vance v Royal Mail Group Plc* EAT 07/04/06, a postman suffering osteoarthritic changes in his hip and chronic back-pain, which meant that he was unable to do housework (although it was conceded that housework was not part of his normal day-to-day activity) without difficulty was held not to qualify as disabled.

Long term effects are defined in Sch.1, s.2 as those which have lasted or are likely to last for 12 months or longer, and subs.2(2) states that if an impairment ceases to have adverse effects on a person's ability to carry out normal day-to-day activities, it is to be treated as continuing to have those effects if the effects are likely to recur.

Under the original 1995 Act, progressive conditions such as cancer or HIV infection may not have been viewed as a disability until such time as the effects impaired normal day-to-day activities; this is no longer the case, progressive conditions are now treated as amounting to a disability if the condition "is likely to result in" such an impairment (Sch.1, s.8).

The Disability Discrimination Act (as amended) is broader than the original 1995 Act; it covers direct discrimination, indirect discrimination (although not stated in similar terms as the SDA 1975, RRA 1976, etc.) and harassment; it applies to all employers (with very limited exceptions) regardless of size of organisation; it specifically includes "non-employees" such as contract or agency workers (s.4B).

Section 4A of the DDA 1995 imposes on an employer a duty to make reasonable adjustments to such things as premises, equipment, allocation of duties, working hours, time off, instructions, etc. Failure to make such adjustments amounts in itself to discrimination (s.3A(2)). Section 18B gives guidance on what factors should be taken into account when determining whether it is reasonable to make such adjustments and what adjustments are reasonable. Section 18B(1) states that when determining whether it is reasonable for a particular employer to carry out such adjustments, regard should be given to such factors as the practicality of the adjustment, the costs of the adjustment, the resources of the employer, and the nature and size of the business. Section 18B(2) lists examples of steps an employer may need to take in order to comply with s.4A:

(a) making adjustments to premises;

(b) allocating some of the disabled person's work to other employees;

(c) transferring the disabled person to an existing vacancy;

(d) altering his hours of work or training;

(e) assigning him to a different place of work or training;

(f) allowing him to be absent for periods of rehabilitation, assessment or treatment;

(g) giving or arranging training or mentoring to the disabled person or to another;

(h) acquiring or modifying equipment;

(i) modifying instruction or reference material;

(j) modifying procedures for testing or assessment;

(k) providing a reader or interpreter;

(l) providing supervision or other support;

As yet, there is very limited case law to fully interpret all the aspects of the law as it now stands in this area, and reliance on older case law may mislead. However, the following may be instructive:

- An employer should plan ahead and consider the needs of future disabled employees (*Williams v Channel 5 Engg Services Ltd* Case 230136/97).

- The treatment afforded a disabled employee should be that treatment with which a reasonable employer would have responded, and the test to be applied is similar to that of the "band of reasonable responses" used in unfair dismissal cases (*Jones v The Post Office* [2001] I.R.L.R. 384, confirmed in *Williams v J Walter Thompson Group Ltd* [2005] I.R.L.R. 376.

- In the case of an employee dismissed for absence brought about by their disability, the proper comparator was a non-disabled employee absent through illness for a similar length of time (*Clark v Novacold Ltd* [1998] I.R.L.R. 420).

- It may be unlawful to select an applicant for redundancy on account of their disability, even where the employer takes the view that they must retain the most flexible workforce in order to meet their obligations (*Morse* v *Wiltshire County Council* [1998] I.R.L.R. 352).

- The duty to make adjustments does not extend to a duty to provide a carer for a disabled employee (*Kenny v Hampshire Constabulary* [1999] I.C.R. 27).

- The duty to make adjustments may only arise once an employer knows or could reasonably be expected to know of the worker's disability (*O'Neill v Symm & Co Ltd* [1998] I.R.L.R. 233), this issue is now covered by s.4A(3) and consequently the case of *HJ Heinz Co Ltd v Kenrick* [2000] I.R.L.R. 144 should not be relied upon. However, it is likely that the courts will interpret the phrase "could reasonably be expected to know" purposively.

- It is not necessary to categorise a condition as either a physical or a mental impairment in order to bring the sufferer within the DDA 1995, the impairment may be an illness or a condition arising from an illness (*Millar v Board of Inland Revenue* [2006] I.R.L.R. 112 in which the doctor could find no physical cause for a condition arising following a workplace accident).

- Those suffering from general learning difficulties may also be covered by the DDA 1995 (*Dunham v Ashford Windows Ltd* [2005] I.R.L.R. 608).

It is clear from the above that the treatment afforded to a disabled person may in other circumstances amount to positive discrimination, which in other situations may itself be actionable.

The Disability Rights Commission has produced a "Code of Practice: Employment and Occupation" in 2004 which gives much guidance in this area; it does not have the force of law, but should be taken into account by tribunals.

RELIGION OR BELIEF

There is as yet no authoritative case law in the area of religion or belief; the **5.5** Employment Equality (Religion or Belief) Regulations 2003 (SI 2003/1660) make it unlawful in an employment context to discriminate by way of direct discrimination (reg.3(1)(a)), indirect discrimination (reg.3(1)(b)), victimisation (reg.4) or harassment (reg.5) based on the religion, religious belief or similar philosophical belief. The regulations apply to potential employees (reg.6(1)), employees (reg.6(2)), contract workers (reg.8), agency workers (by the client company reg.8, or by the agency reg.18), those undertaking vocational training (reg.17) and ex-employees (reg.21). The employer will have liability for anything done relevant to these regulations by any employee, whether such action is with or without the employer's knowledge or approval, if it is carried out "in the course of employment" (reg.22). The Regulations use the extended definition of employment, reg.2(3) stating: " 'employment' means employment under a contract of service or of apprenticeship or a contract personally to do any work, and related expressions shall be construed accordingly".

Due to the current lack of authoritative case law it is perhaps unclear how widely the Regulations may be applied, but the DTI has issued "Explanatory Notes for the Employment Equality (Sexual Orientation) Regulations 2003 and the Employment Equality (Religion or Belief) Regulations 2003" which give both direct assistance whilst leaving interpretation of such phrases as "worthy of respect in a democratic society" (para.12) open to the courts to determine.

Prior to the coming into effect of the Regulations, there has been no legislative protection against direct discrimination on the grounds of religion (with arguably two exceptions—Sikhs (*Mandla v Dowell Lee*[1983] I.R.L.R. 209) and Jews (*Seide v Gillette Industries* [1980] I.R.L.R. 427)—since in most cases it will not be possible to differentiate between the religion and the ethnic origin, although should someone not born of, say, the Sikh ethnic origin convert to the Sikh religion it would have been proper for the court to find that they were not covered by the RRA 1976), although discrimination on the basis of religion may have amounted to unlawful indirect discrimination on the grounds of race.

One potentially problematic area of the Regulations is the issue of indirect discrimination. Regulation 3(1) states:

> "For the purposes of these Regulations, a person (A) discriminates against another person (B) if—
> (b) A applies to B a provision, criterion or practice which he applies or would apply equally to persons not of the same religion or belief as B, but—
>
> > (i) which puts or would put persons of the same religion or belief as B at a particular disadvantage when compared with other persons,
> > (ii) which puts B at that disadvantage, and
> > (iii) which A cannot show to be a proportionate means of achieving a legitimate aim."

In effect, although, apart from the limited exceptions contained in reg.7 (exceptions for genuine occupational requirements), direct discrimination will always be unlawful, the Regulations do allow for indirect discrimination if the employer is able to offer justification (reg.3(1)(iii) above). This may mean that if, for example, the courts hold that Rastafarians are covered by the Regulations a ban on a dread-lock style haircut may still, in at least certain circumstances, be lawful. This sup-position is also supported by para.15 of the DTI Notes which suggests that the courts should draw a distinction between the actual religious belief and the man-ifestation of those beliefs; a proposition which may lead either to inconsistencies or potential injustices.

It remains to be seen how the courts will deal with some of the problems and inconsistencies which are almost certain to arise. For example, certain religions are somewhat intolerant of homosexuality, and conflicts may arise over the appli-cation of the Regulations protecting on grounds of religion and those protecting on grounds of sexual orientation; how will the courts deal with the emergence of "new religions", or developing sects of established religions—particularly if the practices of such groups are unconventional by the standards of the majority. Case law over the next few years in this area should prove interesting.

REMEDIES

Anyone who has suffered an act of unlawful discrimination in the field of employ-ment has the right to make a complaint to an employment tribunal within three months of the occurrence of the act complained of (e.g. s.76(1) of the SDA 1975, s.68(1) of the RRA 1976, Sch.3(3)(1) of the DDA 1995), but the tribunal has the power to extend the time limit if it considers that it is just and equitable to do so (s.76(5) of the SDA 1975, s.68(6) of the RRA 1976, Sch.3(3)(2) of the DDA 1995). The three-month time limit also applies to complaints concerning religion or belief and sexual orientation.

5.6

The usual remedy sought is one of compensation. Compensation is payable according to the principles applicable in tort (s.65(1)(b) of the SDA 1975, s.56(1)(b) of the RRA 1976), in other words the award of compensation should seek to put the applicant in the position they would have been in had the dis-crimination complained of not taken place, and there is no upper limit to the amount of compensation that may be awarded (*cf.* awards for unfair dismissal under the ERA 1975). Awards may include compensation for injury to feelings (*cf.* awards for unfair dismissal under the ERA 1975), but exemplary or punitive damages should not be awarded (*Ministry of Defence v Cannock* [1994] I.C.R. 918). A monetary award will not normally be made in cases of unintentional indi-rect discrimination, but in the case of discrimination on the grounds of disability no distinction is draw between either direct or indirect discrimination nor on the basis of the intention of the employer.

A further remedy lies within s.65(1)(c) of the SDA 1975 and s.56(1)(c) of the RRA 1976, whereby the tribunal may make a recommendation that the respondent take within a specified period action to remove from the complainant the adverse effect of the discrimination complained of. Failure by the respondent to comply would allow the tribunal to increase or make an order for compensation.

In specific instances, further remedies may be available.

Chapter 6

Other Statutory Issues

CHAPTER OVERVIEW

CO6   There are a number of pieces of legislation which although directly concerning the employment relationship do not fit easily into other chapters of this book; they have therefore been collected together into this single chapter.

A considerable amount of this chapter is taken up with examination of the new dispute resolution procedures, both the statutory dismissal and disciplinary procedures and the statutory grievance procedures introduced under the EA 2002 and given effect by SI 2004/752. These procedures will have considerable impact on the number of claims being heard by the tribunals.

It should be remembered that there are many other pieces of legislation that have an impact on employment: legislation relating to unemployment benefits, social security issues, aspects of the criminal law, issues concerning immigration law, etc., but they fall outside the scope of a book such as this. It is however important to recognise and remember that not only do other fields of law impact on the "subject" of employment law, but that employment law itself plays a considerable part in many other areas of law; it is both unwise and blinkered to treat any area of law as either "stand-alone" or complete—John Donne wrote that "no man is an island, entire of itself", neither, I would suggest, is any area of law.

NATIONAL MINIMUM WAGE ACT 1998

6.1   The NMWA 1998 was introduced to provide a basic minimum hourly rate of pay for all workers. Section 2(1) enables the Secretary of State to determine and amend the hourly rate at appropriate intervals. The full minimum wage is to be paid to those workers aged 26 or more and who have completed six months minimum continuous service with their employer. A lower rate is to be paid to certain classes of younger workers.

Scope of the Act

6.1.1   The Act applies to all workers, not merely employees, and includes agency workers (s.34) and home workers (s.35)—but specific exclusions cover certain voluntary workers, students on work experience, members of the armed forces, prisoners and certain ship-board workers. The Secretary of State has power under s.4 to add to the list of excluded persons various other categories.

The definition of worker includes not only employees but also any individual working under a contract to personally perform the work; it is therefore theoretically possible for an employer to insert into the individual's contract a "substitution clause" (see Chapter 2) which may have the effect of persuading the court that the individual is not only not an employee but also not a worker and therefore not entitled to the protection of the NMWA 1998. Although possible, it is unlikely that such an argument would be permitted to succeed particularly considering the wording of s.49 which imposes restrictions on contracting out of the legislation and states:

> "(1) Any provision in any agreement (whether a worker's contract or not) is void in so far as it purports—
>
> > (a) to exclude or limit the operation of any provision of this Act; or
> > (b) to preclude a person from bringing proceedings under this Act before an employment tribunal".

Rights under the Act

The Act affords to all of those covered the right to be paid the minimum wage, the right of access to wage records, and the right not to suffer detriment for asserting a right under the Act—the remedy being via a complaint to an Employment Tribunal. An employee who is dismissed for asserting a statutory right will be treated as having been unfairly dismissed (s.104 of the ERA 1990). **6.1.2**

Operation of the Act

Section 1(1) of the Act states: **6.1.3**

> "A person who qualifies for the national minimum wage shall be remunerated by his employer in respect of his work in any pay reference period at a rate which is not less than the national minimum wage".

Regulation 10 of The National Minimum Wage Regulations 1999 states that the pay reference period is one month, or in the case of workers who are paid by reference to a shorter period it will be that shorter period. During any such period the worker's remuneration when averaged out must be at least the minimum rate. In order to determine whether a worker has received the minimum wage, and in view of the fact that payments to workers may be calculated in different ways, four categories of work are recognised by statute: *time work*; *salaried hours work*; *output work* and *unmeasured work*.

"Time work": On this basis, the amount of wages paid is divide by the number of hours worked which gives an hourly rate, which must be at least the minimum wage level. The question has arisen in a number of cases as to exactly which hours count as relevant hours for timed work. In the case of *Walton v Independent Living Organisation Ltd* [2003] I.C.R. 688 the Court of Appeal held that in the case of a carer who worked on a three days on—four days off basis each week, and who on her working days was required to be available at her charge's house for the full 24-hour period (although she was able to rest, watch television and sleep for much of that time), she was not in fact employed on timed work but on unmeasured work. This decision seems to conflict with the decision in *Scottbridge Construction Ltd v Wright* [2003] I.R.L.R. 21 in which a night-watchman, who was permitted to sleep for several of the 14 hours per night that he was on duty, was held to be engaged on timed work for all of his 14 hours, and with *British Nursing Association v Inland Revenue* [2002] I.R.L.R. 480 in which nurses employed to respond from their homes to emergency calls were held to be working for the whole period of their shifts and not just for the actual times they were responding to calls. The Court of Appeal held that had the nurses been working from the employer's premises there would have been no doubt that they were working for the full shift and it should not therefore be relevant that they in fact worked from home. In earlier cases (*SIMAP* Case C-303/98 and *CIG v Sergas* Case C-241/99), the European Court of Justice has drawn distinctions between those situations in which a worker on standby has been required to be physically present at a location, and those in which the worker must be merely contactable, but clearly such distinctions are not always easily drawn in practice.

"Salaried Hours Work": Under this category workers are paid a salary in equal instalments based on a set number of hours per year. Generally, salaried hours workers will be paid for meal breaks, holidays, time off sick, etc., but specific cases may vary depending upon the terms of the individual's contract of employment.

"Output Work": The worker's wage is determined by the number of pieces or products that worker can produce, i.e. on a piecework basis. The employer may choose to either pay at least the minimum wage for each hour worked, or operate an agreed system whereby all such workers performance and output is measured and a rate agreed under which an average worker may by producing the average number of pieces per hour be paid the equivalent of at least the minimum wage.

"Unmeasured Work": Any work which does not fall within the above three categories will be unmeasured work, for example a fixed task contract in which no hourly rate of pay or production is specified. The employer must either pay at least the minimum wage per hour or agree with the worker an average number of hours per week, each of which of course must equal or exceed the minimum wage level.

WORKING TIME REGULATIONS 1998

6.2   The Working Time Regulations are intended to implement the Working Time Directive 93/104/EC and parts of the Young Workers Directive 94/33/EC.

Main Provisions

- A maximum working week of 48 hours, averaged over a 17-week period. **6.2.1**
It is possible to opt out of this restriction for individuals or by way of collective or workforce agreements.

- Night workers to average no more than eight hours work in each 24-hour period, calculated over a 17-week period. It is possible to opt out of this restriction for individuals or by way of collective or workforce agreements.

- Certain night workers—those involved with heavy physical or mental strain, or whose work involves particular special hazards, may work only eight hours in a 24-hour period.

- All night workers are entitled to a health assessment before being required to work nights, and regular check-ups thereafter.

- Adult workers are entitled to one day off per week, 11 continuous rest hours per day, and a minimum break of 20 minutes if the working day is six hours or more.

- Young workers (those over the minimum school leaving age, but under 18 years old) are entitled to two days off per week, 12 continuous rest hours per day, and a minimum break of 30 minutes if the working day is four and a half hours or more.

- All workers are entitled to four weeks annual paid leave. Under the original Regulations there was a 13-week qualifying period, but this was amended following the case of *R. v Secretary or State for Trade and Industry, Ex p. BECTU* Case C-173/99 ECJ, and in the first year of employment holiday entitlement accrues on a monthly basis. Any provision within a contract that claims that "there is no entitlement to paid holidays under this contract" have been held to be void (*The College of North East London v Leather*, EAT 30/11/01).

- Regulation 13(9) states that leave periods may be taken in instalments, but may only be taken in the leave year in which they are due, and that the actual holiday may not be replaced by payment in lieu except where the worker's contract has been terminated.

- Employees absent from work for extended periods are not entitled to holiday pay for those years in which they had not worked (*IRC v Ainsworth* [2005] I.R.L.R. 465.

- Holiday pay should normally be paid as a separate amount before or at the actual time of the holiday. Employers may pay holiday pay as a "rolled-up" figure (included in a total hourly, or similar, rate); but employers must ensure that such an arrangement is clearly notified to and agreed by the employee (*Marshalls Clay Products Ltd v Cauldfield* [2004] I.C.R. 436, and clarified by *Smith v AJ Morrisroes & Sons Ltd* [2005] I.R.L.R. 72). There is a Scottish case, *MPD Structures v Munro* [2002] I.R.L.R. 601, in which the court stated that holiday pay must be paid as a separate and distinct payment at the time of taking the holiday, but such a practice would be unworkable for those working on a part-time basis.

- Claims for holiday pay must be brought under s.30 of the Working Time Regulations and not under s.13 of the ERA 1996 (*IRC v Ainsworth* [2005] I.R.L.R. 465.

"Worker" is defined in the Regulations in the same way as s.230(3) ERA 1996, and includes both those working under a contract of employment (employees) and those working under any other contract to personally provide any work or service to another party, unless the other party's status under the contract is that of client or customer of any profession or business undertaking carried on by the individual. The term "worker" also applies to apprentices, trainees and those on work experience programmes.

Almost certainly "worker" applies to casual workers, particularly following *Carmichael v National Power Plc* [1998] I.R.L.R. 301, but a Privy Council decision in *Chen Yuen v Royal Hong Kong Golf Club* [1998] I.C.R. 131 highlights an instance where, apparently and surprisingly, it was held that no contract of any sort was in existence between golf caddies and the golf club they "worked" for.

Agency workers are specifically included in the definition of "worker", by reg.36, the party responsible under the Regulations being the party who pays the agency worker—in most cases the employment agency.

Exclusions

6.2.2   Certain categories of workers are excluded from some aspects of the Regulations:

- Transport industry: Directive 2000/34 EC excludes mobile workers within the transport industry.

- Carriage of passengers on regular urban transport services (reg.21(c) (viii)).

- Various activities within the railway system (reg.21(f)).

- Junior doctors: Regulation 18(b) excludes all doctors under training.

- Work at sea: including fishing, shipping and offshore working.

- Police and Armed Forces: the Regulations *probably* do not apply in most instances to ambulance service, fire service, prison service, etc.

- Those with autonomous decision making powers as to the duration of their working time: for example, managing executives, those working in family businesses, etc.

- Security work: requiring round-the-clock presence.

- Continuous production processes: including hospitals, prisons, etc., although the exclusion is dependent upon the worker's activities, rather than merely on the place of work.

- Seasonal industries: such as tourism, Christmas business, agricultural activities, e.g. fruit picking.

- Where the worker's activities are affected by: (i) an occurrence due to unusual and unforeseeable circumstances beyond the control of the worker's employer; or (ii) exceptional events, the consequences of which could not have been avoided despite the exercise of all due care by the employer; or (iii) an accident or the imminent risk of an accident (reg.21(e)).

Incorporation of the Provisions into the Individual's Contract

In the case of *Barber v RJB Mining UK Ltd* [1999] I.R.L.R. 308, pit deputies and **6.2.3** colliery overmen at a privatised colliery were being required to work in excess of 48 hours per week. The employer argued that the men were only being asked to work their normal hours and the Working Time Directive was not to be read as forming part of the employment contract. The court held that the Directive, and by implication the Regulations, are a mandatory requirement and apply to all contracts of employment, and it is not necessary that the rights afforded under the WTR are otherwise incorporated into an individual's contract.

CONTRACTING OUT AND COMPROMISE AGREEMENTS

Section 203 of the ERA 1996 states: **6.3**

> "(1) Any provision within an agreement (whether a contract of employment or not) is void in so far as it purports—
>
> > (a) to exclude or limit the operation of any provision of this Act, or
> > (b) to preclude a person from bringing any proceedings under this Act before an employment tribunal."

However, subs.2 then goes on to lay down a number of exceptions to this, notable amongst which is the situation in which a "compromise agreement" has been reached. A compromise agreement is defined as an agreement in writing relating to the particular proceedings covered, made only after the worker has received advice from an independent advisor on the effect of the agreement in regard to the worker's subsequent ability to pursue the matter before an employment tribunal. The independent advisor may be either a lawyer or someone certified by a trade union or advice centre as competent to give such advice, and they must be independent, i.e. not acting for or employed by the employer, nor, in the case of an advice centre, paid for by the worker. The agreement must also state that it complies with the required conditions. The recent case of *Hinton v University of East London* [2005] I.R.L.R. 552 emphasises the importance of the agreement relating to a specific issue or particular proceedings; the Court of Appeal in *Hinton* held that an agreement relating to "all statutory rights" would not be sufficiently specific to amount to a compromise agreement.

MATERNITY RIGHTS

6.4   Particular rights are accorded women in respect of pregnancy and maternity.

Dismissal on Pregnancy-Related Grounds

6.4.1   An employee will be regarded as unfairly dismissed if the reason or principal reason for her dismissal is that she is pregnant or any other reason connected with her pregnancy (s.99(1)(a) of the ERA 1996), and the case of *Webb v EMO Air Cargo (UK) Ltd* [1995] I.R.L.R. 645 demonstrates the accepted approach of the courts. Mrs Webb had been hired by EMO Air Cargo, a small company employing 16 people, as a replacement for one of their staff who was absent on maternity leave. It was envisaged that Mrs Webb would continue to work with EMO once the maternity replacement period was over. Some two weeks after starting work, Mrs Webb discovered that she was pregnant. On learning of this, her employer dismissed her. Mrs Webb brought a claim alleging sex discrimination. The House of Lords made the following points:

> Discrimination on the grounds of pregnancy is sex discrimination. There is no need for the applicant to compare herself to a "sick man". Their Lordships suggested that it was possible that the dismissal may have been held to be a fair dismissal had Mrs Webb been appointed *only* on a fixed term contract (but see the case of *Carunana v Manchester Airport Plc* [1996] I.R.L.R. 378).

Although a similar case today may be brought under s.99 of the ERA 1996—dismissal on the grounds of pregnancy being automatically unfair—a sex discrimination claim may be advantageous because it would also cover the recruitment process, and also, unlike unfair dismissal claims, there is no upper limit on compensation awards for sex discrimination.

An employee will also be regarded as unfairly dismissed if during the period of her maternity leave she submits a doctor's certificate stating that due to illness she will be unable to return to work following the leave period, and she is dismissed for a reason connected with the birth within four weeks of the end of her maternity leave period (s.99(3) of the ERA 1996, and see *Brown v Rentokil Ltd* [1997] I.R.L.R. 445).

It has been held that dismissal on the grounds of a pregnancy related illness after the maternity leave ends may not constitute unfair dismissal (*Hertz v Aldi Marked K/S* [1991] I.R.L.R. 31). However, be aware of the more recent case of *Caledonia Bureau Investment & Property Ltd v Caffrey* [1998] I.R.L.R. 110, in which it was held by the EAT that a dismissal, which occurred after the maternity leave was over, for post-natal depression—a pregnancy related illness—was for a reason connected with the pregnancy and therefore contrary to s.99(1). The problem for the courts is in drawing a line between illness and pregnancy. On the one hand, *Webb v EMO Air Cargo Ltd* makes clear that pregnancy is not to be treated as an illness, and the legislation protects employees from dismissal "on the grounds of pregnancy", and obviously a pregnancy related illness is brought about "on the grounds of pregnancy". If however the courts treat such illnesses as being protected, in the case of long-term illnesses the protection afforded the woman will be much more than that afforded a man suffering from a long term illness (even if that illness is one that affects only or predominately males) and would therefore appear to conflict with the basic principles of sex equality.

The ECJ in the case of *Habermann-Beltermann v Arbeitwohlfahrt, Bezirksverband* (Case C-421/92) held that the dismissal of a pregnant woman night worker on the grounds of national legislation prohibiting pregnant employees from working at nights was unlawful.

Maternity Leave

Legislation concerning provision of maternity leave is complex. Part VIII of the ERA 1996, as amended by ERelA 1999, gives effect to the Pregnant Workers Directive (Directive 82/95) and now provides for a minimum of 26 weeks maternity leave to all pregnant employees without the need for a minimum period of service. The leave may begin no earlier than the eleventh week prior to the expected week of childbirth and no later than the day following the date of the birth. During the maternity leave the employee is entitled to all the normal **6.4.2** benefits which would have accrued under her contract, and, in the absence of any contractual right to pay, if she has a minimum of 26 weeks of continuous service, is entitled to statutory maternity pay.

If the employee has a minimum of one years service at the beginning of the eleventh week before childbirth, she has the right to return to work at any time up to 29 weeks after childbirth. She is entitled to return to work on terms no less favourable than she would have enjoyed had she not been absent.

Time Off for Ante-Natal Care

6.4.3   A pregnant employee has a right under s.55 of the ERA 1996 to time off during the employer's working hours to keep an appointment to receive ante-natal care.

Statutory Maternity Pay

6.4.4   An employee with a minimum of 26 weeks continuous service is entitled to receive statutory maternity pay for the period of her statutory maternity leave. For the first six weeks it amounts to 90 per cent of her average weekly earnings, and for a further twenty weeks at a rate set by statute (SI 1986/1960). Employees without the requisite continuity of service may be eligible for the state maternity allowance. Statutory maternity pay has been held to constitute "pay" under Art.141 (*Gillespie v Northern Health and Social Services Board* Case C-342/93), but could not be used as a basis for a claim for equal pay, even though the employment contract is running for the duration of the payment of the statutory maternity pay and other male workers performing "like work" or "work of equal value" would for that time be paid more than the woman.

PARENTAL LEAVE

6.5   Parents of children under the age of five years who have at least one year's continuous service with the employer are allowed to take up to 13 weeks unpaid leave for the purpose of caring for that child. If the child is eligible for a disability living allowance the right to parental leave extends to the child's eighteenth birthday. The leave may not be taken in less than one-week periods (*South Central Trains Ltd v Rodway* [2005] I.R.L.R. 583), but does not break continuity of employment or seniority issues. If the leave taken is less than a period of four weeks the employer must reinstate the employee in their original position, if the leave is for more that four weeks and reinstatement is not practicable the employer must offer suitable alternative employment.

PATERNITY LEAVE

The Employment Act 2002 makes provision for those employees with 26 weeks **6.6** continuous service to be entitled to a period of at least two weeks paid paternity leave. Such leave is paid at the rate of 90 per cent of average weekly earnings subject to a statutory maximum. To qualify the individual must be either the father of the child or be married to or be the partner (same or different sex) of the mother of the child, and have responsibility for the upbringing of the child.

ADOPTION LEAVE

Statutory adoption leave is available to employees with a minimum of 26 weeks **6.7** continuous service. The entitlement is for 26 weeks of "ordinary adoption leave" which may be followed by up to 26 weeks of "additional adoption leave" and is available to only one person per child, therefore in the case of a joint adoption only one of the parents may opt for adoption leave, although the other may be entitled to paternity leave. Statutory adoption pay is payable for up to 26 weeks at 90 per cent of the individual's average earnings subject to a statutory maximum.

HUMAN RIGHTS ACT 1998

The HRA 1998 has created new, directly enforceable rights against public bodies **6.8** and against quasi-public bodies undertaking public functions. The Act does not however make European Convention on Human Rights (the Convention) rights directly enforceable against a private litigant—an individual or a private business or company.

What the Act does is to give effect to Convention rights by obliging courts to decide all cases compatibly with Convention rights—unless prevented from doing so by primary legislation (s.6), by obliging courts wherever possible to interpret legislation in conformity with the Convention (s.3), and by requiring courts to take account of Convention based case law (s.2).

Generally, if legislation is held to be incompatible with the Convention, procedures are in place whereby the government can implement fast-track legislation to remedy the situation. Certainly in areas of criminal law, particularly evidential rules, the Act is likely to have considerable long-term impact.

Many of the rights directly concerning employment law contained within the convention are already considered under national law and EC law generally—for instance issues concerning discrimination, although it is still not completely clear what overall effect the Act may have in other areas of employment law. Article 8 (right to respect for private and family life) may have further impact on such areas as dress codes, etc., as may Art.10 (freedom of expression), and it is possible that further challenges under Art.11 (freedom of assembly and association) may result in perhaps a positive right to strike (see *Wilson v UK; Palmer v UK* [2002] I.R.L.R. 568 for example).

PUBLIC INTEREST DISCLOSURE ACT 1998

6.9   The purpose of the Act is to protect workers against action taken by their employers in cases where the worker "blows the whistle" on certain actions of his employer.

The Act protects a worker against dismissal, selection for redundancy or any other detriment, if the reason or principal reason for the action is that the worker has made a "protected disclosure".

The term "worker" is given an extended definition by the Act and includes:

- Those working under a contract of employment (s.230(3)(a) of the ERA 1996).

- Those working under a contract to personally or otherwise provide any work or services in a place that is not under the control of the individual—unless that other party is a client or customer of any profession or business carried out by the individual (i.e. unless the individual is genuinely running their own business) (s.230(3)(b) of the ERA 1996, as amended by PIDA 1998).

- Agency workers, being those supplied or introduced by a third party (s.1 PIDA 1998).

- A person providing medical, dental, ophthalmic or pharmaceutical services in accordance with arrangements made by a Health Authority under ss.29, 35, 38 or 41 of the National Health Service Act 1977, or the equivalent in Scotland (s.1 PIDA 1998).

- A person being provided with training or work experience, unless under a contract of employment or as part of a course run by an educational establishment.

Qualifying Disclosure

6.9.1   A "qualifying disclosure" is defined in the Act as being a disclosure of information which the worker reasonably believes shows or tends to show:

- that a criminal offence has been, is being or is likely to be committed;

- that a person has failed, is failing or is likely to fail to comply with a legal obligation;

- that a miscarriage of justice has occurred, is occurring or is likely to occur;

- that health and safety has been, is being or is likely to be endangered;

- that the environment has been, is being or is likely to be damaged; or

- that information concerning any of the above has been, is being or is likely to be deliberately concealed.

It is immaterial whether the relevant failure occurs or would occur in the UK or elsewhere.

However, the disclosure is not a qualifying disclosure if the person making it commits an offence by making it; nor will it be a qualifying disclosure if the information is subject to legal professional privilege, and had been disclosed to the person in the course of obtaining legal advice.

Protected Disclosure

A qualifying disclosure will become a protected disclosure in the following cir-   **6.9.2** cumstances:

- if the worker makes the disclosure to the employer, or to the person the worker reasonably believes is responsible for the relevant failure;

- if the disclosure is made in the course of obtaining legal advice;

- if the worker's employer is appointed by enactment by a Minister of the Crown, the disclosure is made in good faith to a Minister of the Crown; or

- if the disclosure is made in good faith to a person prescribed by the Secretary of State for the purpose of the Act.

A disclosure made to a person other than the employer or a prescribed person may also qualify as a protected disclosure if, but only if, the worker making the disclosure:

- makes it in good faith;

- reasonably believes it to be true;

- does not make personal gain from the disclosure;

- reasonably believes that he would be subject to some detriment if he makes the disclosure to his employer;

- reasonably believes that relevant evidence would be concealed or destroyed if he makes the disclosure to his employer; and

- has already disclosed the same information to his employer or to a prescribed person.

In deciding whether it is reasonable for the worker to make the disclosure, regard will be had to, amongst other issues:

- the identity of the person to whom the disclosure is made;

- the seriousness of the relevant failure;

- whether the disclose relates to a past, present or future failure;

- whether the disclose breaches a duty of confidentiality owed by the employer to another person; and

- where the disclosure has already been made to the employer or a prescribed person, any action taken, or which should have been taken.

Exceptionally Serious Failures

6.9.3   In the case of an "exceptionally serious failure" regard need only be had to whether the worker makes the disclosure in good faith, believing it to be true, does not make personal gain from the disclosure, and in all the circumstances whether it was reasonable to make the disclosure, particularly in respect of the identity of the person to whom it was made.

FIXED-TERM EMPLOYEES (PREVENTION OF LESS FAVOURABLE TREATMENT) REGULATIONS 2002

6.10   From October 1, 2002 these Regulations, brought in under the EA 2002, oblige all employers to treat fixed-term employees no less favourably than comparable permanent employees. Fixed-term employees are those working under a contract for a specific fixed time, for a specific task, or a contract which will terminate upon the happening, or non-happening of some future event. The Regulations also limit the use of successive fixed-term contracts to a maximum of four years, unless objective justification for further periods can be shown by the employer; this is designed to prevent employers avoiding such employment rights as redundancy entitlements by the use of a series of fixed-term appointments. On this point it is worth considering the EAT decision in *Booth v USA* [1999] I.R.L.R. 16—an issue of continuity of employment.

STATUTORY DISPUTE RESOLUTION PROCEDURES

Statutory dispute resolution procedures (statutory dismissal and disciplinary pro- **6.11**
cedures (SDDP) and statutory grievance procedures (SGP)) were introduced by
the EA 2002 and given effect from October 1, 2004 by the implementation of the
EA 2002 (Dispute Resolution) Regulations 2004 (SI 2004/752). The purpose of
these procedures is to reduce the number of cases reaching the employment
tribunals by obliging employers and employees to complete a statutory in-house
procedure to resolve disputes before taking most claims to a tribunal. The theory
behind the statutory procedures is quite straightforward: the parties should take
part in documented meeting and appeal procedures, and only if the dispute
remains unresolved need the issue be brought to a tribunal hearing. The practice,
however, is somewhat more complex.

Statutory Dismissal and Disciplinary Procedures

The SDDP is laid out in Sch.2, Pt 1 of the Employment Act 2002 and may take **6.11.1**
one of two forms, a standard procedure and a modified procedure:

"Chapter 1 Standard Procedure

1
Step 1: statement of grounds for action and invitation to meeting.

(1) The employer must set out in writing the employee's alleged conduct
or characteristics, or other circumstances, which lead him to contemplate dismissing or taking disciplinary action against the employee.
(2) The employer must send the statement or a copy of it to the employee
and invite the employee to attend a meeting to discuss the matter.

2
Step 2: meeting

(1) The meeting must take place before action is taken, except in the case
where the disciplinary action consists of suspension.
(2) The meeting must not take place unless—

(a) the employer has informed the employee what the basis was for
including in the statement under paragraph 1(1) the ground or
grounds given in it, and
(b) the employee has had a reasonable opportunity to consider his
response to that information.

(3) The employee must take all reasonable steps to attend the meeting.

(4) After the meeting, the employer must inform the employee of his decision and notify him of the right to appeal against the decision if he is not satisfied with it.

3

Step 3: appeal

(1) If the employee does wish to appeal, he must inform the employer.
(2) If the employee informs the employer of his wish to appeal, the employer must invite him to attend a further meeting.
(3) The employee must take all reasonable steps to attend the meeting.
(4) The appeal meeting need not take place before the dismissal or disciplinary action takes effect.
(5) After the appeal meeting, the employer must inform the employee of his final decision.

Chapter 2 Modified procedure

4

Step 1: statement of grounds for action
The employer must—

(a) set out in writing—

(i) the employee's alleged misconduct which has led to the dismissal,
(ii) what the basis was for thinking at the time of the dismissal that the employee was guilty of the alleged misconduct, and
(iii) the employee's right to appeal against the dismissal, and

(b) send the statement, or a copy of it, to the employee.

5

Step 2: appeal

(1) If the employee does wish to appeal, he must inform the employer.
(2) If the employee informs the employer of his wish to appeal, the employer must invite him to attend a meeting.
(3) The employee must take all reasonable steps to attend the meeting.
(4) After the appeal meeting, the employer must inform the employee of his final decision."

The standard procedure applies to situations where the "employer contemplates dismissing or taking relevant disciplinary action against an employee" (EADRR 2004 reg.3(1)). "Relevant disciplinary action" is defined in reg.2 as action short of dismissal, other than suspension on full pay or the issuing of oral or written warnings.

The modified procedure applies to instances of summary dismissal, but neither procedure will apply if the dismissed employee presents an application to an employment tribunal before the employer has complied with para.4 of Sch.2 (reg.3(2)(d)).

The procedures apply to all dismissals except those listed in reg.4:

(a) where "all the employees of a description or in a category to which the employee belongs" are dismissed, provided that the employer offers re-engagement to all of those employees before or upon termination of their contracts. It is as yet not clear whether an individual employee may be "all the employees of a description or . . . category", since these terms are not defined in the regulations.

(b) where the dismissal is one of a number in which the employer has a duty to consult with employee representatives under s.88 of the TULR(C)A 1992.

(c) where at the time of the dismissal the employee was taking part in unofficial industrial action.

(d) where the reason for the dismissal was that the employee took protected industrial action.

(e) where the employer's business suddenly ceases to function because of an event unforeseen by the employer.

(f) where the employee could not continue in that employment without the employer or the employee contravening the law.

(g) where the employee is one to whom a dismissal procedure under s.110 of the ERA 1996 applies.

Regulation 5 then states that the parties will be treated as having complied with the SDDP if the employee has applied to a tribunal for interim relief pending the determination of the complaint but at that time the appeals procedures in either SDDP have not been completed.

Statutory Grievance Procedure

Established by the EA 2002 and implemented under the EADRR 2004, the **6.11.2** Statutory Grievance Procedure (SGP) should be used by the employee prior to the instigation of any complaint to an employment tribunal regarding "a complaint by an employee about action which his employer has taken or is contemplating taking against him" (reg.2).

Section 32 of the EA 2002 states that:

"An employee shall not present a complaint to an employment tribunal under a jurisdiction to which this section applies if:

(a) it concerns a matter in relation to which the requirement in paragraph 6 or 9 of Schedule 2 applies, and
(b) the requirement has not been complied with."

The jurisdiction referred to is detailed in Sch.4 as:

- Section 2 of the EPA 1970 (equality clauses).

- Section 63 of the SDA 1975 (discrimination in the employment field).

- Section 54 of the RRA 1976 (discrimination in the employment field).

- Section 145A of the TULR(C)A 1992 (inducements relating to union membership or activities).

- Section 145B of that Act (inducements relating to collective bargaining).

- Section 146 of that Act (detriment in relation to union membership and activities.

- Paragraph 156 of Sch.A1 to that Act (detriment in relation to union recognition rights).

- Section 17A of the DDA 1995 (discrimination in the employment field).

- Section 23 of the ERA 1996 (unauthorised deductions and payments).

- Section 48 of that Act (detriment in employment)

- Section 111 of that Act (unfair dismissal).

- Section 163 of that Act (redundancy payments).

- Section 24 of the NMWA 1998 (detriment in relation to national minimum wage).

- Regulation 30 of the Working Time Regulations 1998 (breach of regulations).

- Regulation 32 of the Transnational Information and Consultation of Employees Regulations 1999 (detriment relating to European Works Councils).

- Regulation 28 of the Employment Equality (Sexual Orientation) Regulations 2003 (discrimination in the employment field).

- Regulation 28 of the Employment Equality (Religion or Belief) Regulations 2003 (discrimination in the employment field).

In all of these cases an employee *must* follow Step 1 of either the standard griev-ance procedure or the modified procedure (whichever is applicable) before pre-senting a claim to a tribunal. Furthermore, under s.32(3) of the EA 2002 the employee may not present the claim to a tribunal unless 28 days have passed since Step 1 of the SGP was complied with.

It would therefore appear that complaints to a tribunal of constructive unfair dismissal should be preceded by an SGP, unless one of the exceptions (below) applies. As with the SDDP, the SGP may take one of two forms, a stand-ard procedure and a modified procedure. These are detailed in Pt 2, Sch.2, EA 2002:

"Chapter 1 Standard procedure

6
Step 1: statement of grievance
The employee must set out the grievance in writing and send the statement or a copy of it to the employer.

7
Step 2: meeting

(1) The employer must invite the employee to attend a meeting to discuss the grievance.
(2) The meeting must not take place unless—

(a) the employee has informed the employer what the basis for the grievance was when he made the statement under paragraph 6, and
(b) the employer has had a reasonable opportunity to consider his response to that information.

(3) The employee must take all reasonable steps to attend the meeting.
(4) After the meeting, the employer must inform the employee of his deci-sion as to his response to the grievance and notify him of the right to appeal against the decision if he is not satisfied with it.

8
Step 3: appeal

(1) If the employee does wish to appeal, he must inform the employer.
(2) If the employee informs the employer of his wish to appeal, the employer must invite him to attend a further meeting.
(3) The employee must take all reasonable steps to attend the meeting.
(4) After the appeal meeting, the employer must inform the employee of his final decision.

Chapter 2 Modified procedure

9
Step 1: statement of grievance
The employee must—

   (a) set out in writing—

      (i) the grievance, and
      (ii) the basis for it, and

   (b) send the statement, or a copy of it, to the employer.

10
Step 2: response
The employer must set out his response in writing and send the statement or a copy of it to the employee."

The modified SGP will apply only where the employment relationship has ceased, the employer was unaware of the grievance before the employment ceased, or was aware but the standard SGP was either not commenced or not completed before the last day of employment, and both parties have agreed in writing that the modified procedure should apply (regs 3(a), 3(b), 3(c) of the EADRR 2004).

Meetings

6.11.3 Various requirements are laid down concerning the meetings for both SDDPs and SGPs: employees have a right to be accompanied (reg.14 of the EADRR states that the meetings are hearings for the purpose of s.10 of the ERelA 1999), timings and locations of meetings must be reasonable, they should be conducted in a manner that enables both parties to explain their cases, and as far as possible, at the appeal meeting the employer should be represented by a more senior manager than attended the initial hearing (reg.13 of the EADRR). All the steps in the procedures should be carried out without unreasonable delay (reg.12 of the EADRR).

   The statutory procedures do not apply or are taken as having been complied with in certain circumstances. Regulation 11(3) of the EADRR details those circumstances as (a) where a party has reasonable grounds to believe that commencing or continuing with a procedure would result in a significant threat to themselves, others or their property, (b) where the party has been subjected to harassment and has reasonable grounds to believe that commencing or continuing with a procedure would result in further harassment, or (c) where it is not practicable for the party to commence or continue with a procedure.

   Should either party be unable to attend a meeting the employer should invite the employee to attend another meeting, if it proves that either party is again unable to attend, the parties will be taken to have complied with the statutory requirement (reg.13 of the EADRR).

Regulation 15 of the EADRR states that where a complaint is presented to a tribunal and either the SDDP or SGP apply, the time limit for presenting that complaint is extended by three months.

Non-compliance with Statutory Dismissal and Disciplinary Procedure

If non-completion of the statutory dismissal and disciplinary procedure is the fault of the employee, any award made by the tribunal must normally be reduced by between 10 per cent–50 per cent.   **6.11.4**

If non-completion of the statutory dismissal and disciplinary procedure is the fault of the employer, any award against the employer by the tribunal must normally be increased by between 10 per cent–50 per cent.

Non-compliance with Statutory Grievance Procedure

An employee is not able to present a complaint to which an SGP applies to an employment tribunal if they have failed to send a copy of the grievance to the employer under the first stage of the procedure (s.32 of the EA 2002). It appears that the courts are willing to take a flexible approach as to the format of this first stage. In the case of *Shergold v Fieldway Medical Centre* [2006] I.R.L.R. 76 the court held that it was sufficient that the grievance should "set out in writing", and in *Mark Warner Ltd v Aspland* [2006] I.R.L.R. 89 a letter from the complainant's solicitor to the employer's solicitor was sufficient. It was stated obiter in *Galaxy Showers Ltd v Wilson* [2006] I.R.L.R. 83 that an employee leaving because an earlier grievance had not been dealt with does not have to raise that grievance again.   **6.11.5**

If non-completion of the statutory grievance procedure is the fault of the employee, any award made by the tribunal must normally be reduced by between 10 per cent–50 per cent.

If non-completion of the statutory grievance procedure is the fault of the employer, any award against the employer by the tribunal must normally be increased by between 10 per cent–50 per cent.

INFORMATION AND CONSULTATION OF EMPLOYEES REGULATIONS 2004

These Regulations (SI 2004/3426) were brought in to give effect to the Information and Consultation Directive 2002/14/EC which seeks to lay down   **6.12** minimum standards regarding consultation and information in all "undertakings" with more than 50 employees. The Regulations presently apply to undertakings of more than 150 employees, but from April 2007 to those with more than 100 employees, and from April 2008 to those with more than 50.

An "undertaking" is defined any public or private undertaking carrying out an economic activity, regardless of whether it is for profit or not (reg.2), and the term "employees" covers only those working under a contract of employment.

The Procedure (a brief overview)

6.12.1 The Regulations are complex and may be overseen by the Central Arbitration Committee (CAC). A request must normally be made to the employer (although it is possible for the employer to instigate the procedure) by either at least 10 per cent of the employees or 15 employees—whichever is the greater, the request must be in writing and if the individual employees making the request do not wish to be identified, the request may be made via the CAC. The employer should then arrange for the election or appointment of negotiating representatives, and then enter into negotiations with them with a view to reaching a negotiated agreement covering and detailing the situations in which the employer must inform and consult. The negotiating representatives are entitled under the Regulations to paid time off to undertake their duties and are afforded protection from dismissal or detriment short of dismissal for the carrying out of those duties.

Chapter 7

HEALTH AND SAFETY

CHAPTER OVERVIEW

Health and safety is another area of employment law which has been developing   **CO7**
rapidly over recent past.

The common law regarding health and safety is basically the tort of negligence: is there a duty of care, has that duty been breached, and has that breach caused the injury. Issues of proximity and remoteness are also relevant, particularly in cases of third party injury. The employer will be liable for his own acts and those carried out by his employees in the "course of their employment".

Statute is becoming more important; not only is the Health and Safety at Work Act 1974 still the major piece of domestic legislation, but it is also used as an enabling act implementing European legislation.

It is worth noting that the common law and the traditional national legislation lay down a "reasonable" standard of care, whereas the standard of care specified by much of the European generated legislation is much higher.

The "growth area" in health and safety has come within the area of psychiatric injury arising from workplace stress, and the guidelines laid down by the Court of Appeal in *Sutherland v Hatton* [2002] I.R.L.R. 263 are particularly important.

It has been suggested that occupational stress is the "new bad back", allowing employees to take time off from work and seek compensation for what in the past would not have been an actionable complaint, but the recent judgments of the higher courts do not appear to support this suggestion—although areas of the *Sutherland* guidelines are perhaps open to interpretation.

The aim of health and safety law is to prevent accidents occurring in the workplace. The enforcement of health and safety legislation differs from most other areas of employment law in that breach of a health and safety statute usually results in criminal liability. However, this does not prevent the injured party from pursuing a claim for damages in the event of an accident.

SOURCES OF HEALTH AND SAFETY LAW

7.1   The main sources of health and safety law in England and Wales are the common law, statute and European Legislation.

Much of the common law regarding health and safety as it relates to the individual employee is contained in the employer's implied term of duty of care.

The major consolidating domestic legislation is the Health and Safety at Work Act 1974 (HSWA), which over the years has been supported and complimented by other legislation, including input from the EC.

The Treaty of Rome includes Art.118A, which states:

> "The Member States shall pay particular attention to encouraging improvements, especially in the working environment, as regards the health and safety of workers, and shall set as their objective the harmonisation of conditions in this area, while maintaining the improvements."

One outcome of this has been the adoption of a Directive to encourage improvements in health and safety in the field of employment—the "Framework Directive"—Directive EC89/391.

COMMON LAW

7.2   At common law, the basis of the employer's duty towards his employees arises from the existence of the contract of employment. There is an implied term in the contract that the employer will take reasonable care to ensure the safety of his employees. Breach of this duty will amount to a breach of contract, and may allow the employee to leave, claim constructive dismissal and bring an action for unfair dismissal as occurred in *Waltons & Morse v Dorrington* [1997] I.R.L.R. 488 in which a secretary for a firm of solicitors repeatedly complained of the smoky—caused by other workers' cigarettes—and unventilated environment in which she had to work. Her employers failed to act appropriately and she left, complaining successfully of constructive and unfair dismissal.

In the case of injury to the employee however, there is normally no advantage to suing in contract, and most claims are brought in the tort of negligence on the principles laid down in *Donoghue v Stevenson* [1932] A.C. 562.

The employer's liability will arise in one of two ways. He will be directly responsible for his own actions or omissions which amount to negligence and he may also be responsible for the negligent actions or omissions of other employees, through the doctrine of vicarious liability.

Employer's Direct Liability

Under the common law it is necessary to ask two questions: **7.2.1**

- Was the injured party someone the employer should have reasonably foreseen would be likely to have been injured if the work had not been carried out properly?

- In all the circumstances, did the employer attain the standard of care expected from a reasonable employer?

The injured party must show three things:

1. That the employer owed a duty of care.

2. That there was a breach of that duty.

3. That the breach was the cause of the injury.

Duty of care

The duty of the employer is owed to the employee as an individual (*Paris v*   **7.2.1.1**
Stepney Borough Council [1951] A.C. 376), and consequently a higher standard of care may be owed to some employees than to others (*James v Hepworth & Grandage Ltd* [1968] 1 Q.B. 94). If, for example, the employer is or should be aware that some or any of his employees may be illiterate or not fluent in written English, it would probably be necessary for him in order to fulfil his duty of care to ensure that warning signs are given in pictorial, rather than merely written, form.

The duty is owed by the employer, and may not be delegated—although the performance of the duty may be (*Wilsons and Clyde Coal Co Ltd v English* [1938] A.C. 57). In other words, even though an employer may sub-contract the provision and enforcement of all health and safety matters to a third party, the liability for any breach will remain with the employer (although, in such a case, depending on the actual terms of the contract, the employer may have a separate action against the third party).

The duty is generally divided into four areas:

(i) Safe Plant and Equipment: reasonable steps should be taken by the employer to provide and maintain safe plant and equipment. In the case of *Bradford v Robinson Rentals* [1967] 1 All E.R. 267, an employee was instructed to make a delivery involving a round trip of some 400 miles in a spell of particularly cold weather, in a van which had no heating and badly fitting windows. He suffered frostbite and brought an action against his employer. The employer was held to be liable for failing to provide suitable and safe plant and equipment. It should however be noted that statute now provides for a strict liability duty on the part of the employer in terms of equipment (see Employer's Liability (Defective Equipment) Act 1969 and the Provision and Use of Work Equipment Regulations 1992).

(ii) Safe Place of Work: the employer has a duty to take reasonable steps to ensure that the workplace is safe, not only for his employees, but also for anyone else who may use the premises (Occupiers Liability Act 1957 and 1984). The duty is only one of reasonableness, as is demonstrated by the case of *Latimer v AEC Ltd* [1953] A.C. 643 in which rain had flooded a factory floor, which had become slippery with a mixture of oil and water. Sawdust was laid over most of the floor, but there was not sufficient sawdust to cover the entire floor. An employee slipped on part of the untreated floor and was injured. The court held that the employer was not liable. Reasonable precautions had been taken, and the court held that the danger was not sufficient to warrant closing the factory entirely.

(iii) Safe System of Work: the employer has a duty to ensure that the methods used to undertake the work are safe. This includes the system, training, supervision, protective clothing, warnings, etc. In some situations it may be sufficient for an employer to show that he acted and operated in a manner consistent with the normal practice within his particular industry, and certainly such evidence would be persuasive on the court in determining whether the employer acted as a "reasonable employer" would. The employer is responsible for ensuring that the system is carried out, and must bear in mind that employees may be forgetful or lazy, however the employer may not be liable in cases of disobedience.

In the case of *McWilliams v Sir William Arrol & Co Ltd* [1962] 1 All E.R. 623 steel erectors working on a building site were provided with safety belts, which they chose not to wear. The belts were removed to another site, and shortly afterwards one of the employees on the first site fell and was killed. The employer was not held liable for the death, as it was shown that the employees had always chosen not to wear them despite instructions from the employer (see also the issue of Causation).

It has recently been suggested (obiter in *Coxall v Goodyear GB Ltd* [2002] I.R.L.R. 742) that in certain circumstances, for example where a risk to the employee's health has been identified by the employer but the employee wishes to continue with the work, the employer may be under a common law duty to dismiss the employee if it can be shown that this would be a reasonable way of protecting the employee's health and safety—although in view of statutory protection against unfair dismissal such a course of action is uncertain.

(iv) Provision of Competent Fellow Employees: the employer has a duty to recruit and train competent fellow employees, this may include the dismissal of incompetent workers—but normally only after training, warnings, etc. (see Chapter 10). The term "incompetent" has also been used to cover situations of horse-play, as in *Hudson v Ridge Manufacturing Co Ltd* [1957] 2 Q.B. 348 in which for a number of years an employee had played practical jokes including tripping fellow employees. On one occasion an employee sustained a serious injury, and brought an action against the employer. Since the employer was aware that the employee had indulged in such horseplay for a number of years but had taken no action to stop it they were held liable.

Breach of duty

The claimant must show that the employer's actions fell below the standard expected of a reasonable employer. Obviously, the greater the risk, the greater the care required (see *Paris v Stepney Borough Council*); and the more likely the risk, the more necessary the care. In deciding how a reasonable employer would have acted in a given situation, the court will take into account the cost of the action necessary (see *Latimer v AEC Ltd* where the only alternative to the employer would have been to close the factory entirely). **7.2.1.2**

Breach as the cause of the injury

The breach must be the cause of the injury. See, for example, *McWilliams v Sir William Arrol & Co Ltd*, where even though the employer was in breach of his duty by removing the safety belts, evidence showed that even if they had been present the employees would not have used them. Thus the employer's breach was held not to be the cause of the injury. **7.2.1.3**

The normal tort rules of remoteness apply, thus if the employer is negligent in respect of a foreseeable type of injury he will be liable for all loss of that type arising from his action.

Defences

There are three main defences available to an employer found to be in breach of their common law duty of care: **7.2.1.4**

- The issue of causation must be proven, as in the case of *McWilliams v Sir William Arrol & Co Ltd*, see above.

- Contributory negligence on the part of the employee, in which case the court has discretion under the Law Reform (Contributory Negligence) Act 1945 to reduce proportionally the damages payable. The employee is under a duty to take reasonable care of his own health and safety, not to intentionally or recklessly interfere with or misuse anything provided in the interests of health and safety, and to use equipment provided in accordance with the employer's instructions and training; breach of any such duties would normally lead to a finding of contributory negligence.

- Consent to the risk by the employee (*volenti non fit injuria*). This is a complete defence, but the courts are aware that in reality employees very rarely give real consent to injury. There are very few recent case examples where the court has accepted *volenti* as a defence. In one of the few examples, *ICI Ltd v Shatwell* [1965] A.C. 656, two shot-firers deliberately broke both statutory regulations and the employer's instructions, resulting in injury to both of them. One of them then brought an action against the employer on the basis of their vicarious liability for the actions of the other shot-firer. In view of the facts of the case it is perhaps not surprising that the court held that the employer was not liable, the complete defence of *volenti non fit injuria* should succeed.

Employer's Indirect Liability

7.2.2   If a third party is injured due to the negligence of an employee, the employer may be liable under the doctrine of vicarious liability, but only if the employee is acting in the course of his employment.

The concept of "in the course of employment" as used in tort is no longer the same as is used in cases of discrimination (see Chapter 5). In discrimination cases, the courts now interpret the phrase in the way that a layman would understand it, following the Court of Appeal decision in *Jones v Tower Boot Co Ltd*. In tort cases however, the phrase is still interpreted more strictly, and is taken generally to mean that the employer will only be vicariously liable for the actions of his employees if the actions are carried out with the authority of the employer—although it is necessary to bear in mind the House of Lords ruling in *Lister v Hesley Hall Ltd* [2001] I.R.L.R. 472, which in at least some scenarios (the case concerns issues of sexual abuse by an employee towards children in the employer's care) redefines and broadens the common law test.

Examples of the traditional approach of the courts include the case of *Kay v ITW Ltd* [1968] 1 Q.B. 140 in which, when a fork lift truck driver found that his way was blocked by a lorry, he moved the lorry himself, although he had no specific instruction to do so, and in so doing injured another employee. The court held that the employer was vicariously liable, since the action was not so extreme as to take it outside of the employee's normal activities. Whereas in the case of *Hilton v Thomas Burton Ltd* [1961] 1 W.L.R. 705 an employee made use of a firm's van to drive to a cafe on an unauthorised work break. In so doing he knocked down and killed a fellow worker. The court held that, although the employee had the general permission of the employer to drive the van, at the time of the incident he was acting outside the course of his employment. Thus the employer was not liable.

Occupational Stress and Psychiatric Injury

The issue of psychiatric injury arising from work-place stress has been a difficult area for the courts. One of the first important cases was that of *Walker v Northumberland County Council* [1995] I.R.L.R. 35. Mr Walker worked for the social services department as a senior manager. Over the years his workload increased considerably, including a large number of child abuse cases. Despite requests from Mr Walker no additional staff were provided to help cope with the workload. Mr Walker suffered a nervous breakdown, but shortly afterwards returned to work. Additional staff were provided to assist him, but after a short while these were withdrawn. After a few months Mr Walker suffered another nervous breakdown and was dismissed by the Council on the grounds of ill health. The first issue for the court was the question of whether the employer's duty of care owed to its employees extended beyond physical injury to the areas of psychiatric injury—the court held that it did. The court then held that the employer had liability for Mr Walker's second nervous breakdown, that it was foreseeable and the council had failed in its duty to provide appropriate support. It should however be noted that the court only considered the question of liability for Mr Walker's second breakdown, they did not consider possible liability for the first one.

The Court of Appeal then considered similar issues in the joined cases of *Sutherland v Hatton; Somerset County Council v Barber; Sandwell Metropolitan Borough Council v Jones; Baker Refractories Ltd v Bishop* [2002] I.R.L.R. 263 in which they laid down 16 point important guidelines:

- There are no special control mechanisms applying to claims for psychiatric (or physical) illness or injury arising from the stress of doing the work the employee is required to do. The ordinary principles of employer's liability apply.

- The threshold question is whether this kind of harm to this particular employee was reasonably foreseeable. This has two components: (a) an injury to health (as distinct from occupational stress) which (b) is attributable to stress at work (as distinct from other factors).

- Foreseeability depends on what the employer knows (or ought reasonably to know) about the individual employee. Because of the nature of mental

7.2.3

disorder, it is harder to foresee than physical injury, but may be easier to foresee in a known individual than in the population at large. An employer is usually entitled to assume that the employee can withstand the normal pressures of the job unless he knows of some particular problem or vulnerability.

- The test is the same whatever the employment: there are no occupations which should be regarded as intrinsically dangerous to mental health.

- Factors likely to be relevant in answering the threshold question include: (a) The nature and extent of the work done by the employee. Is the workload much more than is normal for the particular job? Is the work particularly intellectually or emotionally demanding for this employee? Are demands being made of this employee unreasonable when compared with demands made of others in the same or comparable jobs? Or are there signs that others doing this job suffering harmful levels of stress? Is there an abnormal level of sickness or absenteeism in the same job or the same department? (b) Signs from the employee of impending harm to health. Have they a particular problem or vulnerability? Have they already suffered from illness attributable to stress at work? Have there recently been frequent or prolonged absences which are uncharacteristic of them? Is there reason to think that these are attributable to stress at work, for example because of complaints or warnings from them or others?

- The employer is generally entitled to take what he is told by the employee at face value, unless he has good reason to think to the contrary. He does not generally have to make searching enquiries of the employee or seek permission to make further enquiries of his medical advisors.

- To trigger a duty to take steps, the indications of impending harm to health arising from stress at work must be plain enough for any reasonable employer to realise that he should do something about it.

- The employer is only in breach of duty if he has failed to take steps which are reasonable in the circumstances, bearing in mind the magnitude of the risk of harm occurring, the gravity if the harm which may occur, the costs and practicality of preventing it, and the justifications for running the risk.

- The size and scope of the employer's operation, its resources and the demands it faces are relevant in deciding what is reasonable; these include the interests of other employees and the need to treat them fairly, for example, in any redistribution of duties.

- An employer can only reasonably be expected to take steps which are likely to do some good: the court is likely to need some expert evidence on this.

- An employer who offers a confidential advice service, with referral to appropriate counselling or treatment services, is unlikely to be found in breach of duty.

- If the only reasonable and effective step would have been to dismiss or demote the employee, the employer will not be in breach of duty in allowing a willing employee to continue in the job.

- In all cases, therefore, it is necessary to identify the steps which the employer both could and should have taken before finding him in breach of his duty of care.

- The claimant must show that the breach of duty has caused or materially contributed to the harm suffered. It is not enough to show that occupational stress has caused the harm.

- Where the harm suffered has more than one cause, the employer should only pay for that proportion of the harm suffered which is attributable to his wrongdoing, unless the harm is truly indivisible. It is for the defendant to raise the issue of apportionment.

- The assessment of damages will take account of any pre-existing disorder or vulnerability and of the chance that the claimant would have succumbed to a stress related disorder in any event.

These guidelines were impliedly approved by the House of Lords in *Barber v Somerset County Council* [2004] I.R.L.R. 475 and applied in the joined cases of *Hartman v South Essex Mental Health and Community Care NHS Trust; Best v Staffordshire University; Green v Grimsby and Scunthorpe Newspapers Ltd; Melville v Home Office; Moore v Welwyn Components Ltd; Wheeldon v HSBC Bank Ltd* [2005] I.R.L.R. 293.

In view of the relative lack of authoritative case law in this area it is worth considering these cases in some detail to appreciate the application of the *Hatton* guidelines:

(a) Hartman v South Essex Mental Health and Community Care NHS Trust

Mrs Hartman was a nursing auxiliary in a centre dealing with children with learning difficulties. This was an unqualified post that she had held since 1989. Prior to her employment with South Essex NHS Trust she had a history of sociological problems, culminating in a nervous breakdown in 1988, but had been screened by the Trust's own occupational health department and been passed fit for employment. In 1996, following the accidental death of a child at the centre, she and other members of staff were given two weeks' compassionate leave and offered counselling; she did not take up the offer of counselling. In late 1996, the working practices at the home were changed which involved Mrs Hartman in working longer hours. Management of the Trust were advised of the additional pressures being placed on the staff.

In 1998, Mrs Hartman developed bronchitis, followed by a number of psychological symptoms and she applied for ill-health retirement. Her sick pay ceased in February 1999, but she did not return to work, and her employment was terminated by the Trust in May 1999. The judge at first instance accepted that Mrs Hartman's condition would not have become chronic, nor have lasted so long, but for the accident and the increased pressures at work. He found in her favour and awarded £51,620 damages. The NHS Trust appealed.

The appeal by the NHS Trust was allowed. The Court of Appeal considered three issues:

(i) the information given by Mrs Hartman to the occupational health department in 1989 was confidential, and it was not right to attribute to the Trust in its capacity as employer medical information given in this way. Further, the occupational health department had passed Mrs Hartman fit for work, a finding which was borne out by a further nine years of employment.

(ii) it appeared that Mrs Hartman had recovered from the effects of the accident in 1996, and that she failed to take up the Trust's offer of counseling; and

(iii) the complaints made to the management referred to the demands placed on the qualified staff; Mrs Hartman was unqualified. In the light of these findings it could not be found that the injury to Mrs Hartman was foreseeable, nor that the Trust was in breach of its duty of care towards her.

(b) Best v Staffordshire University

Mr Best was employed by the university in 1986 as a senior lecturer. Apart from his duties of lecturing and tutoring he was responsible for the department's lecture timetabling. Evidence was given of increasing workloads and complaints by Mr Best of the effect of such workloads. In 1998 he broke down at work with symptoms of anxiety and was prescribed anti-depressants. He was off work for six months, returned to work in August 1998, but from January 1999 was off work again until September 2000, at which point he retired on grounds of ill-health, aged 46. Mr Best claimed compensation from the university for their alleged negligence which he claimed had resulted in his retirement on health grounds. The judge at first instance gave judgment against the university on the issue of liability.

The Court of Appeal found that certain evidence had not been given proper weight at first instance hearing. There was evidence that colleagues of Mr Best who worked closely with him were surprised by his breakdown, that Mr Best had himself applied for promotion shortly before his breakdown and that Mr Best was well aware that the university operated a counselling service, but made no attempt to contact or use the service. For these reasons it could not be held that Mr Best's breakdown was foreseeable, and thus the university could have no liability.

(c) Green v Grimsby & Scunthorpe Newspapers Ltd

Mr Green had worked for the newspaper publishers for over 40 years. In 1989 he was moved from the news section, because he was unable to cope with frequent short deadlines, to the features department where he worked as chief sub-editor, where one of the duties was the sub-editing of a monthly magazine. He claimed that from 1999 new working practices within the company resulted in him having an increased workload, meaning that he had to work through his lunch break and occasionally work late. The company, in response, argued that he worked less hours than anyone else, always took a half-hour coffee break immediately on arriving at the office and very rarely if ever worked late. In June 1999, Mr Green wrote a memo to the editor complaining of the long hours and expressing the opinion that having to edit the monthly magazine was causing "constant worry to . . . the point where it is beginning to affect my health". One morning, some days later, at around 9.00am the editor went to see Mr Green to discuss the memo but found that Mr Green was absent from his office taking a coffee break. On Mr Green's return there was an exchange of views at which point Mr Green left the office. The following day he consulted his doctor who diagnosed depression. Mr Green did not return to work and retired on health grounds in February 2001. Mr Green claimed damages for personal injury and loss resulting from psychological injury caused by the negligence of his employers. His claim was dismissed and he appealed.

Mr Green's appeal was dismissed. The court stated that nothing "said by the House of Lords in *Barber* was intended to alter the practical guidance given in *Hatton*". They then addressed the argument that the memo sent by Mr Green should have put his employer on notice of his health problems and that the employer's response to this memo was inadequate. The court agreed with the recorder at first instance that this contention was "unrealistic", and that the case did not come close to meeting the requirements identified in *Hatton*.

(d) Melville v Home Office

Mr Melville was employed as a health care officer at HM Prison Exeter from 1981. One of his duties was the recovery of bodies of prisoners who had committed suicide. From 1981 until 1998 he had attended eight such suicides. Care teams had been set up by the Home Office to counsel and advise staff following their involvement in such situations; however, it appears that such teams had not contacted Mr Melville during his employment. From 1998, he started to suffer nightmares and flashbacks which were diagnosed as stress related illness, and he retired on ill-health grounds in 1998 at the age of 49.

The question of foreseeability was addressed as a preliminary issue at first instance and found in favour of Mr Melville. The Home Office appealed but their appeal was dismissed. The Court of Appeal stated that the provision of an occupational health scheme does not necessarily show that the company has foreseen the risk of psychiatric injury to any employee or class of employee; on the other hand, if such a scheme exists but an employee chooses not to make use of it, that will not in itself be fatal to an employees claim. Likewise, the provision of such a scheme by one employer does not necessarily indicate that other employers within the same industry will necessarily be liable if they do not provide a similar scheme. Each case must be judged on its facts, although dicta from *Hatton* does indicate that, if such a scheme is in place and operating efficiently, the employer is unlikely to be found in breach of their duty of care. In the instant case, although a scheme was in place, it was apparently not operated effectively.

(e) Moore v Welwyn Components Ltd

Mr Moore had worked for 25 years as an accountant for Welwyn Components. In 1975, he had been admitted to a psychiatric hospital suffering from severe depressive illness causing him to be absent from work for several months. Following various changes to working practices, he was again absent from work in 1988, in 1990, and in 1994; after each of these periods of illness Mr Moore appeared to have made full recovery and returned to work. Evidence was accepted that from 1996 Mr Moore was the recipient of sustained bullying by the company's financial director. The effect on Mr Moore of the bullying was brought to the attention of the financial director in 1997, but apparently the bullying continued. Mr Moore retired due to ill health in 1998. At first instance the case was found for Mr Moore, but permission to appeal was granted only on the grounds that the judge had not addressed the question of apportionment of damages awarded.

The issue here was only the question of apportionment of damages. The court in *Hatton* stated that damages for breach of duty resulting in psychiatric injury will be reduced to reflect the fact that causes other than the breach would, or could in any event have caused a degree of injury. The Court of Appeal in the instant case stated that a similar principle applied in cases of loss of earnings; if there was a reasonable prospect that Mr Moore's mental state might result in him retiring early as a result of non-negligent stress, then an appropriate reduction in damages should be made. The court, however, agreed with the judge at first instance. Although Mr Moore was, according to psychiatric evidence, "a vulnerable individual", he had always returned to work following any absences for illness, and no evidence was adduced by the employer that Mr Moore would not otherwise have continued at work until retirement. The employer's appeal was therefore dismissed.

(f) Wheeldon v HSBC Bank Ltd

Mrs Wheeldon was employed from 1982 to 2000 by HSBC on a part-time, average 17.5 hours per week, basis. She was in joint charge of one of the bank's sub-branches. From the mid-1990s pressure of work increased; there were staff cut-backs, changes in working procedures, closure of a nearby branch and an almost constant requirement for overtime to be worked. In 1997 she complained to her line manager about the pressure of work. In 1999 she had a panic attack at work, was diagnosed as suffering from depression, returned to work, suffered a breakdown, was prescribed anti-depressants and was seen by the company's occupational health department on her return to work in 2000. The occupational health department's report suggested that Mrs Wheeldon was suffering from stress brought about by pressure of work. A copy of this report was apparently sent to her GP with a recommendation that she should be referred to a consultant psychiatrist before any decision as to her future could be taken. On her next visit to her GP, Mrs Wheeldon appeared to be improving and it was decided not to refer her to a consultant psychiatrist. In the summer of 2000, Mrs Wheeldon was off work for a non-stress related medical issue. When she returned the pressure of work had increased and Mrs Wheeldon again suffered panic attacks. When she contacted the company occupational health department she was told that her file had been closed. Mrs Wheeldon resigned in October 2000. At first instance the judge found for Mrs Wheeldon, holding that although the bank had acted quite properly until early March 2000, from that date they had not acted responsibly on the information they had regarding her condition. The bank appealed against this decision.

The conclusion of the judgment of the Court of Appeal is as follows:

"Mrs Wheeldon had problems coping at work. When her mental condition deteriorated she was off work for a period. Following her return, the bank was made aware of her condition by its own occupational health department and the steps it needed to take in the light of that condition. It failed to take those steps and her psychiatric injury resulted. The judge correctly applied the law and there is no basis for interfering with his decision".

One issue that was raised by the Court of Appeal in *Wheeldon* was brought about by the fact that Mrs Wheeldon worked only on a part-time basis. It was stated, ". . . it will only be in exceptional circumstances that someone working for two or three days a week for limited hours will make good a claim for injury caused by stress at work". It is however suggested that this statement must be viewed in conjunction with the statement in *Melville* (above) that each case should be considered on its own facts, otherwise it may appear to amount to indirect sex discrimination.

There are occasions when, although the resulting injury amounts to occupational stress, the rules governing compensation may not apply. Such a case was *Essa v Laing Ltd* [2004] I.R.L.R. 313 where the psychiatric harm had been caused by racial discrimination; the court reiterated that in racial discrimination cases it was not necessary to examine the issue of foreseeability, since compensation was available for all harm which flowed directly from the unlawful act.

The Tort of Breach of Statutory Duty

7.2.4   There is no automatic presumption that all breaches of statutory duties are actionable in the civil court (*Cutler v Wandsworth Stadium Ltd* [1949] A.C. 398). Many recent statutes make clear that a breach will give rise to an action for breach of statutory duty (e.g. s.47(2) of the HSWA 1974) which states that breach of Regulations made under the Act in its role as an enabling Act will give rise to such an action, unless the Regulation specifically states otherwise), and following the decision in *Groves v Lord Wimborne* [1898] 2 Q.B. 402 there was a presumption that a breach of safety legislation would enable an injured worker to bring an action, but the issue has been less clear with some of the older legislation and with legislation regarding the more general topics of health and welfare.

There are four elements to the tort. The first is that the Claimant must show that he is within the class of person the legislation was designed to protect; second, that the injury sustained is of a type that the legislation was intended to prevent; third, that the company, the defendant, is actually in breach of the duty; and finally, the question of causation must be satisfied.

STATUTE

7.3   The main and most important piece of domestic legislation is the Health and Safety at Work Act 1974 (HSWA). It is a complex and detailed piece of legislation, which when introduced had far reaching consequences for health and safety in the workplace.

The Act imposes a duty on employees to act reasonably. Sections 7 and 8 state that the employee should take reasonable care, both for his own safety and for the safety of others. The employee is also under a duty to cooperate with the employer in carrying out the Health and Safety policy, which each employer must prepare under s.2(3).

The main thrust of the Act, however, is aimed at the employer. Section 2 states that it is the duty of every employer to ensure, so far as is reasonably practicable, the health, safety and welfare at work of all his employees, including the maintenance of safe systems of work, safe place of work, safe working environment and adequate training.

"So far as is reasonably practicable" does not mean that the employer has an absolute duty to eliminate all risks and an example of this may be seen in the case of *West Bromwich Building Society v Townsend* [1983] I.C.R. 257, in which an HSE inspector alleged that the employer had not taken reasonable steps to ensure the protection of its staff by failing to erect bandit screens on its counters. The court however held that since the danger of attack was relatively slight, the staff had all been trained not to resist attack, and the screens would appear contrary to the society's customer friendly image, the society had done everything that was "reasonably practicable".

Section 3 of the Act places a duty on the employer:

> "to conduct his undertaking in such a way as to ensure, so far as is reasonably practicable, that persons not in his employment who may be affected thereby are not exposed to risks to their health or safety".

It is perhaps possible to discern a move away by the courts from the traditional common law health and safety approach (which at times appears somewha "black letter" or "literal") to the more purposive approach favoured by the EC in interpreting statutes, by briefly considering two recent important cases:

(a) RMC Roadstone Products Ltd v Jester [1994] I.R.L.R. 330

Independent contractors were engaged to carry out repairs at a factory, and were left alone by the defendant company to operate their own systems and methods of work. One of the contractors fell from a roof and suffered fatal injuries. The court was required to determine the liability of the defendant under s.3 of the HSWA 1974. The Divisional Court held that the defendants mere capacity or opportunity to exercise control over the independent contractors was not in itself sufficient to bring the activities of the contractors within the meaning of "conduct his undertaking" for the purposes of the Act, and consequently the defendant should have no liability.

7.3.1

(b) R v Associated Octel Ltd [1997] I.R.L.R. 123

Independent contractors were engaged by the defendant company to carry out maintenance works including the cleaning and repair of chemical tanks. The contractors were required to obtain from the defendants safety equipment and a "permit to work" for each task they carried out. During work on one of the tanks a contractor was severely injured. The question for the court was one of liability under s.3 of the HSWA 1974. On appeal to the House of Lords it was held that the defendants did have liability. The House stated that when an employer engages independent contractors for such purposes as routine maintenance he must take such precautions as are reasonable to safeguard the health and safety of those contractors. Whether a particular task amounted to part of the employer's undertaking for the purposes of s.3 of the HSWA 1974 was a question of fact for the jury.

7.3.2

Additionally, the Act provides for:

7.3.3

- The establishment of the Health and Safety Commission, an advisory body appointed by the Secretary of State to secure the health, safety and welfare of workers. It also proposes new legislation and standards.

- The establishment of a unified enforcement procedure under the Health and Safety Executive (HSE), which has a staff of over 4500, including inspectors, policy advisors, technical and medical experts. The HSE also publishes a number of Approved Codes of Practice and Guidance Notes.

If an HSE inspector is of the opinion that an employer is contravening the Act, ss.21 and 22 gives him the power to issue an improvement notice requiring that the problem be remedied, or in the case of serious danger, a prohibition notice requiring that an activity be discontinued until the situation is remedied.

Furthermore, the Act is an enabling Act, and has been used to implement EC Directives.

EC Framework Directive

7.3.4   EC Directive 89/391 concerning the harmonisation of health and safety legislation in Europe, along with six other directives concerning specific subjects were implemented by a series of regulations introduced at the beginning of 1993:

- Management of Health and Safety at Work Regulations 1992—the framework regulations, imposing a duty on employers to carry out risk assessment measures, put into practice preventative measures, and nominate health and safety representatives.
- Provision and Use of Work Equipment Regulations 1992.
- Manual Handling Operations Regulations 1992.
- Workplace (Health, Safety and Welfare) Regulations 1992—replacing much existing legislation concerning work environment, provision of workplace facilities, etc.
- Personal Protective Equipment at Work Regulations 1992.
- Health and Safety (Display Screen Equipment) Regulations 1992.

The standard of duty of care laid down by the Regulations is much higher than the "reasonable" standard normally adopted in common law, as demonstrated in the case of *Stark v The Post Office* [2000] I.C.R. 1013. Mr Stark worked for the Post Office as a postman delivering letters, for which purpose the Post Office provided him with a bicycle. One day the front brake on the bicycle broke, causing the wheel to jam and Mr Stark to be thrown to the floor, where he sustained injuries. Both parties accepted that a prior examination of the bicycle would not have revealed the defect, and consequently there was no way in which the employer could have had prior warning of the accident. However, it was argued for Mr Stark that reg.6 of the Provision and Use of Work Equipment Regulations 1992 imposed an absolute obligation on the employer to ensure that the equipment was maintained in good repair. The court held that although the Directives (Work Equipment Directive 89/655 and Framework Directive 89/391) may be read as laying down a less than absolute duty, the same could not be said of the Regulations, which had been drafted so as to impose an absolute duty on the employer.

Chapter 8

TERMINATION OF EMPLOYMENT

CHAPTER OVERVIEW

As with any other contract, the contract of employment will at some stage come to an end. In this chapter we consider the ways by which this may occur.

CO8

Termination by way of contract is when the contract is terminated using a term of that contract—a notice period written into the contract. If no term is expressed in the contract, one is imposed by statute.

Almost all contracts of employment will, for example, include a term permitting the employer to dismiss an employee for "gross misconduct".

Termination in breach of contract occurs when the employee is dismissed by the employer for a reason which is not a contractual term.

Termination by methods external to the contract considers particularly the contract law doctrine of frustration and its effect on the employment relationship.

TERMINATION BY WAY OF CONTRACT

Every contract of employment will contain as a term of the contract details of how the contract may be lawfully determined by either party. Except in certain circumstances this will involve one party giving notice to the other party. Such notice period should be no less than the statutory minimum laid down in s.86 of the ERA 1996.

8.1

Under s.86 minimum notice periods are as follows:

i) Employed for between one month and two years—one week's notice.

ii) Employed for between two and twelve years—one week for each year of employment.

iii) Employed for over twelve years—twelve weeks notice;
and these will apply where either no notice period is quoted in the contract, or the notice period stated in the contract is less than this. If the contractual notice period is longer, the longer period will apply.

It is, of course, possible for the employee to determine the contract for any reason by giving the required amount of notice. Failure to give such notice would allow the employer to bring an action for breach of contract (but see below).

Statute has imposed certain restrictions and obligations on the part of the employer when seeking to determine the employment contract and so dismiss the employee. Not only does the employee have the right to certain minimum notice periods (s.86 of the ERA 1996), there is also a right not to be unfairly dismissed (s.94 of the ERA 1996), and a right to compensation if the reason for dismissal is redundancy (s.135 of the ERA 1996).

TERMINATION IN BREACH OF CONTRACT

8.2 If the contract of employment is terminated by the employer—in other words if the employee is dismissed—in circumstances or for reasons outside of the contractual terms, the dismissal will constitute a breach of contract by the employer. This will allow the employee in many cases to bring an action for either wrongful dismissal or unfair dismissal (see Chapters 9 and 10).

In theory, if the employee were to terminate the contract in circumstances or for reasons outside of the contractual terms, this would allow the employer to bring an action for breach of contract. However, in practice this very rarely happens. Most companies would not wish to sue an ex-employee for damages in such circumstances, partly because the chances of financial success are in reality small, and partly because such action would probably give rise to adverse publicity.

A further factor is that s.236 of the TULR(C)A 1992 states:

"No court shall, whether by way of—

a) an order for specific performance or specific implement of a contract of employment, or

b) an injunction or interdict restraining a breach or threatened breach of such a contract, compel an employee to do any work or attend at any place for the doing of any work."

Thus the courts may not enforce a contract of employment against an employee so as to force the employee either to work or to attend for work. On occasion however the courts have enforced a contract of employment against an employee; such occasions have usually involved cases of "garden leave" wherein an employee wishing to leave and join another, usually rival, company is prevented from doing so until his contractual notice period has expired. During the notice period the company is obliged to continue paying wages but does not have to allow the employee to actually attend for work. An example of such an instance is the case of *Evening Standard v Henderson* [1987] I.C.R. 588, in which an injunction was granted to the employer preventing Henderson from breaching his contractual term which required him to give one year's notice of termination. In recent years the courts have appeared more reluctant to enforce such "garden leave" clauses, and in such cases as *William Hill Organisation Ltd v Tucker* [1999] I.C.R. 291 have refused to do so.

TERMINATION BY METHODS EXTERNAL TO THE CONTRACT

Since in many respects the employment contract is similar to any other contract, the doctrine of frustration of contract applies to it. **8.3**

Frustration

Frustration may be defined as an act external to the contract which is not caused by the fault of either party, and which was not foreseen by the parties to the contract (and thus not planned for within the contract), which has the effect of fundamentally altering the contract, or making it impossible to perform. **8.3.1**

The effect of frustration on the contract of employment is that the contract is held to be immediately terminated without a dismissal taking place, indeed there is no need for the employer to indicate or announce that the contract is terminated since the contract will be terminated automatically by operation of law. Since, in law, no dismissal has taken place, the ex-employee will be unable to claim either wrongful dismissal or unfair dismissal. The Law Reform (Frustrated Contracts) Act 1943 will apply and thus the employee will be entitled to any wages due before the frustrating event occurred and/or to payment for tasks completed if the court treats those tasks as severable, or for payment for non-severable work done, on a *quantum meruit* basis at the discretion of the court.

In order to decide whether the employment contract has been frustrated and, to an extent, to mitigate the harshness to the employee in such situations, a number of factors for consideration were laid down in the case of *Egg Stores (Stamford Hill) Ltd v Leibovici* [1977] I.C.R. 260, including length of previous employment, nature of the job, nature and effect of the disabling event, the requirement for a replacement, whether a reasonable employer could be expected to wait any longer, etc.

Examples of frustration of the contract of employment include:

- Imposition of a prison sentence (*FC Shepherd & Co Ltd v Jerrom* [1986] I.R.L.R. 358). It has been argued that the imposition of a prison sentence must amount to the fault of the employee, thus it cannot constitute frustration. Although there is some logic in this, if it were accepted it would mean that an employee sentenced to imprisonment would be able to sue for wrongful dismissal if given no notice period, or even for unfair dismissal; whilst an employee whose contract was frustrated through illness would have no such recourse. This would give a situation in which the employee at fault is in a better position than the employee whose contract is terminated through no fault of their own. The court in *Shepherd v Jerrom* considered such a situation to be "an affront to common sense", and, partly agreeing with the reasoning of Lord Denning in the earlier case of *Hare v Murphy Bros Ltd* [1974] I.C.R. 603, stated that imprisonment could lead to frustration—holding either that it was not the commission of the offence which was the frustrating event, but the imposition of the prison sentence—had the criminal court imposed a suspended sentence or a fine the contract would not have been frustrated, although there may in such cases be grounds for a fair dismissal; or alternatively that the legal rule concerning frustration was that no party could rely upon their own misconduct when claiming frustration of contract—in this case the employer was not relying on their own misconduct, but on the employee's.

- Medical evidence that the worker could probably never work again (*Notcutt v Universal Equipment Co Ltd* [1986] I.R.L.R. 218). In cases of long term sickness, the court will consider such factors as how long the employee is expected to be absent, the need of the employer to obtain a replacement, how long the employee has been employed, the provision of sick pay within the contract, etc. Long-term absence from work will not automatically constitute frustration, and indeed if the contract provides for enhanced sick pay schemes it would hardly be possible for the company to argue that event had not been foreseen.

The courts are unwilling to find frustration of employment contracts too readily; in *Williams v Watson Luxury Coaches Ltd* [1990] I.R.L.R. 164 it was stated that frustration in employment would be a rare occurrence, and the doctrine should be severely limited.

Death of the Employer

At common law, the death of the employer would have the effect of terminating **8.3.2** the contract of employment without giving rise to a dismissal—the reason being that the identity of the persons is fundamental to an employment contract; consequently, again at common law, the death of the employee would have a similar effect on the contract. In similar circumstances, however, statute now intervenes and in the case of death of the employer would deem a dismissal by reason of redundancy to have taken place (s.136(5)(b) of the ERA 1996).

If the employer is a company as opposed to an individual the legal position is both confusing and complex. If a compulsory winding-up order is served or if a company goes into voluntary liquidation there will generally be a dismissal, and the winding-up order will amount to the giving of notice to the employees.

Chapter 9

WRONGFUL DISMISSAL AND OTHER COMMON LAW CLAIMS

CHAPTER OVERVIEW

Chapter 9 looks at issues of wrongful dismissal and other common law claims. **CO9**
   Students are often confused by the relationship between wrongful dismissal and unfair dismissal. Wrongful dismissal is a common law concept, it is a remedy at common law for the breach of the employment contract (the unlawful termination of the contract by the employer) and is concerned not with the manner of or reasons for the termination, but only with the fact that insufficient notice of termination has been given to the employee. The remedy is damages which amount only to monies in lieu of the notice which should have been, but which was not, given. Unfair dismissal on the other hand will award a remedy for contracts which are terminated by the employer for a reason which is not "fair" or for the manner in which the dismissal was carried out.
   Students are strongly recommended to read the House of Lords judgment in *Johnson v Unisys Ltd* [2001] I.R.L.R. 279 and some of the opinions and criticisms of that case by academics and other writers. Although the statutory remedy of unfair dismissal (see Chapter 10) is generally regarded as a positive aspect of

employment law, one effect of *Johnson* is that statute very much restricts what the common law could otherwise do in favour of the employee—and that is probably not what the legislators intended when the remedy of unfair dismissal was first introduced some 30 years ago.

The Basic Position

9.1   An action for wrongful dismissal is a common law action for damages to compensate the ex-employee for losses suffered for the wrongful termination of the employment contract. Generally this will only amount to monies to which the employee would have been contractually entitled had the contract been lawfully terminated, in effect, monies in lieu of notice. The leading case is *Addis v Gramophone Co Ltd* [1909] A.C. 488, in which Mr Addis's contract provided that he would be paid part salary and part commission, and in the event of termination would be entitled to six months' notice. His contract was terminated by his employers and he was given six months' notice, but was not allowed to work out his notice period. The question arose as to the damages to which Mr Addis was entitled. It was accepted that he was entitled to his basic salary for the six-month period, but could he also claim for the commission he would have earned, or for either the fact of or the manner of his dismissal? The House of Lords held that he was entitled only to the wages for the six-month notice period, plus the commission he would have earned had he been permitted to work for those six months. He was not however entitled to damages as compensation for injured feelings, nor for "the loss he may sustain from the fact that his having been dismissed of itself makes it more difficult for him to obtain fresh employment."*per* Lord Loreburn L.C.

Thus compensation for wrongful dismissal amounts only to monies to which the employee would have been entitled under the contract. It will not include any purely discretionary bonuses or pay rises (but be aware of the approach of the courts in cases such as *Cantor Fitzgerald v Horkulak* [2004] I.R.L.R. 942).

Normally such damages will be limited to either wages for the minimum statutory notice period, or the notice period stipulated by the contract, whichever is the longer. Thus, an action for wrongful dismissal concerns only whether the correct contractual notice period has been given, as such, the reason for the dismissal is irrelevant. Remember, of course, that in a number of circumstances an employer may summarily dismiss an employee quite lawfully, e.g. for gross misconduct (see *Sinclair v Neighbour* [1967] 2 Q.B. 279, *Pepper v Webb* [1969] 1 W.L.R. 514), in which case the dismissal takes place immediately and the only monies payable are those wages due up to the time of dismissal.

Monies in lieu of Notice

In most circumstances, the employer will be able to discharge their obligations **9.1.1**
under the contract by paying money in lieu of notice, and not requiring or not
allowing the employee to work a notice period. There are, however, some situations where such action may in itself constitute a separate breach of contract,
e.g. actors or others whose work requires them to be exposed or displayed to the
public. In such cases the courts have been prepared to award separate damages
for damage to reputation (*Herbert Clayton & Jack Waller Ltd v Oliver* [1930] A.C.
209).

Monies paid in lieu of notice will either be treated as damages for breach by the
employer of the contractual term to give the requisite notice period (*Delaney v
Staples (t/a De Montfort Rceruitment)* [1992] I.C.R. 483), or as a taxable emolument arising under the contract if there is a term in the employment contract
specifically permitting the employer do so (*EMI Group Electronics Ltd v Coldicott
(Inspector of Taxes)* [1999] I.R.L.R. 630) but in neither case may the amount be
reduced in reliance on the employee's duty to mitigate. This is demonstrated in the
case of *Cerberus Software Ltd v Rowley* [1999] I.R.L.R. 690, in which the
employee was entitled under his contract to six months' notice period or money
in lieu of notice on dismissal. Mr Rowley was dismissed without either the notice
period or money in lieu. When he sought to recover those monies the employer
argued that, since Mr Rowley had obtained a new and better paid job within five
weeks of his dismissal, when awarding damages for the company's breach of contract' the court should take into account the employee's duty to mitigate his loss,
which they argued amounted to the monies he had received from his new employment. The EAT dismissed the company's argument holding that the company was
under an obligation in the employment contract to pay the full amount.

CLAIMS FOR OTHER THAN WRONGFUL DISMISSAL

In the case of *Malik v BCCI SA* [1997] I.R.L.R. 462 the House of Lords held that **9.2**
where the manner of the dismissal constituted a breach of the contractual term
of mutual trust and confidence and this caused financial loss, that loss may be
recoverable in an action for wrongful dismissal (*cf. Addis* above). In that case, Mr
Malik was dismissed through redundancy, following the collapse of the bank due
to the bank's "dishonest and corrupt business" practices. Mr Malik claimed
damages for the disadvantage his association with the bank would place him
under in trying to obtain further employment. It was argued that, following
Addis, such damages were not available, but the House of Lords held that *Addis*
did not preclude the award of damages in a situation such as this, since the
damages in *Malik* were in respect of the employer's breach of the contract term
of mutual trust and confidence. At the time of *Addis*, this contract term had not

been recognised, whereas today it is implied into every employment contract; accordingly damages should be assessed for the breach of the term in line with accepted contract principles. On the particular and somewhat extreme facts of this case, the decision would appear to be both sensible and fair, and reflect current business realities. Although the House of Lords implied that this apparent extension to *Addis* was confined to the unusual and particular facts of the *BCCI* case, it was thought that the case may prove useful precedent in future cases if only to assist those employees who were unable to claim for unfair dismissal to receive some financial compensation for the fact or manner of their dismissal; this however has not proved to be the case. Although on a slightly different issue, the House of Lords in *Johnson v Unisys Ltd* [2001] I.R.L.R. 279 refused to extend the remedies available in the common law where statute already provided a remedy by way of compensation for unfair dismissal. In the *Johnson* case, Mr Johnson had worked for Unisys from 1971 until 1987, when he was made redundant. From 1985 he had suffered from work related stress requiring him to take time off from work. In 1990 he was re-employed by Unisys until 1994, when he was dismissed on the grounds of misconduct. He made a successful complaint of unfair dismissal for which the tribunal awarded him compensation.

Mr Johnson then made a further complaint for wrongful dismissal claiming that the manner of his dismissal had caused psychiatric injury and a loss of some £400,000 in earnings. The House of Lords upheld the dismissal of his claim. In somewhat conflicting opinions (two of their Lordships were prepared to depart from the accepted ratio of *Addis*), the majority upheld *Addis*, and distinguished *BCCI* on its facts. It was held that, since parliament had intended that claims concerning manner of dismissal were dealt with as statutory unfair dismissal claims and had placed a financial ceiling on such claims, it was not for the court to undermine the intention of parliament. It is therefore necessary (although sometimes by no means easy) to distinguish between:

(a) a breach of contract which forms part of the dismissal and for which the remedy is a statutory claim for unfair dismissal; and

(b) a breach which does not form part of the dismissal and for which the remedy may be a common law claim for breach of contract.

It will generally be financially beneficial for an applicant to claim under unfair dismissal legislation, but in the case of Mr Johnson and some others this will not be so—Mr Johnson sought some £400,000 damages but was able to claim only the statutory maximum for unfair dismissal which was (at that time) £11,000.

The *Johnson* approach was followed in *Eastwood v Magnox Electric Plc* [2004] I.R.L.R. 733 HL, but in that case, since the actions by the employer had started before the dismissal procedure began and therefore did not form part of that dismissal procedure, the employee was able to bring a separate claim for a common law breach of contract (that the actions of the employer in carrying out a campaign to "demoralise and undermine" the employee had resulted in the employee suffering psychiatric injury).

As stated above, the problem for the courts is to differentiate between those actions which form part of the dismissal procedure—for which the remedy is the statutory claim for unfair dismissal, and those actions which amounted to a breach of contract but did not form part of the dismissal procedure—for which the common law may provide a separate remedy. It is not possible, following *Johnson* to bring a claim for a breach of contract which forms part of the dismissal procedure; the only remedy would be one of an unfair dismissal claim, which is financially capped by statute (presently at some £58,000).

Compensation for the Loss of the Right to Claim Unfair Dismissal

There is authority, suggested in *Stapp v Shaftsbury Society* [1982] I.R.L.R. **9.2.1** 326, and followed in *Raspin v United News Shops* [1999] I.R.L.R. 9, that if the employer unlawfully terminates an employee's contract so as to deny that employee sufficient continuity of employment to claim unfair dismissal, the employee should at common law have a claim for compensation for the loss of his right to claim unfair dismissal. This appears a just remedy—to argue otherwise would, in many cases, allow the employer to gain financially through their own wrongdoing. However, in the case of *Harper v Virgin Net Ltd* [2004] I.R.L.R. 390, where but for the wrongful summary dismissal of Ms Harper she would very likely have been eligible for a successful claim for unfair dismissal, the court considered itself bound by the House of Lords decision in *Johnson v Unisys Ltd* [2001] I.R.L.R. 279 which held that it was the intention of Parliament that compensation available only under statute (i.e. compensation for unfair dismissal under the ERA 1996) should not be extended to common law situations; in this case Ms Harper was not able to satisfy the statutory requirements and therefore had no entitlement to the statutory compensation.

THE EFFECT OF THE REPUDIATORY BREACH

It is sometimes necessary to decide whether the terms of the employment contract **9.3** can exist once the repudiatory breach—the wrongful dismissal—has taken place; in other words, does the breach itself bring the contract to an end (the automatic or unilateral theory), or is it necessary for the innocent party, the employee, to accept the breach to make it effective and end the contractual relationship (the elective or bilateral theory). Common sense might suggest that the employment relationship is at an end and thus the contract is terminated once the dismissal has taken place; but the general law of contract makes it clear that the breach will only become effective on the contract once it has been accepted by the innocent party. Much of the case law relevant to this issue has concerned instances where the employee has sought to restrain the employer from terminating the contract until a contractually agreed disciplinary procedure has taken place, consequently it is perhaps not surprising that the courts have inclined towards the elective or bilateral theory in order to keep the contract alive whilst correct procedures are followed by both parties (*Gunton v Richmond upon Thames LBC* [1980] I.C.R. 755, *Thomas Marshall (Exports) Ltd v Guinle* [1979] Ch. 227, etc.). However, it must surely also be true that the employment relationship is of a purely personal nature, and as such the contract cannot continue to exist once the relationship has been effectively terminated by a repudiatory breach. Authority to support this automatic or unilateral theory may be found in *Sanders v Ernest A Neale Ltd* [1974] I.R.L.R. 236 and as obiter dicta in *Boyo v Lambeth London Borough Council* [1995] I.R.L.R. 50.

A method of viewing this problem which has the effect of reconciling at least some of the otherwise conflicting case law is to consider that in contract law an innocent party may only refuse to accept a repudiatory contract breach if they have a "legitimate interest" in maintaining the contract. Thus, maintaining the contract during disciplinary procedure may well be a "legitimate interest"; wishing to continue to draw wages whilst not having to work, may not be.

The court in *Irani v Southampton and South West Hampshire Health Authority* [1985] I.C.R. 590 chose not to address this issue, but granted an injunction preventing a dismissal in order to allow time for a disciplinary procedure to take place, in circumstances where it was held that mutual trust and confidence between the parties still existed.

PUBLIC LAW REMEDIES

9.4   Certain public employees may be entitled to public law remedies against their employer, by way of judicial review. This may result in a quashing order (previously known as an order for "certiorari"), quashing the decision of the employer, or a mandatory order (previously known as "mandamus"), an order requiring an employer to perform a duty. There are two main advantages to such a course of action for the individual: firstly, the granting of either a quashing order or a mandatory order has the effect that the dismissal has not taken place in law (*cf.* re-instatement or re-engagement under statute which even if ordered may not be factually possible), and secondly, it is not necessary for the applicant to show continuity of employment, or indeed to prove employee status.

The problem however with a public law remedy is predicting when it may be available to any individual or group of individuals (again *cf.* unfair dismissal claims which may not be brought as group actions). In *R v East Berkshire Area*

Health Authority, Ex p. Walsh [1984] I.C.R. 743 the Court of Appeal held that judicial review would only be available where either the matter concerned public rather than private law or where the employment relationship is not defined in contractual terms; since the employment relationship of employees generally (both public and private sector) is defined by the contract of employment, they would be excluded from a public law remedy, unless they could argue that the issue was one of public rather than private law. It is accepted that public law remedies should be available to "office holders" (rather than employees) and much of the available case law concerns police officers (see *Ridge v Baldwin* [1964] A.C. 40) who are considered not to have contracts of employment and who are excluded from most of the provisions within the ERA 1996, and prison officers (see *R v Secretary of State for the Home Office Ex p. Benwell* [1985] I.R.L.R. 6), who until recently were considered "in police service", but are now covered by both TULR(C)A 1992 and ERA 1996. Other holders of public office may be entitled to public law remedies, but only if, following *Ex p. Walsh*, they do not work under a contract.

On the other ground, namely that the matter is one of public rather than private law, it is difficult to envisage when this would apply in an employment law context—although Gillian Morris writing in the Industrial Law Journal (The Human Rights Act and the Public/Private Divide in Employment Law—I.L.J. 27 1998) did consider the situation where a specific right granted under the ECHR was under threat.

Chapter 10

UNFAIR DISMISSAL

CHAPTER OVERVIEW

Unfair dismissal is the one topic that has occurred on every employment law **C010** examination paper I have ever seen, and certainly on every examination paper that

I have ever set. Fundamentally it simply states that, unless a dismissal of an employee is for one of the five potentially fair reasons and is carried out procedurally correctly, then that dismissal will be unfair. However, neither the statute which governs it, nor the body of case law that has built up around it, have proved to be quite that straightforward.

It is however a topic that may be dealt with successfully if a basic format is learned, understood and logically applied; as with all areas of employment law, case law is essential in explaining the way in which the statute operates, but much of the statute is contained in just a few sections of one Act. The importance for a student in understanding what unfair dismissal legislation is and how it operates cannot be overstated. In one guise or another, "unfair dismissal" is likely to occur in almost every other topic of employment law, and thus can almost never be avoided in an examination.

The first point to recognise is that unfair dismissal is a statutory concept; the common law would not normally recognise a dismissal as being "unfair", only as being unlawful in a contractual sense, i.e. only if the dismissal amounted to a breach of contract—and since all contracts of employment will contain either an express or an imposed term concerning the notice period to be given in the case of dismissal, a successful action at common law would normally only result in the remedy of damages amounting to the monies that would have been paid under the notice period (see "wrongful dismissal" in Chapter 9).

Once you have understood how both wrongful dismissal and unfair dismissal operate, you may care to consider the following problem:

> "If a contract of employment contained an express term that the contract may only be terminated by the employer for a specific reason but expressly stated that it may not be terminated for any other reason, but it was then terminated for a reason which was not the specific reason (thus it was terminated in specific breach of contract), would the dismissed employee be able to bring an action for common law breach of contract; and if so, on what basis should damages be awarded?"

As a starting point, consider the House of Lords decision in *Johnson v Unisys*, and remember that we already have case law stating that a common law breach of the implied term of mutual trust and confidence brought about by dismissal may not give rise to a common law action. (Bear in mind also that this is merely an academic exercise since it is almost inconceivable that any employment contract would contain such terms!)

Since this particular question has, as far as I am aware, not been asked of the courts, we can only surmise of the answer. If the ruling in *Johnson* is followed it would appear that since the breach is directly related to the dismissal the only remedy would be by way of an action for unfair dismissal, and presumably this would be the case even if the applicant were not entitled to apply for unfair dismissal (if for example they were not able to fulfil the one year continuous employment requirement); however, if the contract was a contract for services, rather than a contract of service (in other words if the applicant were an independent contractor rather than an employee), presumably a common law remedy would be available, which may be considerably more beneficial in financial terms than the equivalent unfair dismissal remedy which is of course capped by statute.

Thus, the relationship between the remedies afforded by the common law and by statute is at times a difficult one to both comprehend and justify.

Unfair Dismissal is a statutory concept consolidated almost wholly within the Employment Rights Act 1996. *"An employee has the right not to be unfairly dismissed by his employer."* s.94(1) of the ERA 1996.

Unlike a common law claim for wrongful dismissal, which in almost all cases would only entitle the applicant to receive damages amounting to money in lieu of any notice period not given, a successful claimant for unfair dismissal may receive monies from their ex-employer by way of compensation awarded by a tribunal in respect of not only notice period not given, but also for the reason for and the manner of the dismissal. The total amount awarded is capped by statute and periodically revised.

Unfair dismissal is one of the cornerstones of employment protection legislation. Although founded on statute, much of its interpretation has depended on case law and it is therefore natural that, since its inception, a considerable body of such case law has built up around it.

Different writers and commentators have used various formats in order to explain and try to simplify the issue of unfair dismissal. It overlaps into several other areas, and can appear a daunting subject to many students. However, approached properly it is one of the most straightforward topics in employment law.

Issues of unfair dismissal may be approached by logically working through the following four steps in order:

    i) Can the applicant claim?

    ii) Can a dismissal be identified?

    iii) The reason for the dismissal.

    iv) The fairness of the dismissal.

CAN THE APPLICANT CLAIM?   10.1

Is the Applicant an Employee?

It is necessary that the applicant prove their employee status as considered in   **10.1.1**
Chapter 2 in order to qualify for unfair dismissal rights. However, be aware that

under the ERelA 1999 powers have been granted to the relevant Minister to extend existing employment rights to categories of workers not presently covered.

Following recent case law (*Montgomery v Johnson Underwood Ltd*; *Dacas v Brook Street Bureau*; etc.) it is unlikely that agency workers will qualify as employees, but casual workers may (*Carmichael v National Power Plc*) although they may well have problems in showing sufficient continuity of employment to qualify for unfair dismissal. Part-time workers are treated in the same way as full-time workers following *R v Secretary of State for Employment, Ex p. Equal Opportunities Commission* [1994] I.R.L.R. 176 and the subsequent legislation SI 1995/31 (Employment Protection (Part-time Employees) Regulations 1995).

Does the employee belong to an excluded group?

10.1.2   Certain categories of employees automatically fall outside the protection of the Act, these include:

- those over normal retirement age (s.109(1) of the ERA 1996)—this is generally held to be 65 years of age for both men and women, and s.109(1) states that s.94 will not apply if the applicant has attained:

"(a) in a case where—

(i) in the undertaking in which the employee was employed there was a normal retiring age for an employee holding the position held by the employee, and

(ii) the age was the same whether the employee holding that position was a man or a woman,

that normal retiring age, and

(b) in any case, the age of sixty-five."

And case law suggests that in certain circumstances a contractual term specifying a lower age may be accepted (*Brooks v British Telecom Plc* [1992] I.C.R. 414). It is important to remember that the Employment Equality (Age) Regulations 2006, at the time of writing still at draft stage, are due to be implemented by October 2006 and are intended to remove the upper age limit for unfair dismissal claims.

- the armed forces (although provisions are in place to change this), the police, and in certain circumstances crown servants;

- those protected by collective agreements regulating dismissal procedures *may* be exempted—such procedures must be approved by the Secretary for State as operating as a substitute for the statutory scheme (s.110 of the ERA 1996). At present no such schemes are in operation.

It must be remembered at this stage that, if the Statutory Grievance Procedure laid down in The EA 2002 (Dispute Resolution) Regulations 2004 (SI 2004/752) applies and the applicant has failed to carry out the first stage of that procedure, the applicant will be unable to pursue his claim.

Does the Employee have the Minimum Required Length of Continuous Service?

Following The Unfair Dismissal and Statement of Reasons for Dismissal (Variation of Qualifying Period) Order 1999, SI 1436, the minimum period of continuous employment required in order to claim for unfair dismissal is one year. In some circumstances it will be necessary to consider what is meant by the term "continuous employment". **10.1.3**

Continuity of Employment may be considered under two sub-headings: continuity within the contract of employment, and continuity outside the contract.

Continuity within the contract

Weeks which count towards continuity are "any week during the whole or part of which the employee's relations with the employer are governed by a contract of employment" (s.212(1) of the ERA 1996). Thus continuity may be maintained should the terms of the contract change, the place of work or job function change, and even across a series of consecutive contracts with the same employer. Any term of the contract purporting to waive continuity rights would be void under s.203 of the ERA 1996. There is a statutory presumption (s.212(5) of the ERA 1996) that continuity exists and it is therefore for the employer to disprove this. **10.1.3.1**

Continuity outside the contract

Statute protects continuity in certain circumstances where no contract of employment is in force; these are for up to 26 weeks of sickness or injury, due to a temporary cessation of work, or in circumstances whereby through custom or arrangement such absences are not regarded as breaking continuity (s.212(3) of the ERA 1996). **10.1.3.2**

Examples of such situations include:

- Continuity was preserved for a lecturer working under a series of contracts each year from September to July, even though for the months between there was no contract subsisting. The House of Lords held that the summer months constituted a "temporary cessation of work" (*Ford v Warwickshire County Council* [1983] I.R.L.R. 126).

- Workers laid off and taken back on again, possibly on a number of occasions over several years, due to seasonal demand may also have continuity of employment (*Flack v Kodak Ltd* [1986] I.C.R. 775).

- In deciding whether gaps in employment are sufficient to break continuity, the court in *Ford* adopted a mathematical approach by comparing the period of the break with the periods of work on either side of it, to determine whether it was "temporary". The court in *Flack*, however, used a broad-brush approach to determine overall whether continuity had been preserved, rather than to examine each instance of cessation of work in its own right. Although these two methods of approach appear to be in conflict, the EAT in the case of *Sillars v Charrington Fuels Ltd* [1988] I.C.R. 505 suggested that the mathematical approach should be used when gaps are regular, but the broad-brush approach was appropriate where gaps were irregular.

- On occasion the courts have taken a broad view of continuity, particularly when issues of ill health are present. In the case of *Donnelly v Kelvin International Services* [1992] I.R.L.R. 496 continuity was not broken when an employee resigned due to health problems but was re-employed over a month later—despite the fact that during the intervening period he had been employed elsewhere.

- Some doubt was cast on the issue of preserving continuity of employment with the EAT decision in *Booth v United States of America* [1999] I.R.L.R. 16, in which it was stated:

  ". . . whilst it is generally desirable that employees should enjoy statutory protection during their employment, Parliament has laid down the conditions under which that protection is afforded. If, by so arranging their affairs, an employer is lawfully able to employ people in such a manner that the employees cannot complain of unfair dismissal or seek a redundancy payment, that is a matter for him. The courts simply try and apply the law as it stands."

This decision may weaken the line of authority from *Flack, Ford* and *Sillars*, although it should be noted that the *Booth* case was heard before the implementation of the Fixed-term Employees (Prevention of Less Favourable Treatment) Regulations 2002.

- Weeks lost through industrial action will neither count towards nor break continuity of employment (s.216 of the ERA 1996).

Effective date of termination

In some situations another factor which may affect the qualifying period of service is the question of the effective date of termination of the contract.   **10.1.3.3**
   The effective date of termination (EDT) is defined in s.97 of the ERA 1996 as:

a) where notice is given, the date on which that notice expires;

b) where no notice is given, the date on which the termination takes place; or

c) in the event of a fixed term contract not being renewed, the date on which the contract expires.

Some confusion has arisen in determining the EDT in cases of termination with money in lieu of notice. The traditional approach in *Dedman v British Building and Engineering Appliances Ltd* [1974] I.C.R. 53 was to treat money in lieu of notice as a summary dismissal and hold that the EDT was on the date the termination takes place, i.e. the final day of employment. However the case of *Adams v GKN Sankey Ltd* [1980] I.R.L.R. 416 suggested that the EDT should depend upon the true construction placed on the dismissal; if the dismissal was expressed as summary dismissal, but with monies in respect of possible damages for wrongful dismissal, then the EDT should be the date of termination; if, on the other hand, the dismissal was with notice, but monies representing wages in lieu of notice were given, then the EDT should be the date on which the notice would expire. Although there is no binding authority on the point, *Adams* is to be preferred.
   In cases where the contract is terminated by the employer and the minimum notice periods provided for by s.86 of the ERA 1996 would, if given, expire on a later date than the EDT, statute (s.97(2) of the ERA 1996) will intervene to hold that the later date is the EDT for the purpose of calculating the qualifying period of employment under s.108(1) (the right not to be unfairly dismissed contained in s.94), s.119(1) (the calculation of the basic award of compensation) and s.227(3) (the statutory maximum amount of a week's pay).

Has the Claim been Brought within Time?

Section 111 of the ERA 1996 states that claims of unfair dismissal must be brought before the tribunal within three months of the EDT, although s.111(2)(b)   **10.1.4**
allows such further time as the tribunal considers reasonable if it considers that it was not reasonably practicable for the applicant to bring the case earlier. The courts have tended to interpret s.111(2)(b) strictly:

• Ignorance of ones rights will not normally be sufficient (*Dedman v British Building and Engineering Appliances* [1974] I.C.R. 53).

- Incorrect advice from a skilled advisor may not be sufficient (*Riley v Tesco Stores Ltd* [1980] I.C.R. 323).

- Waiting for the outcome of a relevant event, e.g. a criminal trial, may not be sufficient (*Norgett v Luton Industrial Co-op Soc Ltd* [1976] I.C.R. 442).

- Waiting for the outcome of an internal appeal system undertaken following termination may not be sufficient (*Palmer v Southend-on-Sea Borough Council* [1984] I.C.R. 372). In such circumstances the applicant should either enter an application to the tribunal immediately following termination, or should advise the tribunal office that an investigation is being undertaken.

- The Court of Appeal in *London International College v Sen* [1993] I.R.L.R. 333 stated that whether it was reasonably practicable for an applicant to present the application in the time scale was a question of fact based on the applicant's state of mind at the time.

- In the recent case of *Marks & Spencer Plc v Williams Ryan* [2005] I.R.L.R. 562 the court took a somewhat relaxed view of an applicant who on the advice of the Citizen's Advice Bureau awaited the outcome of an internal appeal and by so doing submitted her claim to the tribunal after the three month period had expired. The court accepted that although the applicant had received the tribunal leaflet in good time, she had "more pressing considerations" on her mind at the time.

- In *Fishley v Working Men's College* (2004) E.A.T., an application faxed to the tribunal offices 11 minutes after the three month time limit had expired was rejected.

The three-month time restriction is of course considerably shorter than the six-year limitation period imposed by the Limitation Act 1980 which applies to actions for common law breach of contract claims.

Under reg.15 of the The Employment Act 2002 (Dispute Resolution) Regulations 2004, for those dismissals where either the statutory dismissal and disciplinary procedure or the statutory grievance procedure applies the time limit is extended for a period of a further three months.

CAN A DISMISSAL BE IDENTIFIED?

10.2   Section 95 of the ERA 1996 states:

"(1) For the purposes of this Part an employee is dismissed by his employer if (and, subject to subsection (2), only if)—

(a) the contract under which he is employed is terminated by the employer (whether with or without notice),

(b) he is employed under a limited-term contract and that contract terminates by virtue of the limiting event without being renewed under the same contract, or

(c) the employee terminates the contract under which he is employed (with or without notice) in circumstances in which he is entitled to terminate it without notice by reason of the employer's conduct.

(2) An employee shall be taken to be dismissed by his employer for the purposes of this Part if—

(a) the employer gives notice to the employee to terminate his contract of employment, and

(b) at a time within the period of that notice the employee gives notice to the employer to terminate the contract of employment on a date earlier than the date on which the employer's notice is due to expire;

and the reason for the dismissal is to be taken to be the reason for which the employer's notice is given."

In many situations there will be no problem in identifying the dismissal—"You are fired", "I'm afraid I must give you a month's notice", etc. However, in some cases the situation is much less clear.

Words and Actions

- If the words are clear and unambiguous the tribunal should treat them as such (*Sothern v Franks Charlesly & Co* [1981] I.R.L.R. 278).   **10.2.1**

- If the words are ambiguous, if they have been said in the heat of the moment, or as part of an argument or row, the tribunal may look behind the actual words used to ensure that what has taken place really is a dismissal (*Chesham Shipping Ltd v Rowe* [1977] I.R.L.R. 391).

- Language that may constitute a dismissal in one industry or situation, may not have the same meaning in another (*Futty v D and D Brekkes Ltd* [1974] I.R.L.R. 130).

- It may often be possible for words said in the heat of the moment to be withdrawn (*Martin v Yeoman Aggregates Ltd* [1983] I.R.L.R. 49), but in some cases the mere saying of the words may destroy the contractual term of mutual trust and confidence.

- An employee prompted to resign by the threat of dismissal, may be held to have been dismissed (*East Sussex County Council v Walker* (1972) 7 I.T.R. 280).

- However, if the resignation is prompted not by threat of dismissal, but by the offer of a severance package, there will not be a dismissal (*Birch v University of Liverpool* [1985] I.C.R. 470).

Resignation whilst under Notice of Dismissal

10.2.2   If an employee is under notice of dismissal, but then gives notice of resignation to take effect before the dismissal, statute provides that for the purposes of any unfair dismissal claim the employee shall be taken to have been dismissed (s.95(2) of the ERA 1996).

Dismissal whilst under Notice of Resignation

10.2.3   Clearly, if an employer dismisses an employee during the period of notice given by that employee to resign, then the court will be justified in finding that a dismissal has taken place. This was demonstrated in the case of *Glycosynth Ltd v Proctor* (2005) (unreported) in which the employee stated his intention to resign during a heated exchange with his employer. When the employee handed his resignation letter to the employer later that day, the employer asked the employee to leave immediately. The Court of Appeal held that a dismissal had taken place during the employee's notice period.

Dismissal whilst Continuing in Employment

10.2.4   Under normal circumstances, once a dismissal takes place the employment relationship will end. However, this is not always the case. In the case of *Hogg v Dover College* [1990] I.C.R. 39, Mr Hogg a full time teacher suffered an illness and was subsequently offered part time work at a reduced salary. He worked part time under protest but also lodged a complaint of unfair dismissal. The EAT held that he had been dismissed from his full time position and that his part-time work was being performed under a new contract.

It is unclear how widely this approach may be used by employees to fight unilaterally imposed changes to the contract of employment; by arguing that the change imposed by the employer has caused a dismissal under the original contract, and that by continuing to work under the new terms, the employee is in fact working under a new contract. Thus, a claim for unfair dismissal could proceed, even though the employee continues in employment (see *Alcan Extrusions v Yates* [1996] I.R.L.R. 327).

Expiry of Limited-Term Contract

Prior to the implementation of the Fixed-term Employees (Prevention of Less   **10.2.5**
Favourable Treatment) Regulations 2002 it was necessary to differentiate between
fixed-term contracts (those contracts for which an expiry date may be pre-
determined) and both fixed-task contracts (those which would automatically
expire upon the completion of the particular task, e.g. *Wiltshire County Council
v NATFHE* [1980] I.C.R. 455) and contracts which are determinable upon the
happening or non-happening of a future event (*Brown v Knowsley Borough
Council* [1986] I.R.L.R. 102), since only the expiry of a fixed-term contract would
give rise to a dismissal. However the 2002 Regulations now define a fixed-term
contract as "a contract of employment that, under its provisions determining how
it will terminate in the normal course, will terminate:

(a) on the expiry of a specific term;

(b) on the completion of a particular task; or

(c) on the occurrence or non-occurrence of any other specific event other
than the attainment by the employee of any normal and bona fide retiring age in the establishment for an employee holding the position held by
him."

Section 95(1)(b) of the ERA 1996 uses the phrase "limited-term contract",
whereas the 2002 Regulations use the phrase "fixed-term contract", as does
Directives 91/383 and 99/70EC. This is probably due to the difference that used
to exist between fixed-term contracts and task contracts, but which was removed
by the Regulations; it may now be accepted that there is no difference between the
phrases "limited-term" and "fixed-term", and they may be used interchangeably.

The fact that a fixed-term contract may include provision for the contract to be
terminated by notice by either party prior to the expiry of the fixed term does not
preclude the contract from being a fixed-term contract (*Dixon v BBC* [1979] Q.B.
546). Following the introduction of the ERelA 1999, it is no longer possible
for employees working on fixed-term contracts to waive their rights to claim
unfair dismissal, and following the Fixed-term Employees (Prevention of Less
Favourable Treatment) Regulations 2002 it is, since October 2002, no longer possible to waive rights to redundancy payments.

Self-dismissal

Under the general principle of contract law, if the employee commits a repudia-   **10.2.6**
tory breach of contract, that breach will only be effective on the contract once it
has been accepted by the innocent party, the employer. Thus, it is the action of

the employer that terminates the contract, and thus there is a dismissal (*London Transport Executive v Clarke* [1981] I.C.R. 355). This is not, of course, to suggest that the dismissal is unfair; indeed if the employee has committed a repudiatory breach the dismissal is likely prima facie to be fair.

In the case of *Igbo v Johnson Matthey Chemicals Ltd* [1986] I.R.L.R. 215, Mrs Igbo was permitted to take extended holiday on condition that she signed an agreement that should she not return to work on the agreed day her employment would automatically terminate. When she returned from holiday she was ill, so instead of returning to work she sent in a medical certificate. Her employers invoked the agreement and declared her employment terminated. The Court of Appeal, however, held that the automatic termination agreement was invalid as being contrary to s.203(1) of the ERA 1996 which makes void any term of the contract which seeks to exclude or limit any provision of the ERA 1996—and thus a dismissal had taken place.

Frustration

10.2.7   Any contract which is terminated by frustration does not give rise to a dismissal (*Egg Stores (Stamford Hill) Ltd v Leibovici* [1977] I.C.R. 260).

Mutual Consent

10.2.8   Because of the perceived inequality of bargaining powers in the employment relationship, and due to the operation of s.203 of the ERA 1996, termination by mutual consent not resulting in a dismissal will always be difficult to establish, particularly in a statutory context. Cases in which the courts have found termination by mutual consent include *SW Strange Ltd v Mann* [1965] 1 All E.R. 1069, *Lipton Ltd v Marlborough* [1979] I.R.L.R. 179, both concerning restraint clauses, *Birch v University of Liverpool* [1985] I.C.R. 470 and *Scott v Coalite Fuels Ltd* [1988] I.C.R. 355 both concerning voluntary early retirement schemes—it should be stressed though that these cases are very much the exception to the rule, and mutual consent is rarely established.

Constructive Dismissal

10.2.9   ". . . an employee is dismissed by his employer if . . .
the employee terminates the contract under which he is employed (with or without notice) in circumstances in which he is entitled to terminate it without notice by reason of the employer's conduct." (s.95(1)(c) of the ERA 1996)

The question to be asked is, do the actions of the employer constitute a fundamental breach of a term of the contract—if they do, then the employee can leave and claim constructive dismissal.

The leading case—*Western Excavating (ECC) Ltd v Sharp* [1978] Q.B. 761—confirms that the correct test to be applied to determine whether the actions of the employer permit the employee to terminate the contract and claim constructive dismissal, is a "contractual test" not a "reasonableness test". In other words—"is the action taken by the employer in accordance with the terms of the contract?"—not "has the employer acted reasonably?"

Constructive dismissal may therefore be said to be where the employee terminates the contract due to the employer either committing a fundamental breach of the contract, or evincing clear intentions not to be bound by it.

Although this appears quite straightforward, case law has resulted in some decisions that on the face of it do not appear consistent, and the following principles may be helpful:

- an employer cannot be in breach of a contract term by invoking that term—however unreasonable his actions may be (*Western Excavating v Sharp*); but,

- by invoking a contract term in an unreasonable manner or for an unreasonable purpose an employer may be in breach of the fundamental term of "mutual trust and confidence" (*United Bank Ltd v Akhtar* [1989] I.R.L.R. 507).

The question of what exactly amounts to a "fundamental" breach has been addressed by the courts. In the leading case of *Western Excavating* Lawton L.J. stated:

"... I do not find it either necessary or advisable to express any opinion as to what principles of law operate to bring a contract of employment to an end by reason of the employer's conduct. Sensible people have no difficulty in recognising such conduct when they hear about it [. . .] and what is required for the application of this provision is a large measure of common sense".

Thus the question of whether a breach is repudiatory or not amounts to a finding of fact by the tribunal, on which an appellate court would therefore normally have no jurisdiction to interfere, as long as there was evidence on which the tribunal had based their decision (*Pederson v Camden LBC* [1981] I.R.L.R. 173) and the decision reached was not perverse (*Edwards v Bairstow* [1956] A.C. 14). In the case of *Josiah Mason College v Parsons* (2005) (unreported) a teacher employed to teach caring and nursery nursing claimed constructive dismissal when her employer insisted that she should teach religious instruction, for which she was qualified to do. The employer had consulted with her before insisting on the change and further argued that under the conditions of service handbook they had the right to effect the change. The EAT held that she had been constructively dismissed: her contract made a number of specific references to her specialisation, including her job title, and the reality of the situation was that she had been employed to teach her particular subject. A requirement for her to teach another subject amounted to a breach of a fundamental term of her contract.

In the case of *Kerry Foods Ltd v Lynch* [2005] I.R.L.R. 680 the employer wished to make changes to the working week and the employee who did not wish to agree to those changes was faced with an "accept or we will terminate your contract and offer re-engagement on new terms" situation. The employee left and claimed constructive dismissal. The EAT stated that the giving of lawful notice by the employer could not amount to a breach of contract, and in such situations the employee should have waited for the notice to take effect and then claimed unfair dismissal (although it is perhaps unlikely based on case law such as *Hollister v NFU* [1979] I.R.L.R. 238, that such a claim would have succeeded).

A breach of the duty of mutual trust and confidence will almost invariably amount to a repudiatory breach (*Morrow v Safeway Stores Ltd* [2002] I.R.L.R. 9). This duty of mutual trust and confidence has over the years grown in both scope and importance, and for the purposes of constructive dismissal, has included:

- Use of abusive language by the employer (*Isle of Wight Tourist Board v Coombes* [1976] I.R.L.R. 413).

- Failure to allow an employee reasonable access to a grievance procedure (*WA Goold (Pearmak) Ltd v McConnell* [1995] I.R.L.R. 516).

- Refusing to investigate a health and safety complaint (*British Aircraft Corp v Austin* [1978] I.R.L.R. 332).

- Failure to take seriously a complaint of sexual harassment (*Bracebridge Engineering Ltd v Darby* [1990] I.R.L.R. 3).

- "Arbitrarily" and "capriciously" refusing an employee a pay rise (*FC Gardiner v Beresford* [1978] I.R.L.R. 63).

- Insisting on relocating an employee in the absence of any contractual mobility clause (*Aparau v Iceland Frozen Foods Ltd* [1996] I.R.L.R. 119).

- Disproportionate punishment of an employee for a minor offence (*BBC v Beckett* [1983] I.R.L.R. 43).

Although constructive dismissal is usually brought about by a single serious act of the employer, a series of minor incidents may be sufficient (*Woods v WM Car Services (Peterborough) Ltd* [1981] I.C.R. 666, *Omilaju v Waltham Forest LBC* [2005] 1 All E.R. 75).

A finding of constructive dismissal is not the same as a finding of unfair dismissal. Usually a finding of constructive dismissal will also lead to the finding of an unfair dismissal, but on occasions the courts have found a constructive dismissal to be fair (*Savoia v Chiltern Herb Farms Ltd* [1981] I.R.L.R. 65).

Following the implementation of The Employment Act 2002 (Dispute Resolution) Regulations 2004, it appears that before bringing a claim of constructive unfair dismissal a claimant must first have completed the statutory grievance procedures (see Chapter 6).

THE REASON FOR THE DISMISSAL

Statute identifies only five potentially fair reasons for dismissal (s.98(1)(b)), and **10.3** to successfully defend a claim of unfair dismissal an employer must initially establish that the reason for dismissal falls within one or more of these categories.

The potentially fair reasons are:

• capability or qualifications;

• conduct;

• redundancy;

• contravention of a statute;

• some other substantial reason.

It is for the employer to put forward and show the reason for the dismissal. The tribunal must be convinced that the reason given is the real reason and that it falls within a s.98 reason. If the employer gives a number of reasons for the dismissal and one or more of those reasons is not accepted by the tribunal, the employer must then show that those one or more reasons did not amount to the main or a significant part of the actual reason for the dismissal, and that those reasons accepted by the tribunal amounted in themselves to a sufficient reason for the dismissal. Cairns L.J. stated in the case of *Abernethy v Mott, Hay and Anderson* [1974] I.R.L.R. 213:

"A reason for the dismissal of an employee is a set of facts known to the employer, or it may be of beliefs held by him, which cause him to dismiss the employee."

This statement emphasises the subjectivity of the issue; it would not necessarily be fatal to the employer's defence that the beliefs genuinely held by him were not factually correct. This is supported by the recent case of *Scott & Co v Richardson* (2005) (unreported) in which the EAT stated that it was not for the court to satisfy itself that the commercial decision taken by the employer was correct, only that the employer had genuinely believed it to be so.

Capability or Qualifications

10.3.1 This category may include such issues as skill, aptitude, general ability or ill-health. If the issue is one of incompetence, even one instance may constitute sufficient grounds (*Taylor v Alidair Ltd* [1978] I.R.L.R. 82). On occasion the categories of capability or qualifications and conduct may appear to overlap; in the case of *International Sports Co Ltd v Thompson* [1980] I.R.L.R. 340, Ms Thompson was off sick for a total of some five months during the last 18 months of employment with International Sports. Her medical certificates ranged from dizzy spells, to viral infections and flatulence. In agreement with the trade union the company issued a series of warnings to her, and reviewed her medical history that consisted of a series of unrelated, transitory complaints, and finally dismissed her for unsatisfactory performance. She then claimed unfair dismissal. The court held that the dismissal was fair. The company had carried out reasonable investigation into her absences, given her an opportunity to respond, issued warnings, and in the absence of any improvement in her attendance, were justified in dismissing her. Although this case was considered on the grounds of conduct, in cases such as this, dismissal will normally be on the grounds of capability, since the company would probably not wish to prove that the employee was actually malingering.

Much of the previous case law concerned employees dismissed for absence due to serious and prolonged illness (e.g. *East Lindsey District Council v Daubney* [1977] I.R.L.R. 181).

Conduct

10.3.2 Conduct has been held to include dishonesty (*British Home Stores v Burchell* [1978] I.R.L.R. 379), fighting at work (*Meakin v Liverpool CC* (EAT/142/00), refusal to obey instructions (*Atkin v Enfield Hospital* [1975] I.R.L.R. 217), breach of health and safety regulations (*Wilcox v Humphries & Glasgow Ltd* [1975] I.R.L.R. 211), etc. Breach of almost any of the express terms of the employee's contract, any of the implied terms of the contract, or any of the work rules may amount to a potentially fair reason for dismissal under the heading of "conduct"—although it may be necessary to show that it was a deliberate breach on the part of the employee.

In the recent case of *Perkin v St George's Healthcare NHS Trust* [2005] I.R.L.R. 934, the Court of Appeal held that although an individual's "personality" may not in itself amount to grounds for dismissal, the manifestations of that personality may amount to potentially fair reasons for dismissal under either "conduct" or "some other substantial reason".

Redundancy

Dismissal on the grounds of redundancy is a potentially fair reason for dismissal. **10.3.3**
This issue is dealt with more fully in Chapter 11.

Contravention of a Statute

This category would include both the situation in which the circumstance of the **10.3.4**
employee changes so that his continued employment would become unlawful, e.g.
a driver who is subsequently banned by the courts from driving, and also the rare
situation where the law changes, making it unlawful to continue to employ that
employee in that particular job.

Some Other Substantial Reason (SOSR)

This category has been variously termed a "catch-all" or "dustbin" category. The **10.3.5**
court in *RS Components Ltd v Irwin* [1973] I.C.R. 535 stated that this category
should not be construed *ejusdem generis* with the other categories, and it has
therefore been viewed broadly, including such issues as:

- Failure by an employee to adapt (*Cresswell v Board of Inland Revenue*
  [1984] I.C.R. 508).

- Clash of personalities (*Treganowan v Robert Knee & Co Ltd* [1975] I.C.R.
  405).

- Mistaken belief that employee did not have work permit (*Bouchaala v
  THF Hotels Ltd* [1980] I.C.R. 721).

- Failure by employee to disclose medical history when asked at interview
  (*O'Brien v Prudential Assurance Co Ltd* [1979] I.R.L.R. 140).

- Refusal of an employee to accept a new contract term which the employer
  held "necessary" (*RS Components v Irwin* [1973] I.C.R. 535).

- In the case of *Forshaw v Archcraft Ltd* [2005] I.R.L.R. 600 it was held that
  the refusal of an employee to sign a restrictive covenant which was unreasonably wide could not amount to a potentially fair reason for dismissal
  under SOSR, however in the later case of:

  - *Willow Oak Developments Ltd (t/a Windsor Recruitment) v
    Silverwood* [2006] I.R.L.R. 28 the court declined to follow *Forshaw*
    and stated that the correct approach is not to consider the unrea-
    sonableness of the covenant or term until addressing the issue of
    reasonableness of the dismissal.

- Pressure from a third party (*Saunders v Scottish National Camps Association* [1980] I.R.L.R. 174—although on the facts of this case the issues would fall within the ambit of the Employment Equality (Sexual Orientation) Regulations 2003).

- Refusal of an employee to accept a drop in wages from £130 to £90 per week negotiated with the trade union (*Sycamore v H Myer & Co Ltd* [1976] I.R.L.R. 84).

- Refusal by an employee to cease wearing a badge which was held to be offensive to both fellow employees and customers (*Boychuk v HJ Symons Holdings Ltd* [1977] I.R.L.R. 395.

The list is by no means exclusive.

Automatically Unfair Reasons

10.3.6   Certain reasons for dismissal (or for selection for redundancy) are automatically unfair:

- *Assertion of statutory right (s.104 of the ERA 1996).* Section 104 of the ERA 1996 makes a dismissal automatically unfair if the reason, or principle reason for it is that the employee had brought proceedings against the employer to enforce a "relevant statutory right". Such rights are any of the rights contained in the ERA 1996 for which the remedy is via a complaint to an employment tribunal, the right to a minimum notice period, and rights relating to deductions from pay, trade union activities and time off contained in TULR(C)A 1992. There is no minimum qualifying period necessary to bring a claim.

- *Pregnancy and maternity (s.99 of the ERA 1996).* Dismissal of a worker on the grounds of pregnancy is automatically unfair, there is no qualifying period necessary to bring a claim, and probably no defence available to the employer (but see *Webb v EMO Air Cargo (UK) Ltd* [1995] I.R.L.R. 645).

- *Dismissal for Family Reasons (s.99 of the ERA 1996).* Section 99 also makes unfair dismissal under prescribed circumstances (those prescribed by the Secretary of State) of an employee where the principle reason for the dismissal relates to:

   (a) pregnancy, childbirth or maternity;
   (b) ordinary, compulsory or additional maternity leave;
   (c) ordinary or additional adoption leave;

(d) parental leave;

(e) paternity leave; or

(f) time off under s.57A (time-off for dependants);

and may also relate to redundancy or other factors.

- *Trade union membership or non-membership (s.137 TULR(C)A of the 1992)*. It is automatically unfair to dismiss a worker for joining, being a member of, refusing to join or refusing to remain a member of a trade union. There is no minimum qualifying period necessary to bring such a claim.

- *Dismissal of striking employees (ERelA 1999)*. The dismissal of an employee for taking part in official industrial action is automatically unfair if it occurs within the first eight weeks of such participation. A dismissal after that period may also be unfair if the employer fails to take reasonable steps to resolve the dispute.

- *Employee representatives (s.103 of the ERA 1996)*. Dismissal of an employees' representative (under Ch.II, Pt IV of the TULR(C)A 1992) or a candidate for election to such a position is automatically unfair if the principle reason for such a dismissal relates to the activities of the role.

- *Health and safety (s.100 of the ERA 1996)*. Particular protection is afforded by s.100 of the ERA 1996 to health and safety representatives and members of health and safety committees, and also to workers in companies in which there is no health and safety representative or committee, to make automatically unfair any dismissal on the grounds that the employee was carrying out health and safety duties. No qualifying period is necessary to bring such a claim.

- *Making a protected disclosure (s.103A ERA)*. Dismissal of an employee is automatically unfair if the principle reason for the dismissal is that the employee has made a protected disclosure.

- *Sunday work (s.101 ERA)*. Certain groups of shop workers are protected against dismissal for refusal to work on Sundays (Pt IV of the ERA 1996).

- *Transfer of undertakings (TUPE 1981 as amended by 2005 Regs)*. Dismissal by reason of the transfer or for a reason connected with the transfer which is not an "economic technical or organisational reason" will be automatically unfair.

- *Trustees of occupational pension schemes (s.102 of the ERA 1996)*. Protected if the reason or principle reason for the dismissal is that the employee performed any function as such a trustee.

THE FAIRNESS OF THE DISMISSAL

10.4   Once it has been shown that the applicant is qualified to make a claim, that a dismissal has taken place, and that the employer has put forward a potentially fair reason for the dismissal, only then is it necessary to consider the fairness of the dismissal.

Statute states that:

> ". . . the determination of the question whether the dismissal is fair or unfair (having regard to the reason shown by the employer) depends on whether in the circumstances (including the size and administrative resources of the employer's undertaking) the employer acted reasonably or unreasonably in treating it as a sufficient reason for dismissing the employee, and shall be determined in accordance with equity and the substantial merits of the case." (s.98(4) of the ERA 1996)

The fairness of the dismissal may be divided into two broad headings, both of which must be satisfied in order to prove a fair dismissal: the *band of reasonable responses* and *procedural fairness*.

Band of Reasonable Responses

10.4.1   "[The] tribunal must consider the reasonableness of the employer's conduct, not simply whether they (the members of the industrial tribunal) consider the dismissal to be fair; in judging the reasonableness of the employer's conduct an industrial tribunal must not substitute its decision as to what was the right course to adopt for that of the employer; in many, though not all, cases there is a band of reasonable responses to the employee's conduct within which one employer might reasonably take one view, another quite reasonably take another; the function of the industrial tribunal . . . is to determine whether in the particular circumstances of each case the decision to dismiss the employee fell within the band of reasonable responses which a reasonable employer might have adopted." (*Iceland Frozen Foods v Jones* [1983] I.C.R. 17, *per* Browne-Wilkinson J.)

Thus in summary, the tribunal must not ask, "What would we have done in that situation?", but instead, in effect, "Could a reasonable employer have done what was done?", if so, at this stage, the dismissal will be fair.

The issue is illustrated in the case of *Weatherford UK Ltd v Aitken* [2005] S.C. 360 in which Mr Aitken who worked for the appellants on North Sea oil-rigs was summarily dismissed for gross misconduct in that he failed to turn up for an offshore assignment. His contract of employment stated that an example of gross misconduct would be: "Failure to report for a check-in time for travel offshore without due notice and an acceptable reason . . .". It appears that he was experiencing domestic difficulties brought about by his protracted periods offshore, and that his employers were aware of this. He refused to undertake an assignment that would have involved him flying out on the same day that his previous assignment had ended, consequently he would have been unable to return home between the two assignments. At a disciplinary hearing Mr Aitken stated that he had never before refused an assignment, and admitted that with hindsight he should have explained his reasons more fully at the time of his refusal. He did not however explain what his "domestic problems" were, nor did his employer enquire. The employment tribunal (the majority disagreeing with the Chairman), found that a reasonable employer would have enquired further into Mr Aitken's domestic problems and, having done so, a reasonable employer would then have accepted that Mr Aitken's domestic difficulties did in fact amount to an acceptable reason for his failure to check in for the second assignment.

On appeal the EAT held that the tribunal had misapplied the "band of reasonable responses" test. An employer is entitled to act on the information known to or believed by him at the time, and if an employee chooses not to fully explain a set of facts, the employer would not normally be under a duty to investigate further. By stating what *this* employer *should* have done, the tribunal had in effect substituted its own opinion, rather than asking what *a reasonable* employer *could* have done.

Obviously, the range of reasonable responses may be very broad, and have included:

- The dismissal of an attendant at a boys' camp solely on the grounds of his homosexuality (*Saunders v Scottish National Camps Association* [1980] I.R.L.R. 174). (Be aware that such grounds would now fall foul of the Employment Equality (Sexual Orientation) Regulations 2003.)

- The dismissal of a rail steward of 14 years service for having in his possession food, in contravention of a regulation prohibiting employees engaging in business on their own account (*British Railways Board v Jackson* [1994] I.R.L.R. 235).

- The dismissal of both employees where it was believed that one was guilty of theft, but it could not be ascertained which (*Monie v Coral Racing Ltd* [1981] I.C.R. 109).

Thus, the range of reasonable responses to a situation of, say, horseplay at work could range from an informal rebuke, a formal warning, to dismissal—each of these responses may be considered fair.

It is necessary for the courts, when applying the "band of reasonable responses" test to take into account factors specific to the particular case, for example the employee's work history. In the case of *Donnelly v Charnos Plc* [2001] W.L. 1479728, Mr Donnelly and two other employees were dismissed for allegedly leaving their workplace for three hours and spending that time in a public house. The employer conducted an internal investigation, including the collection of witness statements. Those statements were treated as confidential by the employer and the identity of the authors was not revealed. The appellants, who had employment records of long service and good conduct, maintained that the decision to dismiss fell outside the band of reasonable responses. On appeal the EAT held that the tribunal had erred by not properly considering the issue of fairness in the light of those facts known to the employer at the time. No consideration had been given to the appellants' work history nor to other courses of action available to the employers. The case demonstrates the difficulties a court may have in applying the reasonable responses test without substituting their own opinion, whilst at the same time taking into account specific factors of each case—certainly in this case the employers' decision to keep the witness statements confidential, whilst understandable, went some way to weakening their case.

Doubt was cast on the band of reasonable responses test by the EAT in the case of *Haddon v Van Den Bergh Foods Ltd* [1999] I.R.L.R. 672, who considered that because of the ease with which the test may be satisfied by an employer, the test was "a test of perversity". These views were, however firmly overruled by the Court of Appeal in the joined cases of *Post Office v Foley; HSBC (formerly Midland Bank) v Madden* [2000] I.R.L.R. 827 who confirmed that the band of reasonable responses test should continue to be applied in accordance with binding case law.

Procedural Fairness

10.4.2   It has been possible for a dismissal for a fair reason, which is within the range of reasonable responses, to be found unfair if it failed the test of procedural fairness. ACAS have a Code of Practice, revised in 2004 to take into account The Employment Act 2002 (Dispute Resolution) Regulations 2004, which, whilst not having the force of law, may be relied upon as a blueprint for an employer's own disciplinary code; the Code lays down a system of warnings for misconduct, etc., and follows the principles of natural justice. If an employer abides by the ACAS Code it is most unlikely if not almost impossible that a tribunal would hold that a dismissal was procedurally unfair.

The House of Lords in the case of *Polkey v AE Dayton Services Ltd* [1988] I.C.R. 142, stressed the importance of following an agreed procedure in disciplinary hearings, holding that a failure to follow such procedure was likely to result in a finding of unfair dismissal, unless "the employer could reasonably have concluded in the light of circumstances known at the time of dismissal that consultation or warning would be utterly useless".

However, from October 1, 2004 a major change to the issue of procedural fairness has been introduced by the EA 2002 by way of the EA 2002 (Dispute Resolution) Regulations 2004 (SI2004/752) which has amended s.98 of the ERA 1996 by the introduction of s.98A and introduced a statutory dismissal and disciplinary procedure.

The standard statutory dismissal and disciplinary procedure is set out in Sch.2 of the 2002 Act and consists of three steps:

- Step 1—the employer must set out in writing the issues which have caused the employer to contemplate taking action, and send a copy of this statement to the employee inviting him to attend a meeting.

- Step 2—the meeting should take place before action is taken, and the employee should take all steps to attend. After the meeting the employer should inform the employee of the decision and notify him of his right of appeal.

- Step 3—if the employee wishes to appeal, a further meeting should be arranged at which the parties should attend, and after which the employee should be notified of the outcome. The dismissal or other disciplinary action decided upon in Step 2 may be instigated prior to the second (appeal) meeting taking place.

There is also a modified procedure detailed in Ch.2 , Sch.2 of the Act (see Chapter 6, above).

Failure by the employer to complete the procedure will result in a finding of unfair dismissal if "the non-completion of the procedure is wholly or mainly attributable to failure by the employer to comply with its requirements" (s.98A(1) of the ERA 1996), and in most cases to an increased compensatory award to the employee. Failure by the employee to follow the procedure will result in them receiving a decreased compensatory award. Section 98A(2) of the ERA 1996 states:

> "Subject to subsection 1, failure by an employer to follow a procedure in relation to the dismissal of an employee shall not be regarded for the purposes of section 98(4) as by itself making the employer's action unreasonable if he shows that he would have decided to dismiss the employee if he had followed the procedure".

Thus, if the dismissal is one to which the statutory dismissal and disciplinary procedures apply the dismissal will be unfair if the employer has not completed those procedures. If, however, the employer has completed those procedures, the fact that they may not have completed any contractual procedure in regard to the dismissal will not in itself make the dismissal unfair. Likewise, if the statutory procedure does not apply to the dismissal, the fact that the employer has not completed a contractual procedure or has failed to follow an ACAS Code of Practice will not in itself make the dismissal unfair.

Generally in assessing the fairness of a dismissal the tribunal may only take into account facts known to the employer at the time of dismissal (*W Devis & Sons Ltd v Atkins* [1977] A.C. 931), but the House of Lords in *West Midlands Co-operative Society Ltd v Tipton* [1986] A.C. 536 held that facts arising out of a post-dismissal appeal may also be taken into account by the tribunal. The effect of this is that if an employee is denied an appeal to which he is contractually entitled, the dismissal will almost certainly be unfair.

In view of the changes made by the 2002 Act to the "fairness" issue, much of the existing case law should be treated with caution, but a drawing together of many of the principles of unfair dismissal may be seen from the case of *British Home Stores v Burchell* [1978] I.R.L.R. 379 in which the employee was dismissed because the employer believed she was stealing on a staff discount scheme.

Ms Burchell fulfilled the requirements necessary for her to make a claim.

The reason put forward for her dismissal was conduct, her alleged theft.

The EAT laid down a three part test:

  (i) that the employer honestly held the belief;

 (ii) that the employer had reasonable grounds on which to sustain that belief;

(iii) that the employer had carried out as much investigation as was reasonable in all the circumstances.

It is important to note that the question for the tribunal did not concern the guilt or innocence of Ms Burchell, but the question of whether in view of the facts as they were known to the employer at the time, the employer acted reasonably both in the decision and the manner of her dismissal. Although *Burchell* is a "conduct" case, the Court of Appeal in *Perkin v St George's Healthcare NHS Trust* [2005] I.R.L.R. 934 stated that the test from *Burchell* should not be limited only to "conduct" cases.

For a further consideration of the *Burchell* test see the case of *Boys and Girls Welfare Society v McDonald* [1996] I.R.L.R. 129, but bear in mind that following the implementation of the EA 2002, the courts would now need to consider whether the parties had followed the statutory dispute resolution procedure, etc.

REMEDIES FOR UNFAIR DISMISSAL

10.5   The tribunal may award any of three remedies as may be requested by the successful applicant: reinstatement, re-engagement, or compensation.

Reinstatement

This requires the employer to treat the employee as if he had not been dismissed, making good arrears of pay, any increments or improvements in terms and conditions to which the employee would have been entitled, etc. **10.5.1**

Re-engagement

This requires the employer to engage the employee on the same or comparable work, on terms and conditions such as the tribunal may require, including such matters as an amount for pay arrears, etc. **10.5.2**

The main problem with orders for both reinstatement and re-engagement is that in most cases by this stage the duty of mutual trust and confidence between the employer and the employee will have broken down, making such orders unworkable.

Compensation

This may take the form of a basic award computed in the same way as a redundancy payment; a compensatory award to reflect the loss sustained by the applicant due to the dismissal (from February 1, 2006 maximum amount of £58,400—SI 2005/3352); an additional award should the employer not comply with a reinstatement or re-engagement order; and a special award payable only in cases of trade union membership or health and safety dismissals. **10.5.3**

Compensation is not available for injury to feelings as such. The case of *Norton Tools Co Ltd v Tewson* [1973] 1 All E.R. 183 has restricted the award of compensation for injury to feelings by requiring the courts to attribute compensation to specific heads of claim. Although in the case of *Johnson v Unisys Ltd* [2001] I.R.L.R. 279 Lord Hoffman suggested that the *Norton Tools* approach was too narrow in respect of "manner of dismissal" awards, the House of Lords in *Dunnachie v Kingston upon Hull City Council* [2004] I.R.L.R. 727 reaffirmed that the *Norton Tools* approach remains good law and that the words of the relevant statute (s.123(1) of the ERA 1996 ". . . such amount as the tribunal considers just and equitable. . .") referred to the amount of the compensation—subject to the statutory maximum—and not to the scope or range of heads of the loss.

The regulations and rules concerning the award of compensation are complex and confusing:

Basic Award

The basic award mirrors the compensation payable for redundancy and (from February 1, 2006) stands at £8700 being based on the maximum statutory figure of £290 per week. The tribunal may reduce this figure by any amount under **10.5.3.1** s.122(2) of the ERA 1996 if it considers that the conduct of the employee prior to the dismissal so warrants. The figure is also reduced (under s.122(4) of the ERA 1996) by the amount of any redundancy pay the applicant may have received.

A minimum basic award of £4000 is payable in cases of dismissal or selection for redundancy for trade union, health and safety, employee representative or occupational pension scheme trustee reasons (s.120 of the ERA 1996).

Compensatory Award

10.5.3.2   Section 123(1) of the ERA 1996 states that:

> "the amount of the compensatory award shall be such amount as the tribunal considers just and equitable in all the circumstances having regard to the loss sustained by the complainant in consequence of the dismissal in so far as that loss is attributable to the action taken by the employer".

From February 1, 2006 the maximum amount is £58,400. In computing the award the tribunal must apply the rule concerning the duty to mitigate one's loss in line with damages recoverable under the common law (s.123(4) of the ERA 1996). There is some confusion as to whether actual earnings from alternative employment for the period during which the previous employer has paid monies in lieu of notice should be deducted from the award made by the tribunal—statute would seem to suggest that they should (s.123(4) of the ERA 1996) whereas some case law suggests otherwise (*Voith Turbo Ltd v Stowe* [2005] I.R.L.R. 228, *cf. Hardy v Polk (Leeds) Ltd* [2004] I.R.L.R. 420).

The tribunal must therefore compute the amount of economic loss suffered by the applicant in accordance with s.123(1), plus an estimation of the amount of economic loss likely to be suffered, including actual expenses incurred and others such as rights under an occupational pension scheme. The tribunal need also consider the effects of the statutory dismissal and disciplinary and grievance procedures introduced under the EA 2002: failure by an applicant to follow the procedures will require the tribunal to reduce the compensatory award by between 10 per cent and 50 per cent, if the failure is on the part of the employer the amount should be increased by between 10 per cent and 50 per cent (s.124A(a) of the ERA 1996, s.31 of the EA 2002). The EA 2002 also provides for an adjustment of between two and four weeks additional pay (subject to the statutory maximum of £290 per week) in the case of a failure to give a statement of employment particulars (s.124A(b) of the ERA 1996, s.38 of the EA 2002).

Under s.123(6) of the ERA 1996 the compensatory award shall be reduced by such proportion as the tribunal considers just and equitable having regard to the employee's contribution to the dismissal. Furthermore if the amount of any redundancy compensation paid by the employer exceeds the amount of the basic award, that excess goes to reduce the amount of the compensatory award (s.123(7) of the ERA 1996).

Chapter 11

REDUNDANCY

CHAPTER OVERVIEW

Read and ensure you understand s.139 Employment Rights Act 1996, the House **CO11** of Lords judgment in *Murray v Foyle Meats* [1999] I.R.L.R. 562, and the Court of Appeal ruling in *High Table Ltd v Horst*, along with the guidelines laid down in *Williams v Compare Maxam Ltd* [1982] I.C.R. 156, and you have the basics of when and how the law relating to redundancy operates. Obviously, there is more to the topic than one section of statute and three cases, but if you understand these basics the other issues and occasional anomalies will fall into place and make sense.

Sometimes companies will offer attractive enhanced redundancy packages and perhaps call for volunteers for redundancy, rather than carry out enforced redundancies.

Redundancy is considered in some academic courses and textbooks as a separate and distinct issue; in fact, of course, redundancy is merely one of the s.98(1)(b) potentially fair reasons for dismissal—although certain distinctive rules and legislation apply to it. One of the original motives behind the introduction of the concept of redundancy and redundancy payments was to allow companies to make use of new technology and, if necessary, to reduce their workforce so as to work more cost-effectively; to this end it was, until 1989, possible for an employer to recover direct from the government much of the redundancy payment paid to its workers.

Lord Denning's explanation of redundancy may be a helpful starting point:

> ". . . a worker of long standing is now recognised as having an accrued right in his job; and his right gains in value with the years. So much so that if the job is shut down he is entitled to compensation for loss of the job . . . The worker gets a redundancy payment. It is not unemployment pay . . . Even if he gets another job straight away, he nevertheless is entitled to full redundancy payment. It is, in a real sense, compensation for long service. No man gets it unless he has been employed for at least two years by the employer; and then the amount of it depends solely upon his age and length of service."
> *Lloyd v Brassey* [1969] 2 Q.B. 98.

DEFINITION

11.1   The statutory definition of redundancy is contained in s.139(1) of the ERA 1996 and states:

> "For the purposes of this Act an employee who is dismissed shall be taken to be dismissed by reason of redundancy if the dismissal is wholly or mainly attributable to—
>
> a) the fact that his employer has ceased or intends to cease—
>
> > i) to carry on the business for the purposes of which the employee was employed by him, or
> > ii) to carry on that business in the place where the employee was so employed, or
>
> b) the fact that the requirements of that business—
>
> > i) for employees to carry out work of a particular kind, or
> > ii) for employees to carry out work of a particular kind in the place where the employee was employed by the employer,
>
> have ceased or diminished or are expected to cease or diminish."

The courts have been very reluctant to interfere with or question the employer's motives in declaring that a redundancy situation exists. In the case of *Moon v Homeworthy Furniture (Northern) Ltd* [1977] I.C.R. 117, the EAT stated that there was no power under s.98(4) of the ERA 1996 to investigate the employer's reasons for deciding to close a factory, and similarly in *James Cook & Co (Wivenhoe) Ltd v Tipper* [1990] I.R.L.R. 386, the Court of Appeal held that it was "not open to the court to investigate the commercial and economic reasons which prompted the closure". However, if the situation does not in law amount to a redundancy situation—see for example *North Riding Garages v Butterwick* [1967] 2 Q.B. 56 (below)—the dismissal may be argued as falling within the potentially fair reason of "some other substantial reason" and in such a circumstance the court may hold that no sound business reason existed (see for example *Orr v Vaughan* [1981] I.R.L.R. 63).

Although, at first glance, the statutory definition in s.139 appears fairly straightforward, there are in particular two areas of concern: what is meant by "work of a particular kind" and what is the "place of work"?

Work of a Particular Kind 11.1.1

Contract Test v Job Function Test v Statutory Test

Different approaches have been adopted by the courts in the past. The earlier "job **11.1.1.1** function test" called on the court to consider whether the overall function of the role, rather than the specific work detailed in the employment contract, had changed. If the function had remained, then any dismissal would not have been on the grounds of redundancy.

An example of this can be seen in the case of *North Riding Garages v Butterwick* [1967] 2 Q.B. 56, in which an employee of 30 years service had worked his way up to workshop manager although he still spent much of his time working as a hands-on mechanic. New owners took over and required the workshop manager to concentrate more of his time on sales and paperwork, which he was unable to do satisfactorily. After some months he was dismissed, and he claimed redundancy. In holding that he was not redundant, the court stated that employees have a duty to adapt to new methods and techniques, and only if the new methods alter the nature of the work required may they be redundant. In the case of Mr Butterwick, his function as workshop manager remained, thus he was not redundant.

The later "contract test" required the court to consider the range of work the **11.1.1.2** employee could be called upon to perform under their contract—rather than merely the actual work the employee has been doing—and if this work had diminished or ceased the employee would be redundant. This may be illustrated by the case of *Nelson v BBC* [1980] I.C.R. 100, in which the employee was employed as a producer and editor for the BBC. He had worked for much of his career in the Caribbean Service and, when this service was closed down, the question arose as to whether Mr Nelson was redundant. The Court of Appeal held that although there was a diminution in the specific work Mr Nelson had actually been doing, there was no such diminution in the work of producers and editors generally, which was the work he was contracted to do; thus Mr Nelson was not redundant.

11.1.1.3   The third, and current, approach—a "statutory test"—was introduced by the EAT in the case of *Safeway Stores Plc v Burrell* [1997] I.R.L.R. 200, as follows:

    i) Was the employee dismissed?

    ii) If so, was there a diminution or cessation in the requirements of the employer's business for employees (not the employee) to carry out work of a particular kind, or an expectation of such in the future?

    iii) If so, was the dismissal of the employee caused wholly or mainly by that state of affairs?

The terms of the employee's contract of employment are not relevant for consideration at the second stage; they will only become relevant, if at all, at the third stage. Application of this "statutory test" allows for the principle of "bumping" whereby an employee may be made redundant, not because his own job is redundant, but because his job has been filled by another employee who would otherwise themselves have been made redundant.

Although this "statutory test" was itself doubted by a differently constituted EAT in the case of *Church v West Lancashire NHS Trust* [1998] I.R.L.R. 4, who stated that the proper test is a "sensible blend" of the contractual and functional approaches, the House of Lords in *Murray v Foyle Meats* [1999] I.R.L.R. 562 has confirmed that the "statutory" test is to be applied, and that both the "contract" test and the "job function" test are themselves redundant and should not be followed. Their Lordships stated that if a dismissal is attributable to a redundancy situation, the dismissal will be by way of redundancy.

This important case both clarifies, and indeed simplifies, the situation and also impliedly confirms the lawfulness of bumped redundancies.

Place of Work

11.1.2   The problem faced by the court has been to decide whether the inclusion of a mobility clause in the employee's contract should be the deciding factor in defining the place of work with reference to redundancy.

If a purely contractual approach is taken, and if the employee's contract contains a general mobility clause, an employer may avoid a redundancy situation by offering the employee work in any location—which considering the case of *Western Excavating* (see "constructive dismissal" in Chapter 10) would perhaps appear to be the correct approach. However, although in the case of *O'Brien v Associated Fire Alarms Ltd* [1968] 1 W.L.R. 1916 the court adopted a contractual test, in the later case of *Bass Leisure Ltd v Thomas* [1994] I.R.L.R. 104 the EAT instead applied a geographical approach, looking at where the applicant had actually worked, rather than at where he could have worked.

This has been supported by the Court of Appeal decision in *High Table Ltd v Horst* [1997] I.R.L.R. 513 which favoured the factual or geographical approach to "place of work". In that case, Ms Horst had worked for High Table, a catering services company, as a waitress for a number of years at the premises of one of their clients, Hill Samuel, in the City of London. Following a down turn in the business between High Table and Hill Samuel in 1993, Ms Horst was made re-dundant. She argued that since her employment contract contained an express mobility clause—which purported to allow the employer to transfer staff on a temporary or permanent basis to any location—her "place of work" was at any of her employer's clients, and not just at Hill Samuels. She maintained that she could and should have been offered work elsewhere, thus was not redundant, and claimed unfair dismissal. The Court of Appeal rejected her argument, coming down in favour of a factual approach, and stating:

> "If an employee has worked in only one location under his contract of employment . . . it defies common sense to widen the extent of the place where he was so employed, merely because of the existence of a mobility clause. Of course, the refusal by the employee to obey a lawful requirement under the contract of employment to move may constitute a valid reason for dismissal, but issues of dismissal, redundancy and reasonableness in the actions of an employer should be kept distinct." *per* Peter Gibson L.J.

Presumably therefore, place of work is factual. Even if the employee has a mobility clause in the contract, if there is a down turn of work in one particular location in which the employer has always worked, this may constitute redun-dancy. On the other hand, should the employer choose instead to transfer the employee to another location, rather than declare him redundant, then following *Western Excavating*, this will be lawful; unless either the reason for the transfer or the manner of the transfer breach the implied duty of trust and confidence (*United Bank v Akhtar*), in which case it may lead to unfair dismissal. The courts do therefore appear to favour a strictly orthodox approach to the interpretation of such contractual terms, allowing the employer to decide whether to enforce and rely on such a term, but denying that same right to the employee. However, it should be remembered that following the House of Lords decision in *Murray v Foyle Meats* this is probably no longer a contentious issue.

Who is Eligible?

The claimant must firstly be an employee, they must have been dismissed (s.136 of the ERA 1996), and they must have a minimum of two years continuous employ-ment (s.155 of the ERA 1996) (*cf.* one year requirement for unfair dismissal) on the "relevant date" (s.145 of the ERA 1996)—the relevant date being either the date on   **11.1.3** which notice expires, or in the case of termination without notice, the date on which termination takes effect. However, in certain circumstances where the minimum notice period required by s.86 of the ERA 1996 would if given have expired at a later date, that later date will be the relevant date (s.145(5) of the ERA 1996).

In addition, certain categories are excluded from redundancy rights including:

- those aged under 20 (s.211 of the ERA 1996) and those over normal retirement age (if no retirement age is specified, those over 65) (s.156 of the ERA 1996). It is important to remember that the Employment Equality (Age) Regulations 2006, at the time of writing still at the draft stage, are due to be implemented by October 2006, and propose to remove the upper age limit for redundancy claims unless the employee has reached the genuine retirement age.

- those dismissed for misconduct or industrial action, (s.140 of the ERA 1996),

Continuity of Employment

11.1.4   As stated above, to be eligible for redundancy, an employee must have a minimum of two years, continuous employment. In certain instances, continuity of employment will be preserved, even though the employee apparently changes employers:

- *Associated Employers*. The business of the employer together with the business of his associated employers will be treated as one (s.139(2) of the ERA 1996), and companies are treated as associated if either one has control of the other, or both are controlled by a third party (s.231 of the ERA 1996).

- *Transfer of Business*. If a trade, business or undertaking is transferred, the period of employment at the time of the transfer counts as a period of employment with the transferee (s.218(2) of the ERA 1996).

In the case of the sale of a business this normally means that there must be the transfer of the business as a going concern—probably including the goodwill—and not merely the sale of individual assets (*Melon v Hector Powe Ltd* [1981] I.C.R. 43).

Procedure

11.1.5   In order to ensure that the redundancy may not be held to amount to an unfair dismissal it is important that the employer should follow a procedure of good industrial practice, such as was laid down in the case of *Williams v Compair Maxam Ltd* [1982] I.C.R. 156:

i) The employer should give as much warning as possible.

ii) The employer should consult with the trade union, particularly regarding selection procedure.

iii) The selection procedure should be objective.

iv) The employer should ensure that the selection procedure is followed.

v) The employer should seek to offer alternative employment.

Additionally, since October 2004, dismissals by way of redundancy fall within s.98A of the ERA 1996 and the statutory dismissal procedures laid down in Sch.2 of the EA 2002 (see Chapter 10).

In relation to the guidelines from *Compair*, the following points should also be considered:

- A redundancy situation may come about when an employer wishes to dismiss and re-employ workers as part of a company re-organisation plan.

- In situations where there is a proposal to make more than 20 redundancies within a period of 90 days or less the employer has a statutory duty to consult with the union or other appropriate representatives within 30 days, and if more than 100 redundancies within 90 days (s.188 of the TULR(C)A 1992). Note, however, that the employer's duty is to consult, not to agree, with the union or other representatives—the final decision is the employer's. The question may arise as to when the proposal to dismiss actually occurs; in the case of *Re Hartlebury Printers Ltd (in liquidation)* [1992] I.C.R. 704, it was stated that "contemplating" collective redundancies (as referred to in 98/59/EC The Collective Redundancies Directive) meant more than merely thinking about the possibility of redundancies, and in the case of *Leicestershire County Council v UNISON* [2005] I.R.L.R. 920 the EAT held that the proposal had been taken by officers of the County Council a month before it was formally ratified by the appropriate Council committee.

- If the employer fails to comply with the requirement to consult, a tribunal may make a protective award of up to 90 days.

- Following the introduction of s.98A of the ERA 1996, the failure by an employer to follow an agreed procedure, other than the statutory procedures, will not necessarily make the redundancy dismissal unfair.

- There is no clear authority on how closely the tribunal may examine the procedure adopted for redundancy selection. Certainly, the more transparent the system (e.g. LIFO—last in first out), the more likely it is that the tribunal will not question it (*British Aerospace Plc v Green* [1995] I.C.R. 1006).

- Certain selections for redundancy will be automatically unfair—e.g. trade union activities (s.153 of the TULR(C)A 1992), pregnancy, etc.

- If the employer makes an offer of suitable alternative employment to an employee before the end of his employment, there are two possible consequences:

  i) if the employee accepts the offer, then subject to a four week trial period, there will be no dismissal; or

  ii) if the employee unreasonably refuses the offer he will be barred from claiming a redundancy payment.

The question then arises, what constitutes "suitable alternative employment"? In the case of *Taylor v Kent County Council* [1969] 2 Q.B. 560, a head teacher whose school was merged with another was offered a post as supply teacher, but at his old salary. The court agreed that the demotion in status was sufficient to make the new position unsuitable.

Likewise, generally a drop in pay or earning potential will make a new position unsuitable, but since suitability is a question of fact for the tribunal, this need not always be the case (see *Sheppard v NCB* [1966] 1 K.I.R. 101).

The second issue for the tribunal is whether the refusal of the offer is unreasonable. Here the test is subjective, and the tribunal may take into account such personal factors as health, family commitments, etc. (*John Fowler Ltd v Parkin* [1975] I.R.L.R. 89).

COMPENSATION

11.2   Redundancy compensation is calculated as follows:

a) For each year worked over the age of 18 but under the age of 22, half a week's gross pay.

b) For each year worked over the age of 22 but under the age of 41, one week's gross pay.

c) For each year worked over the age of 41 but under normal retirement age, one and a half week's pay.

A maximum of 20 years of employment can be taken into account (s.162(3) of the ERA 1996), also be aware of the statutory maximum amount for the basic calculation of "a week's pay" from February 1, 2006 this stood at £290 (SI 2005/3352).

Chapter 12

TRANSFER OF UNDERTAKINGS

CHAPTER OVERVIEW

Transfer of undertakings regulations were introduced to give effect to the **CO12** Acquired Rights Directive (Directive 77/187/EC) which basically stated that the rights of individual employees should not be lost in the case of a transfer of a business or undertaking from one operator or owner to another. Both the Directive and the subsequent Regulations (SI 1981/1794) are relatively complicated and have generated a considerable amount of case law, not all of which appears to sit comfortably together.

Many of the important cases are decisions of the European Court of Justice, which is not of course bound by its own previous decisions. This has inevitably given rise to difficulties for national courts when seeking to apply binding ECJ case law to subsequent situations.

It is a difficult area of law and one that has given rise to and opportunity for considerable discussion and legal argument. The purpose of this chapter is to attempt to lay out in a straightforward manner the law as it presently stands and highlight the anomalies that are current in the interpretation of that law. For in-depth discussion and further explanation students are advised to read some of the commentaries written on the various cases cited in the text.

Common Law Position

12.1   Since the common law holds that the contract of employment is a personal contract and not an asset of the company as such, it follows that the sale or transfer of a business would have the effect of terminating the contract, rather than transferring it. It is uncertain what effect the common law would have on the individual contracts of employment; they may on occasion be determined automatically without breach (*Re General Rolling Stock Co* (1866) L.R. 1 Eq. 346), or they may be terminated by breach giving rise to a claim for wrongful dismissal (*Nokes v Doncaster Amalgamated Collieries Ltd* [1940] A.C. 1014).

However, since the intervention of statute through redundancy, unfair dismissal and more recently regulations governing transfers of undertakings, the common law position has little relevance in practice.

TRANSFER OF UNDERTAKINGS (PROTECTION OF EMPLOYMENT) REGULATIONS 1981 (TUPE)

12.2   At the time of writing, it is understood that amended TUPE Regulations are to be introduced. These may give rise to some renumbering of the present regulations, but will also hopefully go some way to clarifying some of the presently anomalous situations not directly covered by the 1981 Regulations. Unless otherwise stated, all references and numberings of regulations below apply to the 1981 TUPE regulations.

TUPE were introduced to implement EC Directive 77/187 (the Acquired Rights Directive), amended by Directive 98/50 and consolidated in Directive 2001/23 and have themselves since both been amended and given rise to amendments of other legislation. Although the regulations are fairly complex—and certainly much case law has been generated both by the regulations and the Directive—the main thrust of the Regulations is contained in reg.5 (1981):

> 5 (1) ". . . a relevant transfer shall not operate so as to terminate the contract of employment of any person employed by the transferor in the undertaking or part transferred but any such contract which would otherwise have been terminated by the transfer shall have effect after the transfer as if originally made between the person so employed and the transferee."
> 5 (2)(a) "all the transferor's rights, powers, duties and liabilities under or in connection with any such contract, shall be transferred by virtue of this Regulation to the transferee;"

Thus the contracts of employment of all employees of the transferor are automatically transferred to the transferee on the same terms and conditions as were previously enjoyed by the employees. If an employee objects to his contract being transferred he is entitled to refuse, but the effect of this is to terminate the contract *without a dismissal taking place* (reg.5(4A)(4B)).

Only if the proposed transfer would result in a significant and detrimental change to the employee may the employee terminate the contract and claim unfair dismissal via constructive dismissal (reg.5(5)). It is not firmly established whether such a claim would lie against the transferee as well as the transferor (*Unicorn Consultancy Services Ltd v Westbrook* [2000] I.R.L.R. 80 *cf. Mitie Services Ltd v French* [2002] I.R.L.R. 512), although arguably it should, since the employee would have terminated his contract before the transferee assumed responsibility.

"Undertaking"

TUPE defines an "undertaking" as including any trade or business, but this definition has been widened, following the case of *Dr Sophie Redmond Stichting v Bartol* [1992] I.R.L.R. 366, to include non-commercial organisations, for example charities. The ECJ ruling in *Collino and Chiappero v Telecom Italia SpA* (Case C-343/98) indicates that the Regulations will apply in the case of privatisation of state industries. However, "activities involving the exercise of public authority" are not included (*Henke v Gemeinde Schierke und Verwaltungsgemeinschaft Brocken* [1996] I.R.L.R. 701). Regulation 3(5) of the proposed regulations may confirm that TUPE does not apply to either reorganisations within public authorities or transfers of functions between public authorities.

12.2.1

"Relevant transfer"

The ECJ in *Suzen v Zehnacker Gebaudereinigung GmbH Krankenhausservice* [1997] I.R.L.R. 255 held that the transfer must relate to "a stable economic entity whose activity is not limited to performing one specific works contract"; and by so doing apparently overruled the authority of cases such as *Schmidt v Spar- und Leihkasse usw* [1994] I.R.L.R. 302 which had held that the transfer of a single individual employee to a sub-contractor could amount to a relevant transfer. It is possible to view *Suzen* as suggesting that the courts will look to find a transfer of physical assets rather than merely a transfer of labour before holding that the transfer is a "relevant transfer" and falls within the ambit of the Directive and Regulations—and this view was supported by the ECJ in *Oy Liikenne Ab v Liskojarvi* [2001] I.R.L.R. 171—although such a view would appear to be contrary to the purpose of the Directive. It remains to be seen how provisions within s.3 of the proposed amended Regulations will be interpreted.

This is not, however, to suggest that a transfer may take place merely on the sale of an undertaking's assets. The ECJ in the case of *Spijkers v Gebroeders Benedik Abattoir CV* [1986] 2 C.M.L.R. 296 stated that a transfer will only take place

12.2.2

within the meaning of the Directive if the entity in question retains its identity, in other words if the organisation is transferred as a going concern, probably including goodwill. The *Spijkers* case was followed in the case of *Suzen* (see above) which was seen as potentially restricting the operation of the Regulations by appearing to differentiate between the "economic entity" and the "activity" and perhaps making it more difficult to consider a labour-only business as falling within the ambit of TUPE; certainly dicta in *Suzen* made clear that the loss of a single contract to a competing firm would not in itself amount to a TUPE transfer. An example of this may be seen in the case of *Betts v Brintel Helicopters Ltd and KLM Era Helicopters (UK) Ltd* [1997] I.R.L.R. 361. Brintel had provided helicopter services under three contracts to Shell (UK) Ltd. When the contracts expired, Brintel were re-awarded two of them, but the third was won by KLM. KLM did not take over any of Brintel's helicopters or staff, nor did they use the same flying base. Although some of Brintel's staff were re-deployed within Brintel's other operations, some, including Betts, were not. Betts claimed unfair dismissal.

The question for the court was whether there had been a transfer of undertakings between KLM and Brintel, if so the dismissal may well have been unfair under TUPE. The Court of Appeal followed the then recently decided case of *Suzen*, and held that there had been no transfer. It argued that, although the operation of the third contract by Brintel had amounted to an undertaking or economic entity, that undertaking had not been transferred. They reasoned that since very few of Brintel's assets had passed to KLM, there was insufficient evidence to show that the undertaking had retained its identity in the hands of KLM. In this case there is evidence that had Betts and others not claimed for unfair dismissal they may well have been engaged by KLM, arguably this should have strengthened the case that a transfer had taken place.

Other points of note include:

- The Directive and the regulations apply both to the contracting-out of services and to the process of compulsory competitive tendering (CCT) (*Rask v ISS Kantineservice* [1993] I.R.L.R. 133, but consider the possible limitations imposed by *Suzen*).

- Neither the Directive nor the regulations consider as relevant transfers changes of ownership brought about by share purchases.

Some of the post-*Suzen* case law appears confusing and contradictory. The Court of Appeal in the case of *ECM (Vehicle Delivery Service) Ltd v Cox* [1999] I.C.R. 1162 held that the economic entity which was transferred was a contract to do work and the actual work done under that contract, rather than any tangible assets. It may be that the court in this case was particularly influenced by the fact that the company involved specifically attempted to avoid the application of

TUPE. Certainly this case does not appear to sit well with the reasoning in the later case of *Oy Liikene Ab v Liskojarvi* (Case C-172/99) where the court appeared to suggest that a distinction may be drawn between contracts for the supply of labour only, and contracts which may include the supply of labour but also depended upon the supply of other assets; in the second type of contract, the transfer of the labour alone may not amount to a TUPE contract.

Dismissal of Employees

TUPE reg.7 provides that if an employee is dismissed either before or after a rele-   **12.2.3**
vant transfer, and the reason or principle reason for that dismissal is the transfer, that dismissal will be regarded as unfair.

However, reg.7 then allows either the transferor or the transferee the complete defence of "some other substantial reason" for the dismissal on the grounds of "economic, technical or organisational" (ETO) reasons. This may be taken to mean that in such a situation the employee would not even be entitled to a redundancy payment, however the EAT in the case of *Gorictree v Jenkinson* [1985] I.C.R. 51 held that the ETO defence is not synonymous with the s.98 ERA SOSR, and thus entitlement to a redundancy payment would not be lost. An example of this ETO defence and some of the problems it may produce may be seen in the case of *Berriman v Delabole Slate Ltd* [1985] I.R.L.R. 305. Mr Berriman's employers sold their business as a going concern to Delabole Slate, who wished to bring the terms of the new employees into line with their existing staff. This would result in a decrease in guaranteed pay for Mr Berriman, who rejected the offer, left and claimed unfair dismissal. Initially the tribunal held that the dismissal was for an "economic, technical or organisational reason", and did not therefore constitute unfair dismissal. Both the EAT and the Court of Appeal took a different view. They held that the reason for the dismissal was that the new employer wished to change employment terms and conditions of the transferred staff and that, "the reason itself does not involve any change either in the number or the functions of the workforce". The court appears to have adopted a purposive approach, and at first glance this decision appears to afford considerable protection to transferred workers. However, the question that needs to be asked is for how long could this situation continue—at what point would a change in the transferred employee's terms cease to be as a result of the transfer, and become a potentially fair SOSR?

The following points should also be noted:

- The transferee cannot escape liability by arranging that the transferor should dismiss surplus staff before the transfer takes place. In the case of *Litster v Forth Dry Dock and Engg Co Ltd* [1989] I.C.R. 341, the respondent company was in receivership and agreed to dismiss the workforce before the transfer took place, so as to make the transfer more attractive to the transferee by attempting to avoid for the transferee any liability under TUPE, (the transferor being in receivership and with the debtors having realised their security, there were insufficient assets to meet the transferor's liability for unfair dismissal or redundancy claims). The House of Lords adopted a purposive approach to the legislation however, and stated that the regulation should be read as if the words "or would have been so employed if he had not been unfairly dismissed . . ." had been inserted after ". . . a person so employed immediately before the transfer . . .". Thus the dismissed employees were brought within the scope of the regulations, and the transferee became responsible for their dismissal.

- Liability for unfair dismissal may be automatically passed from the transferor to the transferee, even though the transferee may not have been party to any of the prior discussions (*Thompson v Walon Car Delivery and BRS Automotive Ltd* [1997] I.R.L.R. 343).

- It appears that in a TUPE transfer those rights which are protected under the Directive may not be varied by the new employer, even with the express consent of the employee, unless it can be shown that the reason for the variation is not by reason of the transfer (*Foreningen af Arbejdsledere I Danmark v Daddy's Dance Hall* Case 324/86). It is not however clear for how long this prohibition would remain.

Consultation over Transfers

12.2.4   There is a duty under TUPE reg.10 to both inform and consult with representatives of all affected employees prior to any relevant transfer. The grounds for consultation include the timing of the transfer, the reasons for it and the legal, economic and social implications, and if the employer is the transferor he must indicate the measures the transferee will be taking at the time and after the transfer (reg.10(2)).

Employee representatives may be either trade union representatives or non-union worker representatives, perhaps elected solely for the consultation process.

Chapter 13

RESTRAINTS OF TRADE

CHAPTER OVERVIEW

If a contract of employment contains an express clause that restricts what the **CO13** employee may do once the contract of employment has terminated, such a clause is termed a "restrictive covenant" or a "restraint of trade clause".

Such a clause may be enforceable even though the contract in which it is contained is no longer in effect—although it should be noted that the courts would be very reluctant to enforce such a clause if the contract has been unlawfully terminated by the employer (see for example *General Billposting Co Ltd v Atkinson* [1909] A.C. 118 and *Rock Refrigeration v Jones* [1997] I.C.R. 938) since repudiation of the contract by the employer would generally release the employee from any further obligation.

The problem for the courts is to strike the right balance between the rights of the employer to protect their interests and the rights of the employee to engage in their profession or trade without undue restriction. Such a balance is not always easy to achieve, and examination of the case law may suggest that over the years the balance has swayed somewhat.

A distinction must be drawn between competition during the employment relationship, and competition once the relationship has ended.

COMPETITION WHILST EMPLOYED

13.1   Competition during the life of the employment contract will usually fall foul of the implied duty of fidelity imposed on the employee, and amount to a breach of contract by the employee; it may also enable the employer to obtain an injunction against a third party, restraining them from employing that employee whilst the original contract is in force (*Hivac Ltd v Park Royal Scientific Instruments Ltd* [1946] Ch. 169). Many contracts of employment will contain a specific clause either forbidding an employee to work in their spare time in a particular capacity or industry, or requiring that the employee obtain express permission from the employer before accepting part-time work elsewhere.

The situation is less certain in the case of an employee who is working for an employer only on a part time basis. Whilst in theory the employer could seek an injunction to prevent the employee working elsewhere during the period of his contract, since the granting of an injunction is an equitable remedy and thus discretionary, and since the employee is only contracted on a part time basis, it is unlikely that a court would be willing to comply in most cases. Perhaps if the contract reflected the need for particular fidelity, either through a specific express clause or in the level of salary paid, an injunction may be granted.

GARDEN LEAVE

13.2   Although an order of specific performance may not be granted to oblige an employee to work for a particular employer (s.236 of the TULR(C)A 1992), in many cases companies are able to write long notice periods into contracts and then enforce the notice period without requiring the employee to actually attend for work. The effect of this is that the employee is paid to stay at home—"garden leave"—and may be legally restrained from taking up other employment during that notice period (*Evening Standard Co Ltd v Henderson* [1987] I.C.R. 588). Such clauses are now common in the contracts of senior employees; they enable an employer to protect all of their business interests for a period of several months should an employee decide to join a competitor.

In more recent years though the courts have adopted a less consistent approach to the issue of garden leave. Although in *GFI Group Inc v Eaglestone* [1994] I.R.L.R. 119 an injunction was granted prohibiting an employee from taking up new employment before his notice period had expired, in the case of *William Hill Org Ltd v Tucker* [1998] I.R.L.R. 313 the Court of Appeal both declined to grant a similar injunction and doubted that in such situations an injunction enforcing garden leave should be granted, but rather the employer should seek to rely upon a restrictive covenant within the employment contract.

There is a further practical difference to the employee between the enforcement of a garden leave clause and being dismissed with money in lieu of notice: money in lieu of notice is generally treated not as wages but as damages for the employer breaching the contract by not giving the employee the required notice period (*Delaney v Staples (t/a De Montfort Recruitment)* [1992] I.C.R. 483) and is thus not normally taxable; the enforcement of a garden leave clause however results in the employer paying wages during the notice period which is taxable (*Redundant Employee v McNally (Inspector of Taxes)* [2005] S.T.C. 1426. The exception to this situation is demonstrated in the case of *EMI Group Electronics Ltd v Coldicott (Inspector of Taxes)* [1999] I.R.L.R. 630, in which a redundancy payment included an amount of pay in lieu of notice. The Court of Appeal held that the pay in lieu of notice was taxable as the employment contract contained a term which stated: "The company reserves the right to make payment of the equivalent of salary in lieu of notice . . ." and thus the payment should be viewed as an emolument arising under the contract, since it became a payment made "in return for acting as or being an employee" (*per* Lord Radcliffe, *Hochstasser v Mayes* [1960] A.C. 376).

RESTRICTIVE COVENANTS

A restrictive covenant is an express term of the contract of employment which **13.3** purports to extend beyond the life of the contract and restrain the employee from working, post-contract, for a particular employer, in a particular industry, in a particular role, or in a particular location or geographical area, for an agreed length of time. Such terms are common in many employment contracts; their purpose being to prevent ex-employees from taking knowledge, skills, information, etc. to a competitor. However, the doctrine of restraint of trade holds that prima facie such agreements are void. The court will only uphold a restrictive covenant if it is satisfied that the employer has a legitimate proprietary interest to protect, such as a trade secret, a particular manufacturing process, a client base or, perhaps, its existing employees; and then only for as long as is fair and necessary.

In effect, the court has to balance the right of the ex-employee to work and do business, with the right of the ex-employer to reasonable protection. Whilst it is quite proper that confidential information and trade secrets of various types should be protected, it is equally proper that the individual should be permitted to practice and exercise skills and knowledge legitimately gained.

The Protectable Interests

13.3.1   There are generally held to be three areas which the courts recognise as protectable: trade secrets, client base and, more recently, stable workforce. The door has perhaps been left open for the inclusion of further protectable interests by the words of Evans L.J. in *Dawney, Day & Co Ltd v De Braconier d'Alphen* [1997] I.R.L.R. 442, when he stated: ". . . the covenant may be enforced when the covenentee has a legitimate interest, of whatever kind, to protect, and when the covenant is no wider than is necessary to protect that interest."

Trade secrets

13.3.1.1   A distinction must be drawn between the knowledge, often confidential, which an employee has gained whilst employed by a particular employer, which is not protectable, and knowledge of a particularly sensitive nature—"trade secrets"—which may be protectable. It is very difficult to lay down rules as to what amounts to a "trade secret", as the court recognised in the early case of *Herbert Morris v Saxelby* [1916] 1 A.C. 688, and whereas it may be possible to say with some confidence that a secret manufacturing process may amount to a trade secret and thus be protectable, the speed with which industries such as information technology and computer software develop makes it very difficult for the courts to determine whether particular knowledge is protectable or not. In the case of *Lansing Linde Ltd v Kerr* [1991] I.R.L.R. 80, the Court of Appeal stated that in some cases the protectable information need not be of a technical nature, but may be considered protectable as its disclosure to a competitor may significantly harm the company. An example of the approach of the courts may be found in the case of *Faccenda Chicken Ltd v Fowler* [1986] I.C.R. 297. Mr Fowler had worked for Faccenda as sales manager, he left and set up his own business in competition, employing several other Faccenda ex-employees. Between them they had information as to the names and addresses of Faccenda's customers, amounts of their orders and the prices charged. Faccenda argued that this was confidential information, and Fowler should be restrained from using it. The court stated:

> "It is clear that the obligation not to use or disclose information may cover secret processes . . . and other information which is of a sufficiently high degree of confidentiality as to amount to a trade secret. The obligation does not extend, however, to cover all information which is given to or acquired by the employee while in his employment, and in particular may not cover information which is only 'confidential' . . ."

Each case must therefore be decided on its own particular facts.

Client base

This is another problem area; on the one hand companies can only exist if they   **13.3.1.2**
do business with others, be they other companies or individual members of the
public—thus it is only reasonable that a company's client basis should be a protectable interest. On the other hand, especially in the service industry, clients may
choose to do business with a company because of the particular individual
employee with whom they are in contact. In such a situation it may seem
inequitable to prevent an ex-employee and a client company from conducting
business with each other merely because the ex-employer inserted a restrictive
covenant into an employment contract. However the courts accept that if the
individual employee had sufficiently direct contact with the company's clients
then it is reasonable to restrict the employee from canvassing or soliciting those
clients for at least a limited period of time (see for example *SW Strange v Mann*
[1965 1 All E.R. 1069). This restriction may on occasion cover any of those who
were customers of the company at any time during the employee's employment
(*GW Plowman & Sons Ltd v Ash* [1964] 2 All E.R. 10).

Stable workforce

In the case of *Kores Manufacturing Co v Kolok Manufacturing Ltd* [1958] 2 All   **13.3.1.3**
E.R. 65, the Court of Appeal held that a "no poaching" agreement between two
competing companies, under which each agreed not to employ anyone who had
worked at the other company during the previous five years, was invalid—which
suggested that a stable workforce was not as such a protectable interest. However
in recent years the courts have been prepared to uphold restrictive covenants
seeking to protect certain parts of a company's workforce in some situations. In
Alliance Paper Group Ltd v Prestwich [1996] I.R.L.R. 25 a "no poaching" clause
was upheld and, in *Dawney, Day & Co Ltd v De Braconier d'Alphen* [1997]
I.R.L.R. 442, the Court of Appeal enforced a one-year anti-solicitation clause. It
is worth noting that in both *Alliance Paper* and *Dawney, Day* the restraint clause
applied only to solicitation of senior employees, and not, as was the case in *Kores*,
to all employees. It therefore appears that an anti-solicitation clause purporting
to prevent the "poaching" of all and any staff by an ex-employee will be considered too wide to be enforceable; what is perhaps not yet clear is whether such
clauses may be enforceable if they apply to any clearly defined grouping of staff
or whether they will only be enforceable if they apply only to *senior* staff (see also
TSC Europe (UK) Ltd v Massey [1999] I.R.L.R. 22).

Extent of the Clause

If the court accepts that the restrictive covenant does no more than guard a pro-   **13.3.2**
tectable interest, it must then consider the extent of the clause, in terms of scope,

time-scale and geographic location. There is considerable interrelation between these three terms, and it is rarely possible for a court to consider each in isolation from the others.

Scope

13.3.2.1   The issue here is that the scope of the restriction must be no wider than is necessary to protect the protectable interest. Thus, in the case of *Attwood v Lamont* [1920] 3 K.B. 571, a clause in a tailor's contract which purported to prevent him working as a tailor, dressmaker, haberdasher or milliner amongst other things, was held to be too wide to be enforceable.

Time-scale

13.3.2.2   Again this should be no wider than necessary to reasonably protect the employer's protectable interest. A restraint of 12 months for a member of the company's senior management team who had access to business and product development plans was held to be reasonable in the case of *Lansing Linde Ltd v Kerr* [1991] I.R.L.R. 80. Such a time-scale may well be found unreasonable in the case of a less-senior employee or perhaps in a particularly fast moving industry such as computer software.

Geographical area

13.3.2.3   In the case of *Greer v Sketchley Ltd* [1979] I.R.L.R. 445, Mr Greer's contract contained a clause purporting to restrain him from working within a particular scope and time-scale "in any part of the United Kingdom". Since, at that time, Sketchley did not operate in several areas of England, in Wales or in Scotland, the Court of Appeal held that the clause was too wide to be enforceable. In seeking to prevent Mr Greer from working in areas of the UK in which Sketchley had no interest, it could not be said that the clause was the minimum necessary to protect the company's protectable interests. Likewise in *Lansing Linde Ltd v Kerr* [1991] I.R.L.R. 80 since the employee's role was limited to the UK and Europe, the court refused to enforce a clause covering a world-wide restriction.

Multiple Clauses

13.3.3   It is not unusual for an employee's contract of employment to contain more than one restrictive covenant. Sometimes these clauses may overlap, which might prima facie appear to benefit the employer, but the courts will consider each clause in isolation—as demonstrated in *Countrywide Assured Financial Services Ltd v (1) Smart (2) Pollard* [2004] EWHC 1214. Mr Pollard worked for an estate agent and his contract of employment contained a number of restrictive covenants. One of these covenants purported to restrict him from working for any other estate agent within a three-mile radius for a period of three months after the termination of his employment, and another restricted him from soliciting any of Countrywide's clients for a period of six months following termination. Mr Pollard left Countrywide to work for another estate agent in the area, and his former employer sought to enforce the first covenant against him. The court held that since the second covenant restricted Mr Pollard from soliciting Countrywide's clients for a period of six months and since there was no evidence that Mr Pollard had taken confidential information with him to his new employers, there was no separate protectable interest covered by the second covenant. It is therefore clear that the courts will only uphold a specific restrictive covenant if relates to a specific protectable interest, and even then, only in so far as that covenant is reasonable. In this case, the court also made the point that an employer's good will is in itself not an interest capable of protection.

Examples

A bringing together of some illustrations of the above principles from case law **13.3.4** include:

- A promise not to use trade secrets or personal influence over customers may be enforced (*Spafax Ltd v Harrison* [1980] I.R.L.R. 442).

- Refusal by the employee to sign such an agreement may be a fair reason for dismissal (*RS Components v Irwin* [1973] I.C.R. 535).

- A promise not to use details of a secret manufacturing process for a period of five years was enforceable (*Forster & Sons Ltd v Suggett* (1918) 35 T.L.R. 87).

- A promise by an engineer not to work for a competitor for a period of seven years was not enforceable. It was held to be an unreasonable restriction on his knowledge and skill (*Herbert Morris Ltd v Saxelby* [1916] 1 A.C. 688).

- A promise by a negotiator in an estate agent's office not to work in that industry within a certain geographical area for a certain period of time was held not to be enforceable since the business was of a non-recurring type, and thus the agreement would not protect the employer's existing business, but merely restrain the employee from obtaining work (*Bowler v Lovegrove* [1921] 1 Ch. 642).

- An agreement preventing an employee from working within an industry or organisation in *any* capacity will generally be void as being wider than is necessary to protect a proprietary interest (*Commercial Plastics Ltd v Vincent* [1965] 1 Q.B. 623).

However:

- An agreement preventing an individual from working anywhere in the world, in a particular industry for a period of 25 years was held to be valid—since the promise had been bought for the equivalent of millions of pounds! (*Nordenfelt v Maxim Nordenfelt Guns Co Ltd* [1894] A.C. 535).

and:

- An agreement preventing a solicitor's clerk from working for other solicitors within an area of a seven mile radius for the remainder of his life was held to be valid! (*Fitch v Dewes* [1921] 2 A.C. 158)—it is suggested that, except in the most exceptional circumstances, such an agreement would today be held to be far too wide to be enforceable.

Methods of Enforcement

13.3.5   The court will occasionally adopt a "blue pencil" approach to restraint of trade covenants, striking out such parts as are unenforceable, whilst upholding the remainder, assuming of course that the remainder is capable of standing alone (*T Lucas & Co Ltd v Mitchell* [1974] Ch. 129). This is not the normal approach however, since the courts follow the contract doctrine of *contra proferentum*—in cases of doubt or ambiguity interpreting the clause against the party seeking to rely upon it. There are however instances of the courts looking behind the actual words used in the clause to determine the intention of the parties at the time of entering into the agreement. One such example is the case of *Littlewoods Organisation Ltd v Harris* [1978] 1 All E.R. 1026 in which a broadly worded clause was construed narrowly by the Court of Appeal so as to give effect to the (apparent) intention of the parties. It is questionable if, bearing in mind the imbalance of the parties bargaining power when entering into most contracts of employment, this is justifiable; a view supported by the dissenting judgment of Browne L.J. who was of the opinion that the court had no jurisdiction to re-write such a clause.

Public Policy

13.3.6   In the case of *Nordenfelt v Maxim Nordenfelt Guns and Ammunition Co* [1894] A.C. 535, the House of Lords took the view that a restraint of trade clause may only be valid if it is both reasonable between the parties and not contrary to the public interest. The issue of public policy has not often been considered by the courts in respect of restrictive covenants in employment contracts; one of the few cases in which the issue has been raised is that of *Wyatt v Kreglinger and Fernau* [1933] 1 K.B. 793 in which Mr Wyatt was promised a pension if he would agree not to work in the wool trade. Letters were exchanged and agreement was reached. Some time later the company sought to terminate the arrangement, and Mr Wyatt applied to the court to enforce the agreement. On the particular facts, the court were unable to agree whether the agreement amounted to a contract, but they were agreed that in any case the arrangement constituted a restraint of trade and as such could not be enforced on the grounds of public policy. In the later case of *Esso Petroleum Co Ltd v Harper's Garage (Stourport) Ltd* [1968] A.C. 269 the House of Lords suggested that at least some of the cases concerning restraint of trade clauses in employment contracts should have been decided on the grounds of public policy. It is likely that this approach would be relevant if an ex-employee were restrained from performing a socially useful or necessary function by reliance on a restrictive covenant. The issue of public policy is more commonly considered in business to business restraint of trade clauses, the so-called "solus agreements" (see *Esso Petroleum Co Ltd v Harper's Garage (Stourport) Ltd* [1968] A.C. 269).

Chapter 14

TRADE UNIONS

CHAPTER OVERVIEW

For many people the importance and relevance of trade unions has diminished over the past few years; certainly, since 1979 overall trade union membership has dropped by something like 50 per cent. Many unions have chosen, often through necessity, to amalgamate, and very few unions have seen any significant increase in membership in recent times.

    Unions came into being originally in order to give workers an effective voice and some strength in bargaining for better wages and working conditions. At the time (the late 1800s) there was very little in the way of employment protection and much of the legislation and the perceived attitude of the courts appeared to favour the employer. The early trade unions were viewed with both suspicion and alarm, and acceptance came slowly. During the 20th century, trade union power and influence increased steadily (although following the General Strike of 1926 there was considerable anti-union feeling and support dropped), to the point where under the Labour governments of the 1960s and 1970s the trade unions were involved in policy making decisions. At around this time it was perceived that many of the unions were coming under the influence of militant activists;

strikes and industrial unrest increased, and legislative intervention proved ineffective (see for example the Industrial Relations Act 1971). When the Thatcher government came to power in 1979 it set about reforming industrial relations by implementing a series of measures designed to both control and restrict the activities of trade unions; collective labour relations gave way to a new "floor of individual rights" with the emphasis turned towards the individual employee and legislation was passed giving rights to the individual whilst restricting the collective. At this time also it is notable that many of the industries in which trade unionism had traditionally been strong—mining, steel, ship-building, docks, car plants, etc.—were being run down, to the extent that today they barely exist in the UK. With minor exceptions the present Labour government has done nothing to reverse the post-1979 trend, and it has been for the unions themselves to adapt to the situation by, amongst other things, emphasising the role they can play in such areas as the offering legal advice and representation to their members.

Brief Historical Overview

14.1   Legislation prior to 1800 had made the organisation of workers in certain industries illegal, but the Combination Acts of 1799 and 1800 made the combination (or organising together) of any workmen unlawful. Furthermore, laws passed in the 17th and 18th centuries and culminating in the Master and Servant Act of 1823 imposed criminal sanctions on any worker who breached their employment contract by refusing to work. Consequently, the organising of workers into any collective body and particularly the taking of any form of industrial action was, until the repeal of the Combination Acts in 1824, both unlawful and criminal. The position between 1824 and the introduction of the Employers and Workmen Act of 1875 was that trade unions were not unlawful, but breach of the employment contract may in certain circumstances give rise to criminal liability resulting in imprisonment. The 1875 Act removed criminal liability for breach of the employment contract, with certain exceptions regarding workers in the public utilities, but had the effect of allowing or encouraging the courts to expand the number and scope of torts that a trade union may commit by instigating industrial action.

The position changed again in 1906 following the implementation of the Trade Disputes Act which gave immunity to trade unions for the commission of certain torts committed "in contemplation or furtherance of a trade dispute". With various relatively minor amendments this position has remained until the present time.

A more detailed examination of the historical development of trade unions in Britain indicates certain, and at times contradictory, themes and issues; and a proper understanding of the development requires an appreciation of the historical context. Certainly, during the late 18th and much of the 19th centuries much of Europe was subject to civil unrest and revolution, and it is hardly surprising that for those who held power in Britain the idea of giving "power to the people" by allowing collectives of workers to negotiate their own working conditions and wage levels reinforced by a legal threat of refusal to work was an anathema. Furthermore, trade unions and their objectives were viewed as a restraint of trade, and arguably it was trade that had made Britain "Great" and provide it with its Empire. What is perhaps rather more surprising is that for much of the time between the mid-1800s and early 1900s the legislature and the courts often appear to have been in conflict; there are numerous examples of the courts "giving" and the legislature "taking away" and vice versa. It is outside the scope of this book to consider these issues in any detail, but a consideration of the works of such as E.J. Hobsbawm provides interesting social background.

THE PRESENT POSITION

A broad definition of a "trade union" is included in s.1 of the Trade Union and Labour Relations (Consolidation) Act 1992 (TULR(C)A):   **14.2**

"In this Act a 'trade union' means an organisation (whether temporary or permanent)—

a) which consists wholly or mainly of workers of one or more descriptions and whose principal purposes include the regulation of relations between workers of that description or those descriptions and employers or employers' associations; or
b) which consists wholly or mainly of—

(i) constituent or affiliated organisations which fulfil the conditions in paragraph (a) (or themselves consist wholly or mainly of constituent or affiliated organisations which fulfil those conditions), or
(ii) representatives of such constituent or affiliated organisations,

and whose principle purposes include the regulation of relations between workers and employers or between workers and employers' associations, or the regulation of relations between its constituent or affiliated organisations."

The courts have defined this definition strictly in such cases as *Midland Cold Storage v Turner* [1972] I.C.R. 773, in which it was argued that no organisation, in that case a committee of shop-stewards, whose principle purpose was to regulate the relations between workers and employers could fail to have sought recognition by the employer. Since the shop-stewards committee had not sought recognition from the employer, they could not be described as a trade union for the purpose of the legislation.

Section 10 of the TULR(C)A defines the status of a trade union as "quasi-corporate". As such, it is not a company, a provident society or a friendly society. It is, however, capable of:

- Making contracts in its own name.

- Suing and being sued in its own name in any action including actions in contract and tort.

- Having proceedings brought against it for offences committed by it or on its behalf.

Interestingly, and perhaps strangely, it would appear that a trade union may not however be able to bring an action for defamation in its own name (*EEPTU v Times Newspapers* [1980] 1 All E.R. 1097), although this issue is not totally clear (see the earlier case of *NUGMW v Gillian* [1946] K.B. 81).

LISTING OF TRADE UNIONS

14.3   A list of trade unions is kept by the Certification Officer (s.2 of the TULR(C)A 1992). Inclusion on the list is available to all trade unions (s.3 of the TULR(C)A 1992) on presentation of an application and supporting documentation. Inclusion on the list offers certain benefits to trade unions, including relief on various taxes, but primarily that such inclusion is a prerequisite for the granting of a certificate of independence. Refusal by a Certification Officer to include an organisation"s name on the list, or a decision to remove such a name permits that organisation to appeal to an EAT on any appealable question (s.3 of the TULR(C)A 1992).

INDEPENDENT TRADE UNION STATUS

14.4   It is necessary for a trade union to be granted independent status in order for it to gain various statutory rights: automatic employer recognition in certain circumstances, protection of its members against dismissal for union activities, time off for its members to undertake particular union activities, access to information for collective bargaining purposes, etc. An independent trade union is one which is not under the control of, or liable to interference from, an employer. The EAT in the case of *Blue Circle Staff Association v Certification Officer* [1977] 1 W.L.R. 239 laid down a list of guidelines for the Certification Officer when determining the status of a trade union; included in the list are such issues as whether the union is financially independent from the employer, whether the union rule book allows the employer to interfere with, or even control, the union, and whether the union has a "robust attitude in negotiation" with the employer. It is possible for a single-company union to obtain independent status, but both the courts and the Certification officer are likely to appreciate that such unions are more susceptible to influence from the employer than those unions operating over a range of employers.

Before arriving at his decision the Certification Officer should make "such enquiries as he thinks fit and shall take into account any relevant information submitted to him by any person" (s.6(4) of the TULR(C)A 1992). An appeal by a trade union against the decision of a Certification Officer to refuse to grant a certificate of independence, or a decision to withdraw such a certificate may be made to an EAT (s.9 of the TULR(C)A 1992).

TRADE UNION RECOGNITION

Recognition of a trade union by the relevant employer is important. It entitles **14.5** the union to involvement in collective bargaining activities, it may claim disclosure of information for such purposes, its representatives and members are entitled to time off for certain union activities, and the union must be consulted on training issues and opportunities. An employer may choose to recognise a union voluntarily, or under the ERelA 1999 there is automatic recognition by an employer of an independent trade union normally if either a majority of the workers in the bargaining unit are members of the trade union, or 40 per cent of those workers in the bargaining unit vote in favour of recognition. The particular rules governing all aspects of statutory recognition are complex. The process for recognition is supervised by the Central Arbitration Committee.

Voluntary Recognition

It is open to any employer to recognise any trade union for the purpose of col- **14.5.1** lective bargaining. In such circumstances the employer may at a later date choose to de-recognise that union, but must be aware that there may be an express or implied term in the individual employees' contracts regarding the products of the collective agreements entered into.

Occasionally the issue arises as to whether based on previous dealings a trade union has been recognised by a particular employer. In the case of *NUGSAT v Albury Bros Ltd* [1978] I.R.L.R. 504, the Court of Appeal held that the courts would require to see clear evidence that the employer had agreed to negotiate with the union for the purpose of reaching agreement, rather than merely holding discussions, and that such conduct had been carried out over a period of time.

Statutory Recognition

14.5.2   The legal position concerning statutory recognition of a trade union is contained in Sch.A1 of the TULR(C)A 1992, it is a detailed and complex piece of legislation. The procedure may be broken down into a number of steps:

1) The union, which must be an independent trade union, must make a written request to the employer, who must employ at least 21 workers. The request should detail the number of workers covered—the "proposed bargaining unit". If the employer within 10 days either agrees to recognise the union or agrees to enter into negotiations regarding recognition, and within a further period of 20 days or such period as the parties agree, agreement is reached on recognition, there are no further steps to be taken under the Schedule (Sch.A1, paras 4–10 of the TULR(C)A 1992).

2) If the employer rejects the request for recognition or the negotiations are not successful the trade union may apply to the Central Arbitration Committee (CAC) to determine whether the proposed bargaining unit is appropriate and whether the union has the support of the majority of workers in the proposed bargaining unit. However, the union will not be able to call on the CAC if during the first 10-day period of negotiations the employer has requested the assistance of ACAS in the negotiations and the union has rejected ACAS intervention (Sch.A1, paras 11–12 of the TULR(C)A 1992).

3) The CAC will not proceed if it finds either that there already exists a situation under which any union is recognised as already representing any of the workers covered by the proposed bargaining unit (however, such an agreement must be in force at the time—see *R (on the application of NUJ) v CAC and MGN Ltd* [2005] I.R.L.R. 28), or if it finds that less than 10 per cent of the proposed bargaining unit are members of the union making the request (Sch.A1, paras 13–15 of the TULR(C)A 1992). Furthermore, if more than one union makes application the CAC will not proceed unless the unions can show that they are prepared to co-operate with each other in any collective bargaining process (Sch.A1, para.37 of the TULR(C)A 1992).

4) If the CAC accepts the application it must then, unless agreement has already been reached between the parties, seek to determine the appropriate bargaining unit. Problems may arise when the proposed bargaining unit covers workers of different characteristics or at different places of work (Sch.A1, paras 18–19 of the TULR(C)A 1992). At this point the union should take note that, if the bargaining unit determined by the

CAC is different from the originally proposed unit, it may have difficulty winning recognition in the recognition ballot necessary if the majority of the workers in the "new" unit are not members of the union.

5) If the CAC is satisfied that the majority of workers within the determined bargaining unit are members of the trade union, a declaration of recognition for the purposes of collective bargaining will then normally be granted to the union. However, recognition will not be granted at this stage if three qualifying conditions are met:

   a) that the CAC is satisfied that a ballot should be held in the interests of good industrial relations;
   b) that the CAC has credible evidence from a significant number of union members from the bargaining unit that they do not wish the union to conduct collective bargaining on their behalf; and
   c) that membership evidence is produced which leads the CAC to doubt whether a significant number of union members within the bargaining unit want the union to conduct collective bargaining on their behalf (Sch.A1, paras 20–22 of the TULR(C)A 1992).

6) If recognition has not been granted at this stage, the CAC must then order a ballot of the workers comprising the bargaining unit. The ballot must be conducted by a qualified independent person and should normally take place within 20 days of that person's appointment. The employer should provide the trade union with access to the workers affected in order that the union may inform them of the purpose of the ballot and obtain their support. The employer must also co-operate with the CAC, both generally, and specifically by providing names and home addresses of all workers entitled to take part in the ballot, by not inducing workers not to attend meetings with the union, and by not taking or threatening to take action against workers attending such meetings. If the employer fails in any of these duties and an order from the CAC to remedy such a failure is not observed, the CAC may at this stage grant recognition to the union (Sch.A1, paras 23–27 of the TULR(C)A 1992). In the recent case of *R (on the application of Ultraframe (UK) Ltd) v CAC* [2005] I.R.L.R. 641 it was held that a ballot for recognition may be ordered to be re-held by CAC if all workers who would have voted were not given the opportunity to vote.

7) The employer and the union must refrain from "unfair practices" in the conduct of the ballot; such practices include bribery, outcome-specific offers, coercion, threats of dismissal, disciplinary action or any other detriment, or the use of undue influence. The CAC may determine the proportion of the gross cost of the ballot to be borne by each party (Sch.A1, paras 27A–28 of the TULR(C)A 1992).

8) If the result is that the union is supported by a majority of workers voting and at least 40 per cent of the workers constituting the bargaining unit, the CAC must issue a declaration that the union is recognised as entitled to conduct collective bargaining on behalf of that bargaining unit. If the result is otherwise, the CAC must issue a declaration that the union is not entitled to be recognised (Sch.A1, para.29 of the TULR(C)A 1992).

9) Trade union recognition in these circumstances is granted only in respect of the particular bargaining unit specified. If the composition of the bargaining unit changes provision is made in Pt III TULR(C)A for either party to apply to the CAC either to vary the composition of the bargaining unit or to reconsider the issue of appropriateness.

Collective Bargaining

14.5.3   Once recognised, a trade union is entitled to take part in collective bargaining—the negotiating process leading towards a collective agreement. Section 178 of the TULR(C)A 1992 details the issues covered by collective bargaining as:

(a) terms and conditions of employment, or the physical conditions in which any workers are required to work;

(b) engagement or non-engagement, or termination or suspension of employment or the duties of employment, of one or more workers;

(c) allocation of work or the duties of employment between workers or groups of workers;

(d) matters of discipline;

(e) a worker's membership or non-membership of a trade union;

(f) facilities for officials of trade unions; and

(g) machinery for negotiation or consultation, and other procedures, relating to any of the above matters, including the recognition by employers or employers" associations of the right of a trade union to represent workers in such negotiations or consultation or in carrying out of such procedures.

In most cases it is for the parties to the negotiations to determine the actual format and procedures for negotiation, but in the case of statutory recognition either of the parties may request that the CAC determines the method of negotiation (Sch.A1, para.30 of the TULR(C)A 1992).

Disclosure of Information

Section 181(1) of the TULR(C)A states:

14.5.4

"An employer who recognises an independent trade union shall, for the purposes of all stages of collective bargaining about matters, and in relation to descriptions of workers, in respect of which the union is recognised by him, disclose to representatives of the union, on request, the information required by this section."

The required information is detailed in s.181(2) as:

"all the information relating to the employer's undertaking which is in his possession, or that of an associated employer, and is information—

(a) without which the trade union representatives would be to a material extent impeded in carrying on collective bargaining with him, and

(b) which it would be in accordance with good industrial relations practice that he should disclose to them for the purposes of collective bargaining".

However, s.182 then lays down six categories of information that need not be disclosed, consisting of such:

"information—

(a) [as] the disclosure of which would be against the interests of national security, or

(b) which he could not disclose without contravening a prohibition imposed by or under an enactment, or

(c) which has been communicated to him in confidence, or which he has otherwise obtained in consequence of the confidence reposed in him by another person, or

(d) which relates specifically to an individual (unless that individual has consented to its being disclosed), or

(e) [as] the disclosure of which would cause substantial injury to his undertaking for reasons other than its effect on collective bargaining, or

(f) obtained by him for the purpose of bringing, prosecuting or defending any legal proceedings."

Furthermore, the:

"employer is not required—

(a) to produce, or allow inspection of, any document (other than a document prepared for the purpose of conveying or confirming the information) or to make a copy of or extracts from any document, or

(b) to compile or assemble any information where the compilation or assembly would involve an amount of work or expenditure out of reasonable proportion to the value of the information in the conduct of collective bargaining." (s.182(2) of the TULR(C)A 1992).

Advice on the practical operation of ss.181–182 is given in the ACAS Code of Practice No.2.

Training

14.5.5 If a trade union is recognised under the statutory recognition process and the method of collective bargaining has been specified by the CAC, the employer is under an obligation to consult with the trade union on matters regarding the employer"s policy on training of workers. Failure by the employer to fulfil the requirements laid down in s.70B of the TULR(C)A 1992 will allow the trade union to complain to an employment tribunal.

DE-RECOGNITION

14.6 If the original recognition of the union by the employer was voluntary, there is no constraint on the employer from either varying the terms of that recognition or withdrawing it altogether.

If the recognition, although voluntary, was brought about under para.10, Sch.A1 of the TULR(C)A 1992 following a request for recognition by the trade union, the employer may not terminate the recognition agreement, without the consent of the parties, within three years (Sch.A1, para.56 of the TULR(C)A 1992). However, if the recognition was by virtue of a declaration issued by the CAC (statutory recognition), TULR(C)A Pts IV and V lay down the statutory procedures involved with de-recognition. As with much of the legislation concerning trade unions, the legislation regarding de-recognition is complex, but the major issues may be précised as follows:

(a) de-recognition may not take place within a period of three years from the granting by the CAC of the recognition declaration (the "relevant date") (Sch.A1, para.97), unless the union loses its certificate of independence (Sch.A1, para.149–154).

(b) If after the relevant date the employer falls within the "small employer" exception by employing less than 21 workers, the employer may advise the union and the CAC (Sch.A1, paras 99–103).

(c) The employer may after the relevant date request the union to agree to the ending of the bargaining arrangement. If the union fails to agree to the request, the employer may apply to the CAC for the holding of a secret ballot to determine whether the arrangement should be terminated. If the CAC finds that at least 10 per cent of the workers in the bargaining unit favour an end to the bargaining arrangement and a majority of workers would favour an end to the arrangement, a secret ballot must be organised (similar rules apply to this ballot as to the ballot for recognition). If the ballot shows that a majority of the workers voting and at least 40 per cent of the workers constituting the bargaining unit are in favour of ending the bargaining arrangements, the CAC must issue a declaration that those arrangements are ended.

(d) A similar procedure to (c) above is carried out if the request for de-recognition is made by a worker in the bargaining unit.

(e) In the case of a request made by an employer, if the original recognition was automatic, based on majority union membership, if the CAC is satisfied that fewer than half of the workers in the bargaining unit are members of the union after the relevant date a secret ballot will be held to determine whether the bargaining arrangements should be terminated (as in (c) above).

Chapter 15

TRADE UNIONS AND THEIR MEMBERS

CHAPTER OVERVIEW

Freedom of association may be though of as a most basic, fundamental right; and in the UK for many years this has been the case. However, in terms of trade unions, problems have arisen—not in terms of association, but in respect of the converse "right", the freedom not to associate. **CO15**

FREEDOM OF ASSOCIATION

The right to freedom of association is contained in Art.11 of the ECHR. It includes the "right to freedom of association with others, including the right to form and join trade unions . . ." Since 2000, this right has been incorporated into UK national law by the HRA 1998. Since trade unions themselves have been lawful in the UK since the late 1800s, the right to associate, for most workers, has not been a problem. However the right not to associate, in other words the right of individual workers to decide not to be a member of a particular trade union had not been recognised by the law. Prior to 1988, in the UK a "closed shop" **15.1** principle was lawful—in many situations and industries, in order for a worker to get a job they must either be a member of the trade union, or be willing to join a particular union; should they leave the trade union they may not keep the job. This requirement had the effect of boosting trade union membership and trade union power. By the late 1970s, some 55 per cent of workers were trade union members. An example of the closed shop may be seen in the case of *Young, James and Webster v United Kingdom* [1981] I.R.L.R. 408 ECHR. At the time, British Rail operated a closed shop. Employment within British Rail at many levels was only permitted if the employee joined the appropriate trade union; should he refuse to join or subsequently leave the union, his employment would terminate. The three complainants had all refused to join the trade union and had been dismissed by British Rail. They took their case to the European Court of Human Rights. The court held that the right to form or join a trade union is a fundamental aspect of freedom of association. Conversely, therefore, the right not to join or to leave a union must also form part of the basic right of freedom of association. The actions of British Rail supported by domestic legislation in UK therefore breached Art.11 of the Convention on Human Rights. Since the case was heard some years before the UK implemented the HRA 1998, the decision of the court had no direct effect in the UK.This closed shop principle was outlawed by the Conservative government under Margaret Thatcher in a series of legislative measures during the 1980s. The result of this legislation saw trade union membership fall, until by the mid-1990s it was estimated that only some 25 per cent of workers were members of a trade union.

Restrictions for Certain Workers

15.1.1   It should be noted that there are some statutory restrictions concerning the ability of certain groups to either join a trade union or to take part in industrial action; police officers are not permitted to join a trade union, although they are automatically members of the Police Federation; members of the armed forces are not permitted to take part in industrial action; and certain Crown employees have a clause in their contracts of employment by which they agree not to join a trade union.

Inducements concerning Union Membership

15.1.2   In 2002, the European Court of Human Rights (ECtHR) in the case of *Wilson v United Kingdom* [2002] I.R.L.R. 568 heard issues relating to decisions of the House of Lords in the joined cases of *Associated Newspapers v Wilson* and *Associated British Ports v Palmer* [1995] I.C.R. 406. The cases of both *Wilson* and *Palmer* concerned attempts by the employers to terminate existing collective bargaining agreements between the employer and the trade unions, and instead enter into individually negotiated contracts of employment with each individual employee. Pay rises were granted to those employees who agreed the new arrangements, but withheld from those who continued under the collective agreement. The question before the House of Lords had been whether the withholding of a pay rise amounted to "action" short of dismissal for the purpose of deterring or penalising trade union membership contrary to the legislation then in force (s.23(1)(a) of the Employment Protection (Consolidation) Act 1978). In a majority decision, the House of Lords held that, for the purpose of the legislation, an "omission" did not amount to an "action", and found in favour of the employers. The ECtHR, however, held that the actions of the employers breached Art.11 of the Convention. The court stated that by permitting an employer to restrict an individual's right to make use of a trade union's role of collective bargaining by treating such employees less favourably, the right of freedom of association becomes illusionary, and the state has a positive duty to secure such rights. (Although stating that an individual worker has a right to make use of any of the services provided by a trade union, the court did stop short of saying that that would amount to a positive right to strike. On this issue see also *UNISON v UK* [2002] I.R.L.R. 497 (ECtHR) in which although the court held that strike action may fall within Art.11, it also held that the right of the employer under Art.11(2) may permit the prohibition of such action).

Following the introduction of the ERelA 2004, it is unlawful for an employer to offer an inducement to a worker to either join or leave a trade union.

UNION RULES

Since a trade union is capable of making contracts in its own name, membership **15.2** of a trade union will amount to a contract between the union and the individual members. The union rules will form part of that contract between the union and its members, and as such, both the union rules and disciplinary procedures are open to scrutiny by the courts (*Lee v The Showmen's Guild of Great Britain* [1952] 2 Q.B. 329), interpretation by the courts (*Jaques v AUEW* [1986] I.C.R. 683), and are subject to issues of natural justice (*Roebuck v National Union of Mineworkers (Yorkshire Area) No.2* [1978] I.C.R. 676).

Discipline

All individual union members have the right not to be unjustifiably disciplined by **15.2.1** the trade union (s.64 of the TULR(C)A 1992). "Disciplined" is defined in s.64(2) of the TULR(C)A 1992 as:

a) being expelled from the union or branch or section of the union;

b) being obliged to pay a sum or fine to the union;

c) having sums paid by him to the union being treated as unpaid or paid for a different purpose;

d) being deprived of any benefit, service or facilities to which by virtue of his membership of the union he would otherwise be entitled;

e) having another union advised or encouraged not to accept him as a member; or

f) being subjected to some other detriment.

Section 65 then lays down a number of situations which amount to "unjustifiably disciplined" including where the individual fails to participate in industrial action, resigning or proposing to resign from the union, working with workers who are not members of that or another union, and working for an employer who employs non-union labour.

Any union member complaining of unjustified action by the union may present a complaint within three months to an Employment Tribunal.

If the employment tribunal find that the complaint is well founded, the individual may then make application to the tribunal for a compensatory award, which, under s.67(5), may be "such as the employment tribunal considers just and equitable in all the circumstances".

Exclusion and Expulsion

15.2.2   There are only limited reasons for which a trade union may either exclude a worker from membership of the union, or expel an existing union member. These reasons, amended by ERelA 2004, are included in s.174 of the TULR(C)A 1992:

(a) The worker does not satisfy, or no longer satisfies, an enforceable membership requirement contained in the rules of the union.

(b) The worker does not qualify, or no longer qualifies, for membership of the union by reason of the union operating only in a particular part or particular parts of Great Britain.

(c) In the case of a union whose purpose is the regulation or relations between its members and one particular employer or a number of particular employees who are associated, they are not, or are no longer, employed by that employer or one of those employers.

(d) The exclusion or expulsion is entirely attributable to conduct of theirs (other than excluded conduct) and the conduct to which it is wholly or mainly attributable is not protected conduct.

"Excluded conduct" is defined (s.174(4)) as being or not being a member of another trade union, working or not working for a particular employer or at a particular location, and conduct referred to in s.65 regarding the issue of "unjustifiably disciplined".

"Protected conduct" is conduct which consists of the individual being or not being a member of a particular political party (s.174(4A)), therefore a member may not be excluded on the grounds of their membership of a political party, but, under s.174(4B), may be excluded on the grounds of their activities or conduct as a member of a political party. In other words, although an individual's political beliefs and membership of political party may be protected, the manifestation of those beliefs (e.g. taking part in demonstrations, fund raising, giving interviews to the media, etc.) may not be protected, and may therefore give grounds for exclusion or expulsion from the trade union.

ELECTION OF UNION OFFICIALS

Sections 46–61 of the TULR(C)A 1992 lay down specific requirements in terms of certain union office holders. No member of the union executive, the president or the general secretary may hold office for more than five years without being re-elected. No member of the union may be unreasonably excluded from standing for election, and no candidate shall be required to be a member of any political party. All members of the trade union are entitled to vote, but the union rules may exclude certain categories of members, such as those not in employment, those whose membership subscriptions are in arrears, and in certain elections those who fall within classes determined by reference to a particular trade, a particular geographical area, or those which the union rules treat as belonging to a separate section within the union. An independent scrutineer is appointed by the union to oversee the conduct of the election. The ballot should be carried out by way of voting papers sent by post to each individual eligible member. The voting, so far as it is reasonably practicable, shall be carried out in secret. In the case of uncontested elections there is no requirement for a ballot to take place.

    If the above requirements are not carried out any member of the trade union, including any candidate, may apply to the Certification Officer or to the court for a declaration to that effect and both the Certification Office and the court have the power to order a new election to take place.

15.3

TRADE UNION POLITICAL FUND

15.4   If a trade union wishes to contribute towards political ends, such as contributions to political parties, that contribution must come from a separate political fund; the general funds of the trade union may not be used. Contributions to political parties stem from the early days of the Labour Party, at which time Members of Parliament were unpaid, but Labour MPs received money from trade unions. The case of *ASRS v Osborne* [1910] A.C. 87 held that a levy on union members for political purposes was unlawful, but the Trade Union Act of 1913 subsequently allowed a union to set up a separate political fund into which union members could contribute if they wished. This is still the position today and is contained within ss.71–87 of the TULR(C)A 1992, individual members may give notice that they wish to be exempt from contribution to the fund, and in such instances they must not be placed under any disadvantage as a result of their withdrawal from such contributions although they may normally be excluded from the management of that fund. The case of *Birch v National Union of Railwaymen* [1950] Ch. 602 demonstrates the issue:

- The NUR rulebook contained a rule that only those members contributing to the political fund may take part in the management of that fund. Mr Birch, who chose not to contribute to the political fund, was elected as a local branch official, part of whose duties was an involvement in the management of the political fund. The union argued that he was not eligible for office, since he would be unable to fulfil all the required duties. The court held that the rule concerning the political fund offended against, what is now, s.82(1) of the TULR(C)A 1992. Whereas it was reasonable that only those members who contributed to the political fund should have authority to manage the fund, it was quite another thing that the rule should have the effect of disqualifying anyone not contributing to the fund from holding office of almost any sort within the union.

"Political objects" for which only the political fund may be used are defined in s.72 as including any contribution to the funds of, or payment of, expenses incurred directly or indirectly by a political party, the holding of conferences or meetings the main purpose of which is the transaction of business in connection with a political party, and the production, distribution or publication of any literature or advertisement the main purpose of which is to persuade people to vote for or against a political party.

A political fund may only be held by a trade union if the union has in place a political resolution to that effect, and that political resolution must be renewed by ballot each ten years. The rules for such a ballot must be approved by the Certification Officer and the ballot must be supervised by an independent scrutineer.

Chapter 16

INDUSTRIAL ACTION

CHAPTER OVERVIEW

Industrial action is a problematic area both for the legislature and also the courts. **CO16** On the one hand, industrial action will amount to a breach of contract, and breaches of contract are unlawful; on the other hand unless industrial action is permitted by the legislation, the only option open to a disgruntled employee would be to terminate the employment relationship—which in most instances would amount to using a hammer to crack an egg. The legislative approach has therefore been to control the industrial action by way of measures permitting action only if certain, at times somewhat onerous, requirements are observed; otherwise the actions will be unlawful and the trade unions may find themselves liable for considerable penalties.

Thus the right to take industrial action is a conditional right; at the collective level breach of those conditions may lead to financial penalties, whilst at the individual level the "penalty" may involve the removal of the individual's other employment rights (for example, the right to complain to a tribunal of unfair dismissal). It is outside the scope of this book to consider whether "conditional rights" should properly be termed "rights" at all, or to comment on whether the "negative rights" within the UK—the right to do things which are not otherwise prohibited—should be replaced by positive, legally entrenched rights.

BREACH OF CONTRACT

16.1 At common law, all industrial action will amount to a breach of the contract of employment. A strike—withdrawal of labour—will obviously constitute a breach of contract by the individual employees of the contract of employment (*Simmons v Hoover Ltd* [1977] I.C.R. 61), and in organising such action the union will commit the tort of inducement to breach of contract. Perhaps surprisingly, the courts have held that a work to rule, employees working to the strict letter of the employment contract, will also amount to a breach (*Secretary of State for Employment v ASLEF* [1972] 2 All E.R. 949, the argument here being that all employment contracts contain an implied term that the employee will not take any action detrimental to the employer, the "duty to cooperate". This logic has been taken further to include a refusal to work non-contractual overtime (*Faust v Power Packing Casemakers Ltd* [1983] I.R.L.R. 117). It is worth bearing in mind that, in such a dispute between an employer and an employee, the reason for the refusal by the employee will be important; if the reason is to put pressure on the employer, the courts are likely to hold that it amounts to a breach of contract, whereas if there is a genuine personal reason—prior engagement or child care obligations, say—it is unlikely to be viewed as a breach. However, in the event of a breach, statute has intervened to offer an amount of protection to trade unions and their members in certain situations.

It should be understood that there is no positive right to breach an employment (or any other) contract, nor any "right to strike" in UK law, but be aware of dicta in cases such as *Wilson v UK; Palmer v UK* [2002] I.R.L.R. 568, *UNISON v UK* [2002] I.R.L.R. 497.

OFFICIAL AND UNOFFICIAL ACTION

16.2 It is important to distinguish between official and unofficial industrial action. Official action is that which is supported by the trade union; unofficial action is that which the union has repudiated. For action to be deemed unofficial it is not sufficient that the union merely does not support it; the union must actively repudiate the action (*Express and Star Ltd v NGA* [1985] I.R.L.R. 455) by giving immediate notice of repudiation to those organising the action (s.21(2)(a) of the TULR(C)A 1992) and to all union members and their employers who may become involved in the action (s.21(2)(b) of the TULR(C)A 1992). In respect of whether action is "authorised" or "endorsed" by the union, the union will be held liable for actions authorised, endorsed or done by the union president, executive committee and its general secretary, along with any union committee or official of the union (s.20). If such action is official and unlawful (see below) the union may be liable in tort. In the case of *Heatons Transport (St Helens) Ltd v TGWU* [1972] I.C.R. 308 the trade union was held responsible for the acts of an unofficial committee of shop stewards, despite the fact that such were committees were not recognised in the union rules.

One other reason for differentiating between official and unofficial action is that, if workers are dismissed for taking part in unofficial action, the employment tribunal will have no jurisdiction to hear their complaint of unfair dismissal.

The position regarding unfair dismissal for taking part in industrial action is governed by ss.237–239 of the TULR(C)A 1992.

Dismissal for participation in *unofficial* action is effectively automatically fair. Section 237(1) of the TULR(C)A 1992 states: "An employee has no right to complain of unfair dismissal if at the time of dismissal he was taking part in unofficial strike or other unofficial industrial action". **16.2.1**

Dismissal for participation in lawful *official* action is, subject to certain restrictions, automatically unfair. This protection lasts for twelve weeks from the start of the official action (or longer if the employer has failed to take reasonable procedural steps to resolve the dispute, s.238A(6), and in the situation where an employer prevents the employees returning to work by a lock-out the protected period is extended by the duration of the lock-out), after which time the dismissal will be fair, subject to s.238A. A major restriction on this protection is that it covers only action that amounts to the commission of an act which by virtue of s.219 (see below) is not actionable in tort. **16.2.2**

Dismissal where the express reason or principle reason for the dismissal is participation in official action which is unlawful (action not covered by s.219) or has lasted over twelve weeks at the time of dismissal, is automatically fair, unless:

(i) not all current participants in the action have been dismissed; or

(ii) within three months of the dismissals, some or any (but not all) of those dismissed are selectively re-employed (s.238(2)).

In such cases, the employment tribunal would consider the issue of fairness of dismissal by applying the "reasonableness" test.

TRADE UNIONS' LIABILITY IN TORT

The structure of the law in this area is very complex. It is useful to approach this issue by adopting a three-stage approach: **16.3**

i) Has a tort been committed?

ii) If so, is the action protected by the immunity granted by s.219 of the TULR(C)A 1992?

iii) If so, has the immunity been lost by the union's failure to comply with legislation (mainly ss.222–226 of the TULR(C)A 1992)?

Has a Tort been Committed?

16.3.1   In the organising of any industrial action it is inevitable that the trade union will commit unlawful tortious acts; for example, merely by promoting the action the union will commit the tort of inducement to breach of contract (by inducing the employees to breach their contracts of employment).

It is important to identify which torts may have been committed during industrial action. The commission of some torts—the major economic torts—may in some circumstances be granted immunity by statute; but the organisers of industrial action, usually the trade union, will still have liability for those torts which do not attract protection, such as the tort of public nuisance (*News Group Newspapers Ltd v SOGAT '82* [1986] I.R.L.R. 337).

The Major Economic Torts

16.3.2   The scope of these economic torts has been increased over the years by the courts; the major torts are: *inducement of breach of contract, interference with contract, interference with trade or business, intimidation,* and *conspiracy.*

Inducement to breach of contract

16.3.2.1   This tort can take two forms, *direct* or *indirect.*

The direct form occurs when an inducement is made by one party, usually the trade union, to the second party, the employee, to breach a contract which the second party has with the third party, the employer. Generally the contract is the employee's contract of employment, and the breach may be a withdrawal of labour—a strike—(*Simmons v Hoover Ltd* [1977] I.C.R. 61), a "go-slow" or work to rule (*British Telecommunications Plc v Ticehurst* [1992] I.C.R. 383) or other form of industrial action (*Wiluszynski v Tower Hamlets London Borough Council* [1989] I.C.R. 493). The leading case concerning direct inducement to breach of contract is the old case of *Lumley v Gye* [1853] 2 E. & B. 216, in which an opera singer who was under contract to appear at a particular theatre was persuaded by an agent to break her contract and appear instead at a different theatre. The agent was liable for, what was then, the new tort of inducement to breach of contract.

It is important to note that a pre-existing contract must be in place, and that the inducement is directed towards one of the parties to that contract. In the case of *Middlebrook Mushrooms Ltd v TGWU* [1993] I.R.L.R. 232 the trade union, in support of dismissed workers, picketed a number of supermarkets where the employer's products were sold, requesting shoppers to support the dismissed workers by refraining from buying Middlebrook's mushrooms. An action against the union for inducement to breach of contract failed since there was no contract between the shoppers and Middlebrook; had the leaflets been aimed at the supermarket managers the action should have been successful, since contracts were in existence between the supermarkets and Middlebrooks.

Although the common law provides a defence of justification for the tort of inducement to breach of contract, the courts have been very reluctant to accept such a defence in cases of industrial action.

The indirect form of the tort is slightly more complicated. It requires that party A should induce party B to cause a breach of a contract between parties C and D. An example is the case of *DC Thomson & Co Ltd v Deakin* [1952] Ch. 646, in which the trade union called upon workers in several companies to refuse to handle deliveries to a particular company, DC Thomson, who were in dispute with the union. Workers from another company, Bowaters, made it clear to their employer that they would not handle deliveries to Thomson's. Thomson's then sought action against the trade union for the tort of inducement to breach of contract. The court held that the tort would be committed if the following four elements were proved:

(i) if the trade union knew of the existence of the contract and intended its breach;

(ii) if the union did induce a breach of the contract;

(iii) if the employees so persuaded did indeed breach their contracts of employment; and

(iv) if the breach of their contracts of employment did cause the breach of the contract complained of.

The later case of *Emerald Construction Ltd v Lowthian* [1966] 1 W.L.R. 691 makes it clear that it is not necessary that the union should have any detailed knowledge of the contract, merely that it is aware, or should be aware, in general terms of the existence of such a contract. It is said that for the indirect form of the tort of inducement to breach of contract "unlawful means" must be used. These unlawful means need be nothing more than another tort itself. In the case of *DC Thomson* the unlawful means would be the inducement to the workers to breach their contracts of employment—itself the simple or direct form of the tort. To prove the direct form of this tort no unlawful means are necessary. It should be noted that if the "unlawful means" are themselves protected by the immunities under s. 219 of the TULR(C)A 1992, they will not constitute unlawful means for the purpose of this tort (see the section on "immunities").

Interference with contract

16.3.2.2 This is essentially an extended version of the tort of inducement to breach of contract. The important difference is that it is not necessary to prove an actual breach of a contract. According to Lord Denning in the case of *Torquay Hotel Co Ltd v Cousins* [1969] 2 Ch. 106, if a person deliberately interferes with the trade or business of another by any means which are unlawful, then a tort will be committed, even though no actual breach of contract may arise. In the *Torquay Hotel* case, industrial action had prevented the delivery of fuel oil from the supplier to the hotel, but within the contract for the supply of the oil there was a clause excluding liability for non-supply in the case of industrial action. Technically therefore there had been no breach of contract, and consequently the union could not be liable for the tort of inducement to breach as it stood at the time.

Interference with trade or business

16.3.2.3 This may be viewed as either a further extension of the torts of inducement to breach of contract and interference with contract, or an "umbrella" tort of which the two previous torts are merely sub-species. Its existence was confirmed by the House of Lords in *Merkur Island Shipping Corp v Laughton* [1983] 2 All E.R. 189, where it was stated that there was no need to prove interference with any particular or specific contract, thus confirming Lord Denning's dicta in *Torquay Hotel* (above). It would therefore be possible to commit this tort by frightening off potential, rather than actual, customers. As with the tort of interference with contract, however, it must be shown that unlawful means have been employed, which in practice will usually simply mean that the commission of this tort has involved the commission of another tort.

Intimidation

16.3.2.4 Although the courts have long held that the threat of physical violence may constitute an unlawful act, usually a criminal act, it was not until the case of *Rookes v Barnard* [1964] A.C. 1129 that the tort of intimidation was identified through the use of threats of breach of contract. Lord Devlin stated in that case: "I find nothing to differentiate a threat of a breach of contract from a threat of physical violence or other illegal threat." Thus putting pressure on an employer to act in a certain way by threatening to breach a contract, often the contract of employment, will amount to the commission of the tort of intimidation.

Conspiracy

16.3.2.5 If two or more combine to injure another, and their predominant purpose is to injure the other rather than to advance their own legitimate interests, the tort of conspiracy will be committed. This form of the tort has little practical importance following the case of *Crofter Hand Woven Harris Tweed Co v Veitch* [1942] A.C. 435, where it was accepted by the House of Lords that normal trade union purposes were "legitimate interests" as long as they were the predominant motive of the organisers of the industrial action. However, if "unlawful means" are used, the defence of legitimate interests will not succeed; it is not clear whether a simple breach of contract would be sufficient to constitute unlawful means for the commission of this tort.

Is the Action Protected by an Immunity?

Although the commission of torts is, of course, unlawful, some protection is given **16.3.3** by statute to trade unions against liability for some torts committed in the course of organising industrial action.

Section 219 of the TULR(C)A 1992 provides, to at least some extent, immunity from liability in the commission of all of the above torts. This immunity will only apply where the actions complained of are carried out "*in contemplation and furtherance of a trade dispute*"—this is the so-called "Golden Formula".

Section 219(1) states :

> "An act done by a person in contemplation or furtherance of a trade dispute is not actionable in tort on the ground only—
>
> > (a) that it induces another person to break a contract or interferes or induces another person to interfere with its performance, or"
> > [*thus protecting directly against Inducement of Breach of Contract and Interference with Contract and indirectly against Interference with Business by limiting the scope for "unlawful means"*].
> >
> > "(b) that it consists in his threatening that a contract (whether one to which he is a party or not) will be broken or its performance interfered with, or that he will induce another person to break a contract or interfere with its performance."
> > [*thus protecting directly against Intimidation and indirectly against Inducement of Breach of Contract, Interference with Contract and Interference with Business by limiting the scope for "unlawful means"*].

Section 219(2) states :

> "An agreement or combination by two or more persons to do or procure the doing of an act in contemplation or furtherance of a trade dispute is not actionable in tort if the act is one which if done without any such agreement or combination would not be actionable in tort".

[*thus protecting directly against conspiracy to injure without the use of unlawful means and also conspiracy to use unlawful means* except *where it is an agreement to commit a tort*].

The Golden Formula

16.3.3.1   Protection under s.219 is only granted to those actions which are carried out in contemplation or furtherance of a trade dispute.

A "trade dispute" is defined in s.244 of the TULR(C)A 1992 as a dispute between "workers and their employer" which relates wholly or mainly to such issues as terms and conditions of employment.

It would thus exclude disputes where the union is motivated mainly by 'political' considerations, e.g. ideological objections to privatisation (*Mercury Communications Ltd v Scott-Garner* [1984] I.C.R. 741), or refusing to handle mail for South Africa as an anti-apartheid protest (*Gouriet v UPOW* [1978] A.C. 435), as well as disputes motivated mainly by personal spite (*Torquay Hotels Ltd v Cousins* [1969] 2 Ch. 106; *Huntley v Thornton* [1957] 1 All E.R. 234).

Also excluded are disputes between workers and other employers. The term "worker" is defined in s.244(5) to include both employees and those personally performing work, and also includes those no longer in employment if their employment was terminated in connection with the dispute or if the termination was a cause of the dispute.

"In contemplation" requires the dispute to be imminent—*Bent's Brewery Co Ltd v Hogan* [1945] 2 All E.R. 570.

"In furtherance" presupposes a dispute already in existence and not yet over (see, e.g. *Stewart v AUEW* [1973] I.C.R. 128). An action is in furtherance of the dispute if D genuinely believes it will further its interests in the dispute whether or not it will or is capable of doing so and whether or not it is a reasonable means of doing so (*Express Newspapers Ltd v McShane* [1980] I.C.R. 42; *NWL Ltd v Woods* [1979] 1 W.L.R. 1294).

Has the Immunity been Lost?

16.3.4   Once it has been determined whether the torts committed are covered by the statutory immunities, it must then be determined whether that immunity has been lost by the actions or omissions of the union concerned. The statutory immunities contained in s.219 will be lost if any of the requirements contained in the legislation, mainly in ss.222–234 of the TULR(C)A 1992, are breached. The immunity may therefore be lost if the action:

(a) is, or if one of the reasons for the action is, to enforce union membership (s.222);

(b) is taken due to the dismissal of an employee for taking unofficial industrial action (s.223);

(c) amounts to secondary action which is not lawful picketing (s.224);

(d) is pressure to impose union recognition (s.225); or

(e) if the extensive requirements concerning the organisation of the ballot have not been met (ss.226–234)—the rules covering balloting are complex, but have been somewhat clarified by ERelA 1999 and ERelA 2004.

Ballot before union action

In order to amount to protected industrial action, a ballot must be carried out prior to any action by the trade union to induce any person to take part or continue to take part in the action (s.226). Notice must be sent by the union to all employers concerned not less than seven days before the ballot detailing the date of the ballot, the numbers, categories and places of work of those entitled to vote in the ballot, and not less than three days before the ballot a sample voting paper must be sent (s.226A). Entitlement to vote must be accorded to all of those members of the trade union who will be induced by the union to take part in the action, and must not be accorded to others (s.227). Subject to the requirements of ss.228 and 228A, separate workplace ballots may be required. Voting must be by the marking of a voting paper which must: **16.3.4.1**

a) contain the name of the independent scrutineer;

b) be marked with one of a number of consecutive numbers;

c) include a question answerable with either "yes" or "no" as to whether the individual is prepared to take part in the proposed industrial action; and

d) include a notice proscribed by statute advising the individual of his rights and liabilities in respect of the action (s.229).

The conduct of the ballot is regulated by s.230, and the result of the ballot should be made known to those entitled to vote and the relevant employers as soon as is reasonably practicable (ss.231 and 231A). Subsequent to the ballot taking place, any call for industrial action must be made within either four weeks of the date of the ballot, or within a period of not more than eight weeks if agreed between the union and the relevant employers. After such time periods the ballot ceases to be effective (s.234). Section 234A lays down detailed requirements for the union to give notice to any relevant employer.

   If the immunities have been lost, or if torts have been committed which are not covered by the protection afforded by s.219, the trade union may be liable for damages in a civil action for tort.

PICKETING

16.4   Section 220 of the TULR(C)A 1992 states:

> "It is lawful for a person in contemplation or furtherance of a trade dispute to attend—(a) at or near his own place of work, or (b) if he is an official of a trade union, at or near the place of work of a member of the union whom he is accompanying and whom he represents, for the purpose only of peacefully obtaining or communicating information, or peacefully persuading any person to work or abstain from working."

It should therefore be noted that:

a) the picketing must come within the Golden Formula;

b) the picketing must be at or near the pickets' workplace—in the case of *Rayware Ltd v TGWU* [1989] I.R.L.R. 134, the Court of Appeal held that this should be the closest point to their workplace at which the pickets could lawfully assemble;

c) picketing is for clearly defined purposes only—in the case of *Broome v DPP* [1974] I.C.R. 84, a picket was arrested for attempting to stop a vehicle entering his employer's premises.

d) picketing must be peaceful—a large number of pickets could not be said to be "peacefully communicating", their purpose was to intimidate (*Thomas v NUM* [1985] I.R.L.R. 136), in which the court restricted picket numbers to a maximum of six.

The act of picketing will almost certainly involve the commission of torts, which unless immunity is provided by the "golden formula", will attract liability on the part of the union for any actions not repudiated by that union. The issue of criminal liability may also arise for the individual pickets. In for example both the cases of *Broome v DPP* (above) and *Tynan v Balmer* [1967] 1 Q.B. 91 arrests were made for unreasonable use of the highway, although the House of Lords in *Jones v DPP* [1999] 2 All E.R. 257 did allow that peaceful lawful picketing could, depending on the facts of the individual case, amount to reasonable use of the highway. The police have considerable power to control picket behaviour and numbers under public order legislation—these powers have been tested and exercised in such disputes as the miners' strike and the move of various newspapers from Fleet Street to Wapping in the 1980s, both of which saw mass picketing and outbreaks of considerable violence.

Certainly there is relevance within Arts 10 and 11 ECHR to the issue of picketing—Art.10 guaranteeing the right to freedom of expression and Art.11

concerning the right to peaceful assembly, but as yet these have not been fully tested in law.

EMPLOYER'S REMEDIES AGAINST INDIVIDUAL EMPLOYEE PARTICIPANTS

Apart from any remedy, the employer may have against the trade union—generally either injunction or action in tort for damages—the employer may also have remedies against the individual employee who participates in industrial action.   **16.5**

- The courts will not grant the remedy of specific performance against an employee (s.236 of the TULR(C)A 1992).

- Damages may be awarded, but only for the individual's *own* contribution to the loss, so such a remedy is not usually sought in practice (*NCB v Galley* [1958] 1 W.L.R. 16).

- Deductions from wages, amounting in effect to self-assessed damages and permitted under s.14(5) of the ERA 1996, see for example *Miles v Wakefield MDC* [1987] I.C.R. 368 and *Wiluszynski v London Borough of Tower Hamlets* [1989] I.C.R. 493.

- Dismissal at common law may be contractually permitted without notice where, as will usually be the case, employee's action is a repudiatory breach. However, whether or not the action is in breach of contract, the position concerning unfair dismissal is governed by ss.237–9 of the TULR(C)A 1992 which distinguish between official (i.e. backed by a worker's TU) and unofficial action (see above).

APPENDICES

Flow charts and Diagrammatic representations:

(i) EMPLOYMENT STATUS

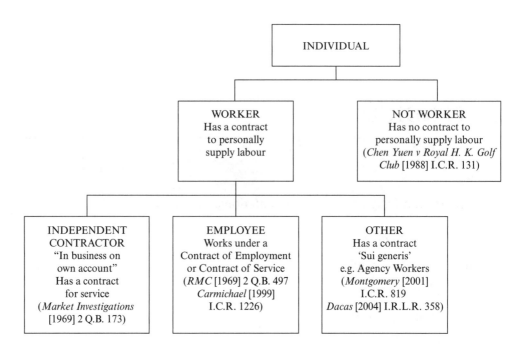

(ii) CONTRACT OF EMPLOYMENT

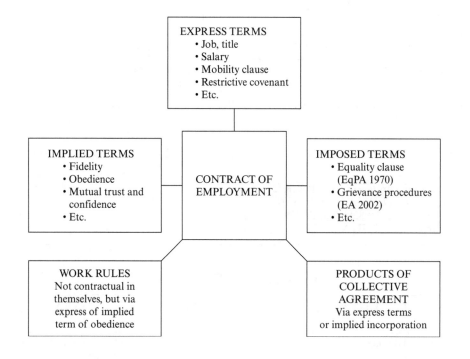

EXPRESS TERMS
• Job, title
• Salary
• Mobility clause
• Restrictive covenant
• Etc.

IMPLIED TERMS
• Fidelity
• Obedience
• Mutual trust and
  confidence
• Etc.

CONTRACT OF
EMPLOYMENT

IMPOSED TERMS
• Equality clause
  (EqPA 1970)
• Grievance procedures
  (EA 2002)
• Etc.

WORK RULES
Not contractual in
themselves, but via
express of implied
term of obedience

PRODUCTS OF
COLLECTIVE
AGREEMENT
Via express terms
or implied incorporation

(iii) CLAIMS

STATUTORY CLAIMS

UNFAIR DISMISSAL	STATUTORY BREACH
• Governed by the ERA 1996.	• Action for breach of Discrimination legislation.
• Action for dismissal and manner of dismissal.	• Action for unlawful deduction of wages, breach of working time legislation, etc.
• Re-installment, re-engagement compensation (capped at £58,000).	• Statutory Grievance Procedure will normally apply.
Western Excavating [1978] I.R.L.R. 27 *BHS v Burchell* [1978] I.R.L.R. 379 *Iceland v Jones* [1982] I.R.L.R. 439 *Devis v Atkins* [1977] A.C. 931	

COMMON LAW CLAIMS

WRONGFUL DISMISSAL	BREACH OF CONTRACT	RESTRAINTS
• Unlimited damages but only in respect of actual economic loss directly due to insufficient contractual or statutory notice period.	• Only if the breach does not form part of the dismissal process.	• Discretionary Interim Injunction.
Addis [1909] A.C. 488 *BCCI v Malik* [1997] I.R.L.R. 462 *Johnson v Unisys* [2001] I.R.L.R. 279	*Eastwood v Magnox* [2002] I.R.L.R. 447	*Irani v Southampton* AHA [1985] I.R.L.R. 203

PUBLIC LAW

JUDICIAL REVIEW
• Available only to office holders and on issues of public (rather than private) law.
Ridge v Baldwin [1964] A.C. 40 *Ex p. Walsh* [1984] I.C.R. 743

(iv) UNFAIR DISMISSAL

1) Can the applicant claim?

    a) Is the applicant an 'employee' as defined in s.230 of the ERA?

    b) Does the applicant have one year continuous service?
- issues of continuity of service and effective date of termination may be important;
- no requirement for minimum service period in cases of discrimination, trade union activities, minimum wage claim, etc.

    c) Is the claim brought within three months?
- tribunal has power to extend the time limit.
- in cases where statutory dispute regulations apply, the time limit is extended by three months.

    d) Is the applicant a member of an excluded group?
- over normal retirement age (but see age discrimination)?

    e) If statutory grievance procedure applies, has applicant complied with ss.6 and 9 (statement of grievance to the employer)?

2) Can a dismissal be identified?
- including Constructive dismissal, non-renewal of limited term contract, etc.

3) Reason for the dismissal
- employer must show one of the five potentially fair reasons;
- automatically unfair reasons.

4) Fairness of the dismissal

    a) 'Band of reasonable responses' test;

    b) Procedural issues (particularly Dispute Resolution regs).

5) Remedies

    a) Reinstatement

    b) Re-engagement

    c) Compensation
- capped at £58,000;
- tribunal may make adjustment if full dispute resolution procedures have not been compiled with.

(v) INDUSTRIAL ACTION

1) What torts have been committed?

2) Are the above torts protected by s.219 'the golden formula'?
   • only certain torts may be protected by s.219 immunity;
   • does the action qualify as a 'trade dispute' s.244?

3) Has the immunity been lost?
   • has the union complied with all the requirements, mainly contained in ss.224–234.

4) If any of the torts committed are not protected under s.219, or if immunity has been lost, the trade union is liable in a civil action.

INDEX

This index has been prepared using Sweet and Maxwell's Legal Taxonomy. Main index entries conform to keywords provided by the Legal Taxonomy except where references to specific documents or non-standard terms (denoted by quotation marks) have been included. These keywords provide a means of identifying similar concepts in other Sweet & Maxwell publications and online services to which keywords from the Legal Taxonomy have been applied. Readers may find some minor differences between terms used in the text and those which appear in the index. Suggestions to sweetandmaxwell.taxonomy@thomson.com.

(All references are to paragraph number)